Innovation and Entrepreneurship in the Public Sector

Innovation and Entrepreneurship in the Public Sector

WENDY D. CHEN
DAVID B. AUDRETSCH

OXFORD
UNIVERSITY PRESS

OXFORD
UNIVERSITY PRESS

Oxford University Press is a department of the University of Oxford.
It furthers the University's objective of excellence in research, scholarship,
and education by publishing worldwide. Oxford is a registered trade mark of
Oxford University Press in the UK and in certain other countries.

Published in the United States of America by Oxford University Press
198 Madison Avenue, New York, NY 10016, United States of America.

Library of Congress Cataloging-in-Publication Data
Names: Chen, Wendy D. editor | Audretsch, David B. editor
Title: Innovation and entrepreneurship in the public sector /
Wendy D. Chen, David B. Audretsch.
Description: New York, NY : Oxford University Press, [2025] |
Includes bibliographical references and index.
Identifiers: LCCN 2025016091 (print) | LCCN 2025016092 (ebook) |
ISBN 9780197679449 | ISBN 9780197679456 epub | ISBN 9780197679470
Subjects: LCSH: Public administration | Government business
enterprises—Management | Public works—Management |
Technological innovations—Government policy | Entrepreneurship
Classification: LCC JF1351 .I4647 2025 (print) | LCC JF1351 (ebook) |
DDC 351—dcundefined
LC record available at https://lccn.loc.gov/2025016091
LC ebook record available at https://lccn.loc.gov/2025016092

DOI: 10.1093/9780197679470.001.0001

Printed by Sheridan Books, Inc., United States of America

The manufacturer's authorized representative in the EU for product safety is
Oxford University Press España S.A., Parque Empresarial San Fernando de Henares,
Avenida de Castilla, 2 – 28830 Madrid (www.oup.es/en or product.safety@oup.com).
OUP España S.A. also acts as importer into Spain of products made by the manufacturer.

MIX
Paper | Supporting responsible forestry
FSC® C008955
FSC www.fsc.org

This book is dedicated to our families and those who care about building a better public sector to ensure a prosperous future.

Contents

Preface

A generation ago, a daunting challenge confronted the developed world. The same stalwart companies and industries that had propelled the post–World War II economies to unprecedented levels of growth and standard of living had run out of steam. The new and strange phenomenon of globalization and technological change, as the second industrial era gave way to its successor, wreaked havoc on what had been a bedrock of stability and prosperity. Economic growth stalled, while unemployment ratcheted upward in a worrisome spiral. When relief, in the form of new vitality and renewed prosperity, finally did come, its source was surprising. The solution to one of the most compelling threats to society did not come as had been expected, from a revival of those traditional manufacturing corporations and industries. Rather, the way forward came from an entirely new and unprecedented direction—entrepreneurial startups ushering in bold new innovations upon which entirely new technologies and industries were built. Before the mid-1980s, virtually no one had ever heard of Bill Gates and Microsoft, or Steve Jobs and Apple Computer. Just a few years later, it would be hard to find someone who had not heard of them. It was entrepreneurship that delivered the bold new disruptive innovations needed to move the economy and society forward again.

Today we face an entirely different set of new and unprecedented challenges—civic participation, global health threats, infrastructure bottlenecks, and natural disaster response—along with a worrisome divisiveness tearing at the fabric of society and military conflicts threatening to erupt into global wars. The gravity of this new wave of threats is well beyond the scope of firms, industry, and the private sector. The point of this book is to explain how and why entrepreneurship and innovation will still, perhaps more than ever, deliver the solutions to the most pressing problems that threaten society. However, just looking to the private sector for entrepreneurship and innovation will not suffice. Rather, resolving the existential crises and challenges threatening society will require entrepreneurship and innovation in the public sector as well.

The public sector, including government and entities controlled by the government, is not where people have generally looked for dashing entrepreneurs to unleash bold innovations. President Ronald R. Reagan used to quip, "I'm from the government, and I'm here to help," and the audience would invariably laugh. They got the joke.

Only today it is no joke. If the public sector is not able to harness the creativity and inspiration inherent in entrepreneurship that provides the catalyst for breathtaking new innovations, society may succumb to the overwhelming challenges posed by the looming social, political, environmental, and economic crises. In fact, as this book will make clear, the successful negotiation from the third to the fourth industrial era, ushered in by computational and digital technologies, was attributable not just to the entrepreneurial and innovative power of the private sector but also the bold thinking and initiatives found in the public sector as well.

The writer Mark Twain once observed about Richard Wagner's music, "It's better than it sounds." When it comes to entrepreneurship and innovation in the public sector, this book documents that they, too, have been better than they sound. Even more importantly, this book makes it clear that to address the challenges posed by the daunting threats confronting contemporary society, public sector entrepreneurship and innovation need to rise to new levels, to be better than they have been. The promise of the public sector is to deliver the requisite entrepreneurship spawning a new era of breathtaking innovations to tackle the pressing issues burdening our society.

Acknowledgments

We thank James Cook, senior editor for economics, business and finance at Oxford University Press; Emily Mackenzie Benitez, the senior project editor; and Mhairi Bennett, the editorial manager, for their strong support and helpful guidance. We also thank the external reviewers for their thoughtful suggestions and guidance in preparing this book manuscript. Additionally, we are grateful to a plethora of partners and organizations in the public sector, spanning both governments and nonprofit organizations, across a broad spectrum of international, national, and local contexts, for sharing their experiences, frustrations, and aspirations with us. Without their own perspectives from the trenches on the ground, this book would have been a sterile exercise in theory, devoid of the blood, sweat, and tears that distinguishes the real from the imagined.

Writing a book is a daunting task. Wendy Chen is profoundly grateful to her family for their unwavering support, encouragement, and understanding, allowing her to continue writing relentlessly throughout the challenging yet rewarding journey of pregnancy and welcoming her and her husband's newborn into the world. Finally, it is our own mentors and colleagues who have impressed and inspired us with the requisite scholarly discipline and research rigor, to take on this task of what many would consider to be an oxymoron: entrepreneurship and innovation in the public sector.

List of Acronyms

AI	artificial intelligence
ARPA-E	Advanced Research Projects Agency-Energy
CIO	chief innovation officer
CCI	Córdoba Smart City
DED	Dubai Economic Department
DOD	Department of Defense
DOE	Department of Energy
EHR	electronic health records
EPA	Environmental Protection Agency
EU	European Union
FAA	Federal Aviation Administration
FbF	forecast-based financing
FFRDC	Federally Funded Research and Development Centers
FSRDC	Federal Statistical Research Data Centers
HITECH	Health Information Technology for Economic Clinical Health
ICT	information communication technologies
IIA	Israel Innovation Authority
IoT	Internet of Things
IPO	initial public offering
IRS	Internal Revenue Service
ISCF	Industrial Strategy Challenge Fund
MBDA	Minority Business Development Agency
NGO	nongovernmental organization
NIH	National Institutes of Health
NPM	new public management
NSF	National Science Foundation
OGP	Open Government Partnership
PII	personal identifiable informaiton
PPP	public–private partnership
R&D	research and development
SBIR	Small Business Innovation Research
SIB	smart impact bonds
SOP	standard operating procedures
STEP	Specialized Training and Employment Programme
STTR	Small Business Technology Transfer
TIA	Technology Innovation Agency
USDA	United States Department of Agriculture

Chapter 1
Introduction

Bold entrepreneurs and dazzling innovations have riveted the attention of the public (Audretsch et al., 2020; Patriotta & Siegel, 2019). They generate new markets, make new products, provide new services, lead to process efficiency, create massive economic growth for society, and build strong regional and international competitiveness. Nevertheless, if you ask anyone, regardless of age or occupation, to name an entrepreneur or an entrepreneurial organization, their response will invariably be the likes of Apple's Steve Jobs, Microsoft's Bill Gates, Amazon's Jeff Bezos, Tesla's Elon Musk, or Facebook's Mark Zuckerberg.

What do all these responses have in common? They all refer to the private sector. We all know that in order for the private sector to compete, they have to innovate. Whether it is the entrepreneur, organization, or innovative product or service, the realm of innovation and entrepreneurship is seemingly restricted to private business or individuals. However, lost in the enthusiasm and urgency of both thought leaders in business and policy as well as scholars across multiple disciplines, to embrace, understand and harness the forces of entrepreneurship and innovation, a key actor or player has been overlooked—the public sector.

The public sector is run by governments and government agencies on all levels including local, territorial, state, or national governments. Different from the other sectors, agencies and organizations of the public sector are responsible for creating regulations and policies that directly impact economy and our daily life, providing vital services such as public transit, police, public education for the public, and defense.

First, the public sector contributes a significant amount to the GDP (about 20%–30%) of developed countries (Arundel et al., 2019), playing a crucial role in economic growth. For instance, one major contribution of the public sector lies in infrastructure development that provides a solid foundation for all economic activities to thrive. According to a study by Aschauer (1989), every one percent increase in public infrastructure spending can

Innovation and Entrepreneurship in the Public Sector. Wendy D. Chen and David B. Audretsch, Oxford University Press. © Oxford University Press (2025). DOI: 10.1093/9780197679470.003.0001

lead to a 0.3% increase in the long-run economic output. These infrastructure investments can include developments in energy facilities, heavy engineering, petroleum and gas, transportation networks, high-tech communication systems, and public utilities. In addition, governments invest in people in the form of education and human capital, leading to long-term positive effects on economic growth. It is found that cognitive skills, measured through international standardized tests, have a consistently positive impact on GDP (Hanushek & Woessmann, 2012). Providing quality public education enables the public sector to prepare individuals with the necessary skills and knowledge to participate more effectively in the labor market in the future.

Similarly, government spending on research and development is another long-term investment that facilitates technological advancement and innovation, both of which are crucial drivers of economic growth. In the US, government agencies like the National Science Foundation often provide public research institutions and universities with government funding to conduct cutting-edge research, which has greatly increased industrial productivity growth.

Another way in which the public sector contributes to the greater economy is perhaps the most direct way—by facilitating employment for public services. Other than providing public education, employment, healthcare, national security, and so on that contributes to economic growth, the public sector also creates a regulatory system that protects consumers and establishes a more stable environment for the market to grow (Djankov et al., 2002; Stiglitz, 2000).

But how did such a significant part of our lives, the public sector, end up seeming out of place if it shares the same sentence with term "innovation"? One of the reasons lies in that unlike the private sector, the public sector lacks competition (Bekkers et al., 2011). We might not even think the public sector should be innovative. In fact, the role of the public sector is viewed exclusively as at best an enabler of, or at worst, an impediment to private sector innovation and entrepreneurship, not as a bona fide actor or source of that innovative and entrepreneurial activity (Jacknis, 2011; Karlson et al., 2021).

Even as the new research fields of entrepreneurship and innovation responded decisively in creating frameworks providing an analytical lens to examine entrepreneurial and innovative activity in the private sector, no analogous frameworks have been developed for public sector entrepreneurship and innovation. An examination of the leading journals and books in these fields reveals that the burgeoning literature, while incorporating the critical role played by government policy, has simply overlooked innovation and entrepreneurship in the public sector context (Audretsch et al., 2020).

The omission of the public sector from the analysis of entrepreneurship and innovation matters. First, extant literature has generally identified entrepreneurship and innovation as crucial drivers of prosperity and economic performance. Neglecting what may be an important source and type of entrepreneurial and innovative activity clouds both the full understanding of entrepreneurship and innovation as well as society to attain its potential. Even a private sector that delivers a vibrant innovative and entrepreneurial contribution to the economy and society may be limited by the absence of a concomitant complementary degree of entrepreneurship and innovation in the public sector context. Additionally, many government agencies across the globe have created Chief Innovation Officer roles indicating that the public sector has started to realize the importance and necessity of innovation and entrepreneurship by the sector. However, the public knows little about this role.

Why should the public sector be innovative? The public sector is often criticized as the major reason for failure in modern society. As we all know, the sector faces new challenges every day, especially over recent years when the world has been severely impacted by the global pandemic, economic downturn, and various large wicked social issues. The changing demographics in all societies due to globalization and aging has also left an indelible impact the nature and scope of public demands. Governments must cope with and respond to these challenges in a timely manner, which has made public innovation and entrepreneurship imperative and critical. They must continuously look for new techniques to innovate.

In the meantime, advancements in technology—such as AI-driven tools, the convenience of online communication, and the ease of mobile shopping—have also raised our expectations for the efficiency and quality of public service delivery. While these new trends undoubtedly bring out challenges, they also present an opportunity for the public sector to take advantage of for innovation so that it can keep up with the pace of change and stay ahead of it. Many of these problems are relatively new but complex, including digital privacy, cybersecurity, an aging population, failed educational systems, and mental health and well-being, which requires alignment between the public sector and other actors to tackle together.

Therefore, traditional methods and regulation procedures that the public sector has long relied on may no longer work. Equally important, without new approaches to addressing these wicked issues, trust and confidence from the public can no longer be guaranteed. According to the Pew Research Center, public trust in the US government has plummeted—from about 75% in 1958 to just 22% in 2024 –with only 2% of Americans saying they trust the government "just about always" and 21% "most of the time".[1] The same downward trend is also found in other Organization for Economic Co-operation and Development countries.[2,3]

More importantly, the public sector is the bellwether of society. As it is responsible for serving citizens and leading policy, government agencies essentially set the tone and act as a role model for the public. If these core establishment bodies embrace and exemplify principles of innovation, entrepreneurship, and other forward-thinking reforms, they could help cultivate a more innovative and entrepreneurial culture. With supportive policies promoting fresh ideas and supporting problem-solving skills, private individuals and businesses would gain greater confidence to take risks in their own innovative endeavors.

But one might ask—is it possible for the public sector to be innovative? Closer inspection from history or even contemporary society raises this puzzling question—what about public innovations such as Greek democracy, Roman legal system, and ancient China's decentralized system of government? Or Vannevar Bush, whose untiring campaign enabled harnessing science for economic, social, and national goals? Or entrepreneurial public organizations, such as Research Triangle Park, which ultimately transformed a region from among the poorest in the United States to one of its most prosperous? The invention of postage stamps, the building of canals, and the formation of national parks were also all innovative ideas championed by public entrepreneurs.

[1] Pew Research Center, 2024. "Public Trust in Government: 1958-2024". https://www.pewresearch.org/politics/2024/06/24/public-trust-in-government-1958-2024/.

[2] Partnership for Public Service. 2022. "How trust in the U.S. government compares with trust in government around the world". https://ourpublicservice.org/blog/how-trust-in-the-u-s-government-compares-with-trust-in-government-around-the-world/.

[3] https://www2.deloitte.com/ie/en/pages/public-sector/articles/govlab-blog/why-should-gov-public-service-innovate.html.

Admittedly, some previous works have discussed government innovation. However, their focus is predominantly on technological innovation. Even many governments share the same belief that innovation is equal to developing new technology. However, history tells us that public innovation is not limited to the adoption of technology. Nor should it be conflated with government spending, as some might argue. Rather, it is a mechanism of value creation that includes new product and service ideas, methods, strategies, and processes. Therefore, innovation does not only include the introduction of new novel products or services but also redesign or changes to the existing ones (Covin & Slevin, 1989). It involves overcoming old fashioned ways of thinking and embracing new ideas to better citizens' lives.[4]

Put plainly, entrepreneurship is creative destruction. Schumpeter (1942) famously attributed the rise of capitalism and new goods as well as new ways of more efficient mass production to innovation and entrepreneurship. He also pointed out that the key component of entrepreneurship lies in opportunity discovery and risk-taking. Every startup must be agile and adaptable to various unforeseen situations. That said, an innovative and entrepreneurial public sector is a first mover instead of an imitator, adopting new perspectives to identify social problems and taking calculated risks to develop bold solutions to ever-changing societal challenges, committing to new approaches to improving human lives, designing new tools to speed up processes, and identifying new solutions to work with different stakeholders. All parties associated with the public sector, including politicians, government agency leaders, and public employees, work together to create new value for the public. Public innovation is an entrepreneurial mindset to identify new opportunities and seek new resources to accomplish public goals and address grand societal challenges. Osborne and Gaebler (1992) pointed out that public sector actors need to "embrace innovation, engage in experimentation, and adopt a proactive and flexible approach to problem-solving." The sector should not only direct new programs to support innovation but create an environment for innovation. On the local and global level, innovation and entrepreneurship by the public sector aims to outperform competitors from other areas and countries to attract more skilled labor and increase economic development and improve life quality.

[4] https://www.oecd.org/gov/innovative-government/embracing-innovation-in-government.pdf.

Most of the time, when we hear about public innovation, it tends to mean the public sector driving innovation rather than being innovative itself. For instance, the US Small Business Innovation Research program has been lauded by many to represent the US government innovation. The program offers high-risk funding support including loans and grants to early-stage companies with beneficiaries including Apple, Intel, and Compaq. They suggest that if the US Defense Advanced Research Projects Agency, under the Department of Defense, had not invested in ARPANET in the 1960s, the internet would not have been born (Mazzucato, 2013). Similarly, many drugs are invented with the help of funding provided by the National Institutes of Health.

This book does not intend to dismiss government's role to simply a deep pocket that can provide finance. Rather, we argue that government itself must be entrepreneurial. We seek to debunk the conventional wisdom that the public sector cannot be innovative, or that innovation from the sector is only government spending. Also, public innovation is not limited to enabling private sector innovation by providing funding like a venture capitalist or investor or like a marketer to push these innovations. In fact, there are various important roles that the public sector plays (or can play) in innovation and entrepreneurship. For instance, developing a new political system that allows the mass population to voice their concerns and to be heard like the modern democratic system was politically innovative and risk-taking. The public sector can also play the role of a public entrepreneur through innovative policies. Building a public transportation system that especially benefits the poor is another example of the government creating new value for the public. Moreover, the public sector can be a supporter of its internal innovation. Various government labs such as Lab@OPM created by the US Office of Personnel Management are excellent examples.

In contrast to the existing research on public innovation, this book does not boast government innovation or contributes all innovations to the government. While it is important for the public sector to innovate, there is limited guidance for the public sector on how to innovate. *Innovation and Entrepreneurship in the Public Sector*, therefore, answers the call by investigating with an unbiased view and a global perspective: What is public innovation and entrepreneurship? Conversely, what is not public innovation and entrepreneurship? Should the public sector innovate? Can it innovate, and how to correctly innovate while mitigating risk? We use real-life examples and large data sources around the world to provide a new view of innovation and entrepreneurship in the public sector. We also provide actionable advice for the public sector to push innovation forward. Admittedly, there are various barriers and risks associated with public innovation. Nevertheless, despite risks and challenges of public innovation and entrepreneurship, we argue that with the right tools and approaches, it is possible for the public sector to lead and create new values for the world.

Just as the twin forces of entrepreneurship and innovation lifted the economy and society on the back of the private sector, igniting entrepreneurial and innovative activity in the public sector may be at least one of the keys to restoring economic and social prosperity in an era of insecurity, doubt, and increased divisiveness.

Chapter 2
Past Wisdom
History of Public Innovation and Entrepreneurship

So where did public innovation truly begin? To understand this origin story, we must first understand the origin of government. Today it is hard for us to imagine that there was once a time when human societies were assembling behind tribal leaders and roaming the earth for food. We've traded tents for towers, spears for satellites, and chieftains for commanders-in-chief. The shift from nomadic lifestyles to settled communities brought about new challenges related to resource allocation, conflict resolution, and social order. These challenges necessitated the establishment of more formalized systems of governance and called for more public innovation. Although in contemporary context government is not typically considered innovative, throughout human history across the world, governments have directly or indirectly impacted innovation and pushed human race forward.

Grassroots of Civilization

But how did we get from those humble origins of chieftains and tribes? Much of the shift away from hunter-gatherer societies and tribalism is attributable to the agricultural revolution, which brought about a fundamental transformation in human societies. As hunter-gatherer groups began to learn the ways of agriculture and settle in communities near fertile lands, their pursuit of food resources via a nomadic lifestyle was no longer required. Instead, they realigned their efforts to focus on cultivating crops and raising livestock.

This agricultural way of life led to several important developments that helped facilitate the emergence of complex social structures and eventual formation of governments. First, the concentration of population in these newly formed agricultural communities fostered the creation of centralized locations where people could congregate and exchange goods, knowledge, and ideas. These hubs cultivated increased interactions between different

Innovation and Entrepreneurship in the Public Sector. Wendy D. Chen and David B. Audretsch, Oxford University Press. © Oxford University Press (2025). DOI: 10.1093/9780197679470.003.0002

groups, helping to pave the way to impactful cultural exchanges, the spread of innovations, and the emergence of more complex social structures.

Additionally, as agriculture became increasingly important as the primary means of subsistence, communities began to shift their mindsets of how best to achieve their goals. One such way was through specialization in agricultural practices and industries. This division of labor led to the foundations on which we have built society today including the development of craftsmen, artisans, and other skilled workers who provided essential services to their communities. Over time, these specialized roles began to transform into more formalized positions within these primitive societal structures, serving as the foundation for new hierarchies and leadership configurations.

Moreover, with the advancements in agriculture, the storage and accumulation of surplus food resources became possible. Thanks to the stockpiles of food and resources, emerging leaders were able to begin consolidating power, effectively enabling greater control over the populace. In essence, they could leverage their control over food stores to ensure loyalty and support from their followers, further solidifying their positions within these complex sociopolitical structures. These types of power plays were some of the early strategies used in nascent government systems.

Ancient Powers and Power Structures: Mesopotamian Region

The word "government" means "to steer," with its roots in Greek and Latin. The first creators of a real government can be traced back to the ancient Mesopotamian region, which broadly includes modern day parts of Syria, Turkey, and Iraq. One group that resided in that area specifically were the Sumerians, dating back to around 5000 BCE with twelve city-states including Eridu, Nippur, Lagash, Kish, Ur, and the first true city, Uruk.[1] The Sumerians had over 3,000 gods, with each city being run by a king who claimed to represent one of these gods and operating more as a city-state rather than as one cohesive country or empire. These rulers were responsible for establishing and enforcing laws, collecting taxes, and maintaining order (Leick, 2001; Podany, 2013).

Eventually, one king triumphed above the rest, giving rise to Sumer as one of the first monarchies in the world. The Sumerian government was

[1] https://www.history.com/topics/ancient-middle-east/sumer.

a theocracy, meaning that the ruler was believed to be guided by divine authority. Each city-state in Sumer was surrounded by a wall and was identified based on their choice of local deity worship, with villages located just outside the walls.[2] They established villages and towns centered around their farming communities.

Sumerian society also exhibited a highly specialized workforce that helped set them apart from their neighbors and allowed their cities to flourish. Once they had developed a steady supply of food via irrigation systems and other advances in agriculture, the Sumerians became one of the first civilizations to utilize specialization in their society including merchants, rulers, artists, and government officials. This specialization afforded the Sumerians a way to develop skills and build the empire, serving as the foundation for what would later be recognized as the first public works program. This included dams, dikes, canals, and walls.

In the realm of ancient civilizations, the Sumerians are renowned for their groundbreaking achievements in various domains, particularly in science and art. Among these accomplishments, they are celebrated for pioneering the first systematized written language: cuneiform. This revolutionary innovation would significantly impact human communication and record-keeping for centuries to come.

The Sumerians are among the oldest and most renowned ancient civilizations because of their innovative contributions to an extensive variety of domains, most notably the arts and sciences. Among their numerous achievements is the invention of cuneiform, the earliest systematized written language. For centuries to come, the impact of this groundbreaking invention on human communication and record-keeping would be immense.

Other early examples of structured governance from around 3000 BCE can be found in ancient Egypt, the Indus Valley, and the Yellow River Civilization in China. These societies were also remarkably inventive when it came to creating colossal constructions, systems of irrigation, and city design. The construction of the Hanging Gardens of Babylon, the pyramids of Giza, and the Great Wall of China stand as testaments to their innovative spirit, which we will cover later in this chapter.

Ancient Egyptian society, much like that of Sumer, was characterized by a centralized political structure with monarchial rulers known as Pharaohs at

[2] https://www.history.com/topics/ancient-middle-east/sumer.

the helm of all decisions. These Pharaohs held two important roles in society as both temporal and spiritual leaders, effectively embodying the divine will of the gods in their governance and religious guidance for their people. The Pharaoh was regarded as a god-king, bestowing upon himself significant power that enabled him to shape laws and policies that permeated Egyptian society.

Pharaohs' divine nature in the eyes of the public extended beyond mere political authority. In fact, they were believed to have a direct connection with the heavens that enabled them to serve as intermediaries between their subjects and the gods, ensuring harmony and balance within the cosmos through their actions. This notion that Pharaohs were not just kings but actually living gods was deeply ingrained in Egyptian culture and mythology. As such, the religious components of Egyptian society were intricately woven into the political structures put in place, allowing for a great concentration of power within the hands of the Pharaoh.

The concept of the divine kingship had its roots deeply placed in Egyptian culture, which is traced back to early Egyptian dynastic times around 3100 BCE. The Pharaohs, as god-kings, were thought to possess the ability to maintain "Ma'at," the cosmic balance and order, through their rule. They performed various rituals and ceremonies to appease the gods and preserve Ma'at, reinforcing their divine role in Egyptian society (Assmann, 2001).

Furthermore, this belief that Pharaohs were closely aligned with the divine had a massive positive influence on the Egyptian state, leading to long periods of the stability and ultimately contributing to its survival for over 3,000 years. But an additional benefit of the divine status of Pharaohs was that it allowed for their rule to extend beyond themselves and to be passed down for generations, ensuring continuity of power and authority through the dynastic lineages (Kahn, 2005).

Political System Innovation

As civilization grew, so too did the needs of the governing and the governed. To that point, it would be hard to talk about government innovation without talking about the Greeks. Beginning back around 680 BCE and eventually reaching their golden age between 480 and 404 BCE (also referred to as the Age of Pericles by historians), the Greek government, particularly in the city-state of Athens, was known for its innovative approach to governance and democracy. This marked a significant departure from earlier forms of government that were more autocratic or hierarchical when power was held by a small group of elites or a single ruler (Herodotus, 1920).

Regarding Greek democracy, some have posited that the seeds of this revolutionary political system were sown from a combination of social, economic, and military factors (Finley, 1999). For instance, Athenian Solon suggested that in civil matters, no one was to remain neutral and must take a side, making it one of the first recorded solicitations for citizens to take a stance on a matter. This development came on the heels of a struggle between the aristocracy and the poor at that time. The Solonian Reforms of 594 BCE introduced greater political autonomy and social equality by transforming poor Athenian farmers who were previously under serfdom by the rich landowners into small landowners (Schwuchow & Tridimas, 2022). This sets the stage for further democratic developments and innovations.

The engine that kept the Greek democracy running was the Ecclesia, which was an Assembly of all free adult males to vote and deliberate on state affairs. Individuals argued their cases and, in the end, actions were passed via a majority vote. The system was revolutionary, as previously only theocracies and despots had been utilized as a form of rule over a people. However, the system did have its flaws as unbridled control over individuals at that time more closely resembled tyranny than liberty as no systems of checks and balances were put in place to protect citizens (Frank, 2019).

Another innovative measure implemented by the Greek government was the establishment of the rule of law. The Greeks held to the notion that the law ought to be based on objective tenets rather than the capricious judgments of individuals or organizations, and that it ought to apply uniformly to all citizens. This new approach made it possible to administer justice in a way that was predictable and unbiased. The Greeks understood that by preserving citizens' rights while providing them certainty that the law would be administered fairly and equitably, this idea would contribute to the preservation of a stable society (Canevaro, 2017).

Subsequently, the Romans built upon the Greeks' foundations. With the establishment of the Roman Republic in 509 BCE, representational features of administration were added, with elected officials standing in for the interests of the people. The new structure aimed to address some of the shortcomings of Greek democracy and achieve a balance of power among the several parts of the government. Eventually, subsequent democratic systems would be built upon the foundation of this new representative government.

Another example of Roman government innovation was their evolution of the Greek rule of law. Compared to the Greeks who placed an emphasis on the transparency and accessibility of objective legal principles, the Romans held that a more pragmatic and hierarchical approach to their legal structure might improve upon the Greek's system. Roman jurists developed a comprehensive body of written legal precedents, known as *ius gentium*, which provided guidance for judges in interpreting and applying the law (and this system for interpreting laws is still applied today). This system enabled greater consistency and predictability, but it also introduced an element of bureaucracy and legal expertise that diverged from the more egalitarian Greek philosophy. Similar to the Greeks, the hope was that implementing the rule of law would help bring about a more stable and peaceful society.[3]

While many in the West would be familiar with the Greek and Roman contributions to government, in the East, the ancient Chinese exhibited many forms of public innovation. The Zhou Dynasty (1046–256 BCE) in ancient China was one of the first systems to experiment with the notion of a decentralized system of government, in which power was divided between the central government and local authorities. Although the king served as the central figurehead, actual governance was carried out by the nobles and their bureaucratic officials. This system, which was known as the feudal system, allowed the Zhou Dynasty to effectively govern a sprawling and diverse territory by delegating some decision-making powers to local leaders (Zhou Li, i.e., "The Rite of Zhou").

Later, the Tang Dynasty (618–907 CE) in China began experimenting with a new political system innovation that began placing heavy emphasis on meritocracy to help develop a more equal and just society. During this time, the Tang recognized the importance of providing pathways for people to improve their life quality and implemented imperial examinations as the primary means of recruiting government officials. This was unique in the sense that these exams were based on people's knowledge and abilities as opposed to their noble birth or connections. The exams were open to all, regardless of social background, and covered a wide range of subjects, including Confucian classics, poetry, calligraphy, mathematics, and astronomy. It was believed that well-rounded individuals would make better public servants.

Because the Tang Dynasty placed such a heavy emphasis on meritocracy, the government began attracting highly talented individuals to government

[3] https://law.gwu.libguides.com/romanlaw.

positions, resulting in an exceptionally capable and competent bureaucracy. This resulted in a flourishing dynasty that experienced great prosperity, cultural achievements, and military strength. The Tang civil service system became a foundational tool for later Chinese dynasties and influenced the development of meritocratic systems in other parts of East Asia, including Korea and Vietnam.

The Roman Republic during its late period (133–27 BCE) was a stark contrast from the opportunities provided in the Tang Dynasty. Although the early Roman Republic relied on a combination of military service and public speaking abilities to obtain political positions, personal connections were still required for many political offices. As Rome grew in power and influence, the problem only became exacerbated and noble birth and family connections increasingly became the primary factor in securing high positions. This eventually led to an increasingly oligarchic system where power and wealth became consolidated among a small group of elites, leading to rampant corruption, debt, and political instability (Hudson, 2023).

Rome's shift to an oligarchic system proved to be a burden too great for the system to shoulder and eventually was one of the factors that toppled the empire. Relying solely on the aristocratic class for leadership positions while neglecting other potential talent from different social classes ultimately led to a harsh lesson about the consequences of allowing innovations to fail.

Seeking to learn from some of these lessons, the founding of the United States government in 1787 was a groundbreaking moment in world history. It was a truly unique event in the sense that it marked a radical departure from all of the traditional government systems that prevailed across the rest of the globe. Unlike the traditional government forms at that time, including monarchies, absolute rule, and other power structures that had existed in antiquity, the US Founding Fathers sought to tie the hands of government with the crafting of the US Constitution while providing the American people with the key to the restraints. This revolutionary concept of having a limited government that operated under the people instead of above them marked a pivotal point for a new governing structure that favored democratic self-rule and individual liberties, placing the United States in a league of its own at the time.

Of course, much of the reason behind this could be found in the beliefs of the Founding Fathers themselves that set us on the road to success. Thomas Jefferson's belief in limited government and individual liberties helped to drastically shape a culture that defied being placed under absolute rule. His belief in the power of education, enshrined in the establishment of the

University of Virginia, fostered a culture of learning and intellectual curiosity. James Madison drafted the influential Virginia Plan, which made the case to create a strong central government with expanded powers and influenced the final version of the US Constitution. George Washington set an essential example for the role of the president as a national unifier and symbolic leader. Then, of course, at the conclusion of the Revolutionary War, George Washington refused to become king and even refused a third term, setting a precedent for future presidency. These extraordinary individuals paved the way for future leaders, igniting the spirit of leaders worldwide and shaping the systems that have been iterated and expanded on today.

Meanwhile, on the other side of the Atlantic, things were drastically different. In Europe, most countries were still ruled by powerful monarchs who held absolute authority over their subjects and practiced hereditary rule. Instead of following these footsteps, American revolutionaries drew upon the ancient Greek and Roman republics as models for self-governance. Admittedly, these systems had significant flaws, such as mob rule and the tyranny of the majority. To counteract these weaknesses, the US Constitution was crafted in such a way that balance was always considered. First, there was an intricate balance between individual rights and collective responsibilities to ensure individuals had their freedoms and individual liberty while still being part of a cohesive country. Additionally, checks and balances were put in place to prevent the newly created executive, legislative, or judicial branches from overpowering the other.

Perhaps one of the largest deviations from nations before it and the most revolutionary aspects of the new government was the Bill of Rights, which was added to the Constitution in 1791 to safeguard American citizens from the government and to guarantee their individual liberties. This charter of "God-given" freedoms included the protection of speech, assembly, press, religion, and the right to bear arms, among others. These protections were unprecedented in their scope and depth, as no other government up until that point had offered such a robust and comprehensive list of guarantees for individual rights. By prioritizing the rights of the individual over the self-interests of their new government, the Founding Fathers showed the rest of the world that the preservation of dignity and autonomy superseded the Old World's values of ledging allegiance to a king and collectivism. This revolutionary approach to governance went on to profoundly shape the course of American history and inspire countless movements for freedom and democracy around the world.

Public Management Innovation

Public innovation can take many forms and has evolved within the verticals of multiple paradigms. Another form of public innovation that has manifested itself is public management innovation. Throughout human history, many governments significantly innovated government management, which has enabled the government to enhance its efficiency and effectiveness and has led to modern governance. This public management innovation has been both internal and external facing, with gains being made in terms of government workers and how they organize themselves as well as offering new standards and improvements in the public's lives.

One such example of this public management innovation can be found in the Qin Dynasty (221–206 BCE) in ancient China. The Qin Dynasty (221–206 BCE) is renowned for its significant innovations in public management and administrative reforms, which produced a drastically different political landscape for China at the time and planted the seeds for the development of a centralized imperial bureaucracy. In contrast to the precursory Chinese dynasties, which were distinguished by their feudalism, decentralization, and fragmentation, the Qin Dynasty implemented a series of innovative measures designed to create an efficient and unified administrative system.

Although the Qin Dynasty was short-lived, there were multiple benefits the dynasty brought that helped to improve the management of China. Some of these improvements included standardization of weights and measures as well as currency. These management improvements helped to promote economic and social cohesion throughout the empire and made it easier for the government to administer and control the population (*Shi ji*, "The Basic Annals of the First Emperor of Qin"). Similarly, the Qin Dynasty also implemented the top-down management structure that allowed for more streamlined communication and resource distribution.

Furthermore, Shang Yang's transformative reforms during the Qin Dynasty addressed a chaotic administration where accurate population records were scarce, hampering effective governance and resource allocation. This problem gave rise to the Household Registration System, a revolutionary concept that at the time and the predecessor of today's Hukou system in Mainland China. This innovative structure organized families into manageable units of five ("Wu") and ten ("Shi"), revolutionizing taxation and conscription processes and fortifying social management. Special county or prefectural officials were tasked with validating the household population every three years. This structure enabled meticulous tracking of details such as conscription and migration regulation. The Qin advancements established a cornerstone for China's imperial bureaucracy and beyond, lasting over 2,000 years as one of the most enduring and impactful political institutions in world history.[4]

The Ottoman Empire (1299–1922) was another civilization that made great strides in the ways of its approach to public management and administrative reforms, leading to new ideas and transformations that spread across the Middle East and Europe during the late Middle Ages and early modern period. Compared to the European feudal system dominated by monarchies and decentralized power structures in place at that time, the Ottoman system could be described as calculated and intentional. Their public management was characterized by its attention to making the bureaucracy run as efficiently as possible, while maintaining centralized authority. In the meantime, the Ottoman system blended many different cultures into one, drawing on influences from Islamic, Christian, and Jewish traditions (Ihsanoglu, 2024). Furthermore, much of the system's success favored meritocracy during a time when much of Europe was still favoring social hierarchy and family connections.

One such notable innovation in Ottoman public management was the creation of a professionalized bureaucracy, comprised of various departments or councils responsible for maintaining order, collecting taxes, providing public services, and administering justice. The Ottoman Imperial Council, or Divan, was structured in such a way that workers were grouped based on function and operated under the supervision of a central authority, leading to improved consistency and efficiency in administration (Yilmaz, 2006). Moreover, the Ottoman government was known for employing a large number of non-Muslims, including Christians, Jews, and Armenians. These individuals were frequently placed in key positions throughout the bureaucracy, reflecting the Ottomans' openness to diverse talent and expertise.

Another significant innovation was the development of a complex system of taxation known as the Timar system (Haque, 1976). Different from the Roman system *ager publicus*, which granted soldiers frontier land upon completion of their military terms or for exemplary achievements, and later the *latifundia*, which granted large swaths of public land to nobles

[4] https://pepchina.com/what-was-the-household-registration-system-in-ancient-china/.

and military officers, the Timar system represented a more systematic and efficient method to granting land to military officers.

Under this system, tax-free land grants were provided to military officers in exchange for their service, providing them with both a source of income and an incentive to defend the empire's borders. The system was widely successful and provided benefits both to the military personnel as well as the empire. First, these grants gave military personnel a place to live and raise their family. The grants were renewable and acted as an inheritance that could be passed down for generations, providing them with a stable source of income while maintaining their loyalty to the empire.

Second, the system also had multiple benefits for the empire. The Timar system ensured that the military remained well-funded and motivated, enabling the Ottomans to control their vast territories and expand their borders. Unlike the Roman Republic's ad hoc approach to providing land to their soldiers and military officers, which had potential to lead to the concentration of power and wealth, the Ottoman Timar system provided means for a more equitable distribution of resources among military personnel while still sustaining the overall efficiency and effectiveness of the empire's military apparatus.

Compared to Europe at the time, where most people were beholden to the whims of the crown under feudal monarchies and religious institutions, the Ottoman model to public management set itself apart by emphasizing efficiency, centralized authority, and a focus on meritocracy. While European kingdoms relied on decentralized power structures and a patchwork of local jurisdictions to carry out the wills of those at the top of these feudal systems, the Ottomans incorporated measures in their administrative system to ensure their effective communication, coordination, and control across their vast territory. The Ottoman innovations not only shaped the development of the Middle East but also impacted their European neighbors in terms of political thought, providing inspiration for later reforms during the Enlightenment period.

Innovation in Public Infrastructure Development and Policies

Public innovation also included various forms of public works projects that enabled the expansion of national infrastructure. These projects included the building of roads for the exchange of resources and ideas, dams for controlling the flow of water, and walls to defend the country from external threats.

The Great Wall

Upon mention of defensive walls, the Great Wall of China is likely to come to mind. Stretching over 13,000 miles (21,196 kilometers) from east to west across northern China, is an iconic representation of ancient Chinese culture. Under China's first emperor Qin Shi Huang, the Wall's construction spanned over 2,000 years beginning in the late Warring States Period (475–221 BCE), and up until the Ming Dynasty (1368–1644 CE), undergoing various improvements and additions over the course of several dynasties. Its primary intent was to keep numerous nomadic groups, especially the Manchus and Mongols, from invading Chinese territory along its northern boundaries.[5]

During his time in power (221–210 BCE), Qin Shi Huang ordered the walls, which originally began as several isolated walls, to be linked into one large defensive construction. However, significant efforts to bolster and extend the wall were not made until the Han Dynasty (206 BCE–220 CE). Although experts debate regarding how much it cost to build and maintain the Great Wall—estimates range from $35 million to over $600 billion in today's US dollars—it is undeniable that the wall represented a remarkable example of massive public ingenuity.

Beyond building walls, multiple other projects were carried out in ancient China. One notable feat of engineering was completed during this period with the building of the Grand Canal. Although its origins may be dated to the Sui Dynasty (580–618), it experienced tremendous growth and transformation during the Warring States Period (475–221 BCE) and the succeeding dynasties. The Grand Canal was essential in enabling the flow of commodities between the central and northern areas, including grain, salt, and lumber. It also provided military leaders with an essential channel of communication, allowing them to quickly transmit orders and communications across the canal.[6]

[5] https://whc.unesco.org/en/list/438.
[6] Ibid.

Roman Aqueducts

With the same theme of controlling and delivering water, the Roman aqueducts were another notable innovative public infrastructure system that aided the Roman empire and allowed it to flourish. Beginning around 312 BCE in Rome itself and eventually reaching over 200 aqueducts spanning over 300 miles across the Roman Empire, the system was an engineering feat that was truly groundbreaking for its time.[7]

The unique trait of the Roman aqueducts was their use of gravity as the mechanism to allow water to flow across long distances. This was accomplished by building them with a slight slope incorporated into them that took impressive engineering skills to calculate and the use of durable materials such as stone and concrete to reach their required height, sometimes reaching over 60 feet to accomplish a steep enough slope to keep the water flowing. To account for difficult terrain, siphons were utilized to channel water across valleys while channels brought water across rivers. Utilizing these methods, the Romans were able to successfully transport water from their sources in the mountains dozens of miles away to areas that otherwise would not have had access to fresh water (Deming, 2020).

No other civilization had the engineering know-how and technological proficiency to build a system of such vast proportions. For most other civilizations, water for most ancient settlements came from nearby springs, rivers, or wells. But as Rome expanded, so too did its thirst for more water. To accommodate its citizens, Rome's built additional aqueducts capable of delivering enormous volumes of water to its residences, baths, fountains, and other locations. Thanks to their ingenuity in solving one of the most basic needs, Rome was able to expand further and more rapidly than its rival nations at the time.

National Parks and Conservation

In more modern times, the establishment of national parks under the Theodore Roosevelt administration was another creative endeavor completed in the United States. Under President Theodore Roosevelt's careful guidance from 1901 to 1909, the United States National Park System was

[7] https://education.nationalgeographic.org/resource/roman-aqueducts/.

launched, marking a historical shift in federal lands management and conservation (Brinkley, 2009). Roosevelt, who considered himself to be an avid lover of the outdoors, was not the first to advocate for government protection of public lands against commercial exploitation, with others including George Perkins Marsh and Grover Cleveland (Clark & Foster, 2002; Taylor, 2016). Roosevelt's measures, however, resulted in the designation of national parks, forests, and monuments covering nearly 230 million acres of public lands (Brinkley, 2009).

The nineteenth and early twentieth centuries were uniquely characterized by multiple factors, making this public innovation a product of its time. One of these factors was the fear of a loss of national treasures and wilderness due to industrialization and settlement of the West (Taylor, 2016). The establishment of Yellowstone National Park in 1872 set an early precedent becoming the first national park, but large swaths of US territory remained unprotected (Sellars, 1997). Roosevelt, a native New Yorker who spent much of his life attempting to prove himself after battling illness as a child, was enamored by the range life and heavily influenced by his experiences ranging the Dakota Badlands as a young man (McCullough 2001; Watts, 2005). This led to Roosevelt having a soft spot for the West and cherishing conservation and outdoor recreation. These priorities showed through in his presidency as evidenced by his leadership in protecting lands and resources from monopoly and destruction (Brinkley, 2009).

Roosevelt established the US Forest Service in 1905 to protect and manage the forests that spanned the country. The Antiquities Act in 1906 allowed presidents to act quickly when they deemed a site or artifact with historic or scientific interest worthy of being declared a National Monument (Sellars, 1997; Watts, 2005). His efforts led to the designation of over 150 million acres of new forest reserves, serving as a prime example for other governments seeking to preserve their natural wonders (Brinkley, 2009).

Public Education

Another important area for public innovation is the promotion of education. Today, we take schools for granted. But for much of history, schools and the prioritization of scientific advancements have witnessed their own evolutionary process. The Han Dynasty in China (202 BCE–220 CE) gave rise to major advances in education and state-sponsored schools. Believing in that education should be accessible to all, education shifted from being reserved for aristocratic elites to becoming accessible to the masses (Bai, 2005). It was with this belief in mind that the Imperial Academy was established by the Han court to train civil servants in Confucian classics, law, math, archery, and horsemanship. This professional school was a first in its time, setting a precedent for national academies across East Asia.

With the first state-run school system being established in 3 CE, local state-run schools also appeared across the rest of China to teach writing and arithmetic to the children (Bai, 2005). To support their education, the government provided resources to these localities, including the schools, teachers, and textbooks to help develop the new generation capable of leading the nation. The students who wished to advance and become government officials could attend the Han Taixue, or Imperial Academy. It was here that students could prepare for the famous civil service exams, which provided them with a pathway of upward mobility through meritocratic recognition. This system proved to be an innovative, systematic effort that helped to provide public education on a society-wide scale. It was this education and examination system that the Tang Dynasty later expanded upon.

Concurrently in the West, education remained private, decentralized, and accessible only to a handful select few. Education was much less formal as official schools did not exist in ancient Greece or Rome (Bonner, 2012). Instead, rich families hired private tutors to teach their children, while the poor received no education. A few centuries later in Europe, monastery schools emerged to provide education to clergy, while it was still a small, privileged group who were able to attend these schools (Gasman, 1971; Lawson & Silver, 2013). In this sense, China led the world in promoting schooling for commoners and bureaucratic aims.

While on the topic of education, in the US, the Morrill Act of 1862 was a revolutionary federal policy that enabled the creation of land grant universities in the United States. Signed into law by President Abraham Lincoln, this act granted federal lands to states to sell to fund public colleges specializing in agriculture, science, and engineering.[8]

The first land grant institution established was Kansas State University in 1863 under the Morrill Act provisions, shortly after being admitted to the

[8] https://www.aplu.org/wp-content/uploads/land-grant-but-unequal-state-one-to-one-match-funding-for-1890-land-grant-universities.pdf.

US in 1861. The Universities of Vermont and Maine were also among the first created after the act passed. Over the next five years, dozens more land grant colleges opened across the country.

These schools were innovative because they made higher education accessible to the working class in fields with practical applications for a rapidly industrializing nation. Although it was in America, traditional higher education was still reserved for classical studies geared for the elite. But the Morrill Act enabled new universities that focused on applied sciences, mechanical arts, and agriculture (Nevins, 1962).

Land grants colleges also spearheaded new academic programs that had not yet existed, from veterinary medicine to engineering that became standards nationwide. These schools helped to contribute to the United States' competitive advantage and helped place the country as a global scientific leader. The ingenuity of the Morrill Act made higher education relevant and available to the masses.

Public Innovation in Supporting New Science

Innovation builds upon itself, known as cumulative innovation. The basic idea is that each new innovation or advancement enables further innovations down the road. There is a cumulative effect where technological progress builds on itself, as each step makes the next step possible. Importantly, innovation accelerates as progress begets progress, and new innovations open new pathways to further innovation (Murray, 2002).

One time period exemplifying this cumulation was the late eighteenth and early nineteenth centuries in the United States. It was during this time that the country saw massive growth in manufacturing and industry, known as the Industrial Revolution. Much of this growth and the improvements people experienced were enabled and accelerated by supportive policies and investments from the federal government.

Although we covered infrastructure before, the importance of the infrastructure improvements at this time and its impact on scientific advancements could not be underscored enough. The government funded canals, roads, steamboats, and especially railroads through land grants and subsidies (Chandler, 1977). The transcontinental railroad system constructed between 1863 and 1869 opened national markets for trade and connected industrial hubs (Stover, 1961). Through this funding, new advancements in technology exploded within the companies that provided the corresponding products and services.

It was during this time that many new patents were filed every day for the inventions that were products of cumulative innovation. The US Patent Office was established in 1802, granting inventors protection for their innovative creations (Khan, 2005). This was an example of public innovation that protected innovation. It was this assurance that helped to incentivize inventors to advance innovation and technology development across industries like transportation, chemistry, and electricity. Patents tripled between 1850 and 1860 as inventors were driven to create and profit from their ideas (Khan, 2005).

Federal investments in science and technology research also catalyzed progress. The newly created land grant colleges that were established through the Morrill Acts of 1862 and 1890 focused on teaching pragmatic skills in practical science, engineering, and agriculture (Williams, 1991). Meanwhile, government armories and labs conducted R&D that was transferred to arms contractors and manufacturers while Americans were eager to be part of the new innovation landscape (Ames & Rosenberg, 1968; Morris, 2012; Trebilcock, 1969). These knowledge transfers powered advances across a plethora of industries.

Meanwhile, the government has also paid for the advancement of sciences directly through grants as well. The Ottoman Empire saw the emergence of state-sponsored scientific grants in the eighteenth century under Sultan Ahmed III, as part of the Empire's broader Tulip Era reforms (1718–1730). Ahmed III set up new royal academies and observatories to aid in the advancement of science and technology (Ihsanoglu, 2024). These institutes received imperial funding and stipends, which they used to pay for research.

One of the recipients of such grants was Ibrahim Muteferrika. In 1727, the Ottoman scholar Ibrahim Muteferrika received direct funding and support from Sultan Ahmed III to establish the first printing press with Arabic movable type in Istanbul. This imperial decree granted Muteferrika the exclusive right to print nonreligious books deemed beneficial for society. After obtaining a fetva (religious approval) emphasizing the value of printing, Muteferrika published approximately sixteen titles. His press produced original scientific and technical works by Ottoman academics as well as translations of European texts. Four separate maps were also printed. Muteferrika's printing enterprise, funded by the sultan's decree, thus introduced vital secular literature and cartography that diverged from the predominant religious publications of the time.[9]

Perhaps one of the most famous early US examples of funding scientific research was Thomas Jefferson's request to Congress to fund the Lewis and Clark expedition. Jefferson asked for funding for the expedition, with Meriwether Lewis receiving $2,776.22 and William Clark receiving $2,113.74, and both men receiving 1,600 acres of land.[10] Although not formally declared a grant, it was a form of government funding that helped set the tone for scientific advancement during a period where many Americans were eager to explore the frontier.

The antebellum period saw more instances of the US government providing direct funding for scientific research through grants. Another one of the earliest examples was the scientific expedition to explore the Pacific Northwest territories authorized by Congress in 1838 (Dupree, 1986; Schwantes, 1996).[11] This expedition led by Charles Wilkes opened new discoveries to scientists like Titian Peale to advance the fields of botany, geology, and naturalism. Wilkes's works were published in 1845 allowing for the discoveries to make their way into future research.

Another pioneering use of science grants came through the United States Exploring Expedition of 1842. The expedition was organized by the Navy and led by Lt. Matthew Fontaine Maury and enabled Maury to produce wind and current charts for the Pacific and to collect data on astronomy and magnetism (Grady, 2015). Maury's publications greatly expanded scientific knowledge in the field of oceanography and demonstrated the value and potential of government-funded research.

New Organizations Supportive of Innovation

"World War II and the prewar Great Depression—an historic combination of two important epochs—caused a vast expansion of government agencies and services at the federal level."[12] The economic crisis of the 1930s followed

[9] https://memorients.com/articles/i%CC%87brahim-m%C3%BCteferrika-%E2%80%93-a-brief-portrait-of-life-and-works-of-an-early-modern-ottoman-intellectual.

[10] https://www.nps.gov/articles/wages-of-the-lewis-and-clark-expedition.htm#:~:text=Meriwether%20Lewis%20received%20a%20total,the%201%2C600%20acres%20of%20land.

[11] https://www.oregonencyclopedia.org/articles/united_states_exploring_expedition_1838_1842_/.

[12] https://www.nsf.gov/about/history/nsf50/nsf8816.jsp.

by US entry into World War II in 1941 dramatically increased the size and scope of federal government activities and services. Facing 25% unemployment during the Depression, President Franklin D. Roosevelt implemented the New Deal domestic programs to provide economic relief through new federal agencies (Fishback, 2014).

The war also pushed the US government into developing innovation policies leading to a plethora of newly funded programs for scientific research (Hooks, 1990). For instance, five years after the war, the National Science Foundation was born. It was created to "develop a national policy for the promotion of basic research and education in the mathematical, physical, medical, biological, engineering, and other sciences; to initiate and support basic scientific research in the sciences; and to evaluate the scientific research programs undertaken by agencies of the federal government.[13] Similarly, the war also greatly expanded the science and technology workforce, leading to the establishment of many federal labs started. These labs, sponsored by various government agencies, fill in the gaps between academic and profit-driven research and develop new products.[14]

Overall, the history of innovation in government is a complex and multifaceted topic that has been influenced by a variety of factors and has had a significant impact on the way governments operate and serve their citizens. These have taken multiple forms from the most fundamental foundations such as the political systems in which we operate to scientific enablement that shapes the world in which we live. One common thread that links all the history of government innovation, however, is its direct impact on each and every one of us.

[13] Ibid.

[14] https://insight.ieeeusa.org/articles/a-brief-history-of-the-u-s-federal-government-and-innovation-part-iii-1945-and-beyond/.

Chapter 3
New Frontiers
Digitalized Contemporary Public Innovation

In the modern world, the rapid development of digital technologies has impacted nearly every aspect of human life. Advancements in computing power, internet, and mobile connectivity have completely revolutionized how information is collected, shared, and used. The convenience that technologies have brought to people such as the ease of communication, collaboration, and accessing information have led to the rise of a new citizenship that is more acquainted with digital tools, especially among younger generations.

Notably, digital technologies have not only affected people's routine lives, but also significantly altered how governments make policies, improve daily operations, and engage with citizens. From big data analytics to e-governance to smart cities, governments have been able to utilize digital tools to predict crises much more accurately, to speed up public service, and to improve citizens' quality of life. Issues that once seemed intractable can now potentially be addressed through the innovative use of digital tools, vast amounts of data, and open government approaches.

In addition, because digital technologies also have brought up new challenges for society including the ease of spreading misinformation online, disrupting labor markets that especially hurt disadvantaged groups, and shifting economic landscapes, we need to have a government that is capable of adjusting and responding to new challenges and increased demands from the public (Acevedo & Dassen, 2016). This is where public innovation began in the digital era.

Governments across the globe are making increased use of digital tools to anticipate and address complicated issues (OECD, 2019). These tools speed up governments' decision-making in various ways on different important issues. As a result, governments have been increasing efforts to advocate and provide support for enhancing digital technology use in public service, which is also referred to as the digital government. The government

Innovation and Entrepreneurship in the Public Sector. Wendy D. Chen and David B. Audretsch, Oxford University Press. © Oxford University Press (2025). DOI: 10.1093/9780197679470.003.0003

of Peru provides an interesting example. In order to curb pollution, the government employs vultures in an innovative way to help tackle Lima's significant waste management challenges. Specifically, ten vultures have been fitted with GoPro cameras and GPS devices to help identify illegal dump sites around the capital city. Monitoring the vultures' movements via GPS allows for the real-time recording of their locations on a live public map, pinpointing the exact coordinates of impromptu dumping grounds.[1]

Open Access to Big Data

Governments worldwide have increasingly embraced open data policies in recent years, aiming to make nonsensitive public datasets freely accessible online. This shift underscores a growing recognition that data held by public entities represents a valuable national asset capable of fostering innovation, transparency, and economic opportunities when released openly with minimal usage restrictions.

With advancing technological capabilities enabling the processing of increasingly vast and intricate datasets, policymakers stand to gain enhanced insights and foresight, leading to more efficient, accountable, and inclusive e-services. This presents numerous opportunities, particularly in the pursuit of complex sustainable development goals. Transitioning from intuition-driven to data-centric policymaking is rapidly becoming not just a viable option but a strategic imperative, as highlighted in the United Nations Department of Economic and Social Affairs' "E-Government Survey 2020 Digital Government in the Decade of Action for Sustainable Development." In fact, countries providing open government data portals surged from 46 in 2014 (i.e., 24% of countries), to 153 in 2020 (i.e., 80% of countries) (Figure 3.1). Alongside this growth in open data portals, 59% of the member states surveyed reported to have open data policy in place, 62% provide metadata or a data dictionary, 57% accept requests from the public for new datasets, 52% offer guidance on using open data, and 49% engage in promotional activities such as data hackathons.[2]

[1] https://www.oecd.org/gov/innovative-government/embracing-innovation-in-government.pdf.

[2] https://digitallibrary.un.org/record/3884686?ln$=$en.

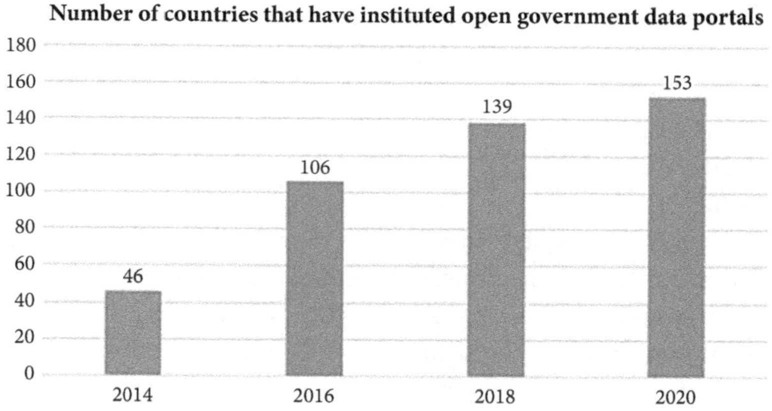

Figure 3.1 Number of countries with open government data portals

Source: United Nations-Department of Economic and Social Affairs Public Institutions, 2020, "E-Government Survey 2020 Digital Government in the Decade of Action for Sustainable Development."

In terms of open data adoption, the United Kingdom was one of the first movers to attempt to make use of open data with their launching of Data.gov.uk in 2010. This served as a milestone that set the stage for thousands of public datasets to be made available and established open data as a top policy priority (Janssen et al., 2012). This initiative produced substantial value, with early analyses suggesting an annual economic boost of around £1.8 billion/year and 6.8 billion/year of indirect benefits.[3] In a parallel move, the United States spearheaded open data initiatives by launching Data.gov in 2009, a significant step toward establishing open data as the default for nonsensitive government-held information. This early action served as a global model, showcasing the innovative potential of open data and setting the stage for subsequent initiatives, including the United Kingdom's Data.gov.uk.

Numerous other nations have followed suit and made their own attempts at developing comprehensive open data strategies to modernize and provide further transparency for their citizens. For instance, India implemented the National Data Sharing and Accessibility Policy in 2012 to harness open data across various sectors including agriculture, resources, and logistics.[4]

[3] https://assets.publishing.service.gov.uk/media/5a7ec24940f0b62305b82ff6/bis-14-946-open-data-strategy-2014-2016.pdf.

[4] https://dst.gov.in/national-data-sharing-and-accessibility-policy-0.

Beyond speaking only at a national level, entities like the Hong Kong government promote transparency and citizen engagement through initiatives like the Data.gov.hk open data portal (Conradie & Choenni, 2014). Similarly, in Africa, countries have begun to make use of open data portals and policies to address information disparities that impede equitable growth.[5]

Open data offers a plethora of benefits to countries willing to implement it. For one, it fosters the growth of startups and applications that utilize public transport schedules or location data to create innovative services (Nikiforova & Zuiderwijk, 2022; Troisi & Grimaldi, 2022). In various science domains, researchers can access datasets to more effectively tackle social, health, economic, and environmental challenges (Fischer et al., 2022; Pereira & Pereira, 2022). Additionally, the opening up of this data gives citizens the opportunity to glean insights into policy processes and governmental actions through analytics of open expenditures, contracts, and parliamentary voting records.

Despite its widespread adoption, open data implementation and the realization of its full value encounter common challenges. One of the primary concerns related to open data is how to protect citizens' privacy as more information becomes available to the public (Solymosi et al., 2023). Another overarching concern has been the quality of the data that is published and whether it is reliable and usable (Grönman et al., 2023). Furthermore, there is a broader debate over the tension that exists between ethics and economic benefits as more data becomes available to a wider audience and how that data will be used (Sieber & Johnson, 2015). Continuous evaluation of use cases and impacts further strengthens the business case for sustained funding of open data programs domestically as more implementations demonstrate the challenges and solutions.

In Slovenia, an initiative called the Big Data Analysis for HR Efficiency Improvement was launched in 2017 to help promote development in the country by utilizing information and communication technologies (ICT) to advance data-driven public administration (Deloitte, 2020). The initiative ran for ten months and was carried out under the Ministry of Public Administration of the Republic of Slovenia (MPA), along with external partner EMC Dell. Its primary objective was to assess the capabilities of a tool designed to handle big data which was deployed on the Slovenian State

[5] https://opendataforafrica.org.

Cloud Infrastructure to analyze HR data within the ministry, with the aim of enhancing its operational efficiency. To achieve this goal, anonymized internal datasets encompassing time management, HR databases, financial records, and public procurement were amalgamated with external data sources utilizing employee postal codes and weather data. The findings underscored significant potential for enhancing HR practices and reducing costs in public procurement processes for the government. Moreover, this initiative underscored the efficacy of big data tools in facilitating predictive analytics, policy planning, and decision-making across managerial echelons within the public administration. The acquired insights highlighted the transformative role of big data analytics in bolstering decision-making efficiency within the MPA through diverse statistical and quantitative analyses. Subsequently, the MPA has continued to expand the project, disseminating newfound knowledge and expertise in big data tools among its workforce while extending support to other ministries and administrative entities within the Slovenian government (OECD, 2019).

Open data policies have emerged as a mechanism to provide access to nonsensitive public datasets, thereby fueling insights and driving innovation within the private sector (Janssen et al., 2012). This approach not only encourages evidence-based policymaking but also amplifies civic engagement and oversight. Additionally, as technology has advanced there have been new opportunities to solicit direct democratic feedback from citizens including the conducting of online polls or collaborative platforms designed to produce new policies (Barber et al., 2014; Eskelinen et al., 2015; Lee, 2023). When implemented deliberately with multiple stakeholders in mind, these initiatives hold the potential to reignite citizen participation in governance processes.

E-Government

Since the emergence and massive penetration of ICTs in everybody's daily lives, the public sector has gradually embraced the convenience of the internet to speed up public service. This notion has several names, sometimes referred to as "digital government," "electronic government," or simply "e-government."[6] E-government is the delivery of public information and services through digitalization 24 hours a day, 7 days per week (Norris

[6] https://www.oecd.org/about/2506789.pdf.

& Moon, 2005; Reddick & Frank, 2007). Some of these initiatives make use of websites, apps, and pull in data from the services that use them to improve the efficacy, efficiency, and transparency of their processes (Coursey & Norris, 2008). These improvements can be both internal and external in the government, either serving the government itself to help process their own internal documents or external and helping to serve the general public. Some examples might be the ability for citizens to renew vehicle registration online or to pay for property taxes via an online portal. An e-government is more accessible, more responsive, more accountable, more transparent, and more efficient than traditional government that used to rely on in-person and mailing services.

When the global pandemic shook the world in 2020, it once again reminded people of the importance of e-government.[7] E-government revolutionizes the way the public sector interacts with their citizens, providing more information and services to its populace than ever before.

At its core e-government offers at least three major benefits including significantly improving administrative tasks delivered by the public sector, increasing public political participation, and providing greater transparency (Figure 3.2).

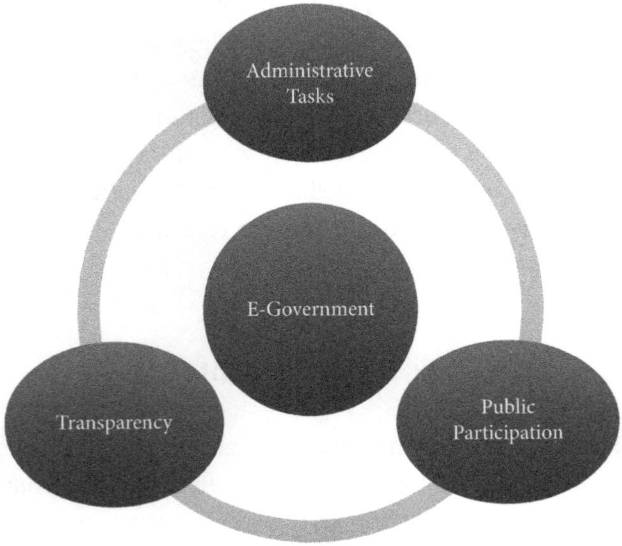

Figure 3.2 Major benefits of e-government

[7] https://publicadministration.un.org/egovkb/en-us/Reports/UN-E-Government-Survey-2020.

Administrative Tasks

In the US, several initiatives have been implemented to help ease the burden of administrative responsibilities on citizens or to provide more straightforward resources designed to aid with the location and participation in federal services. To that end, federal portals like Benefits.gov and USA.gov enable citizens to locate and access a wide array of government services through the internet pertaining to healthcare, retirement, family support, and more. These federal agency websites provide resources that may benefit citizens who need to participate in the agency's services that previously might have only been available through visiting local offices or reaching them via telephone. Some of those resources include providing forms that individuals would need to fill out to participate in their services, eligibility calculators, and other tools that aid in the individual's application for benefits, grants, licenses, or other programs. For example, the IRS website provides tax forms that can help individuals determine their tax and payment options or what tax burden they may owe. Additionally, Benefits.gov provides a consolidated resource for helping citizens find benefits they might be able to use to assist with healthcare, disaster relief, or small business loans.

With all of these services now migrating to a digitalized version, the 2020 UN E-Government survey has estimated that 98% of governmental basic services can now be found online in the US. Shifting public services to digital channels for citizens provides numerous benefits for both citizens and government agencies. For citizens, the implementation of e-government drastically reduces the frequency required to physically visit government offices or spend time in lengthy queues to use public services or fulfill regulatory obligations, saving time and money. For government institutions, digitization can aid in the improvement of overarching operational efficiency and help their workers provide a more effective and responsive delivery of services (UN, 2020).

E-government has taken root outside of the US as well. Gov.uk represents a significant milestone in the evolution of e-governance, serving as the centralized digital portal for the UK government. Since its inception in 2012, this platform has unified a diverse selection of government offerings, providing citizens with a seamless avenue to access vital services and information. Gov.uk is the manifestation of the government's commitment to digital transformation, aiming to provide more opportunities for citizen–government interactions while promoting transparency and efficiency (Kattel & Takala, 2023). Through its interface, the platform facilitates user-friendly engagement with government services, spanning tax submissions, healthcare appointments, and more, thereby providing a more unified view into one's relationship with government services and administrative processes while fostering greater accessibility for citizens.

The implementation of gov.uk yields tangible benefits for citizens, as evidenced by empirical studies in public administration and e-governance (Kattel & Takala, 2023). First, it affords citizens unparalleled convenience by enabling remote access to government services, alleviating the burdens associated with in-person visits to government offices. Second, the platform promotes transparency and accountability by providing citizens with comprehensive and up-to-date information on government operations and policies. Moreover, by digitizing bureaucratic procedures, gov.uk has enabled many of the government services to improve their delivery of services to people, resulting in expedited processes and heightened citizen satisfaction. Succinctly put, gov.uk serves as a pioneering example of how digital innovation can help play a more human-centered role in governance while fostering a more inclusive, responsive, and citizen-centric philosophy to public administration.

The Indian government developed a robust digital platform called India Stack, which serves as a main infrastructure connecting government databases and applications. It enables citizens to access a wide range of public services directly via their mobile devices. India Stack created the sophisticated Aadhaar, which is a system for residents to be uniquely identified via biometric data and to access various welfare programs and services.[8]

E-government has not just been limited to federal governments. In Durham County, UK, their govService digital program has over ninety public services and forms available online, making it easy for citizens to assess public information in one place. Since its implementation, and in collaboration with Better Durham, it is estimated that over $310,000 has been saved annually.[9] Residents can apply for their passports and make appointments for their driving tests and more.

[8] https://blogs.worldbank.org/en/developmenttalk/indias-digital-transformation-could-be-game-changer-economic-development.

[9] Granicus. (2023). How a County saves $310k+ annually after moving services online with govService. https://granicus.com/success-stories/how-a-county-saves-310k-annually-after-moving-services-online-with-govservice/.

The use cases we have discussed up to this point have all focused on governments providing services to their own citizens. Sometimes, however, there is a need to expand services to foreigners as well. Estonia, another top performer in e-government, has an e-residency program enabling anyone including foreigners who are interested in doing business in Estonia digitally. This e-government program was specifically designed for promoting entrepreneurship and economic growth. Entrepreneurs can file taxes and sign legal documents online.

Public Participation

The next area we explore is public participation, which stands as a cornerstone of modern governance. Perhaps an easy way to think of it is a central hub with spokes representing varying voices from disparate groups, all working together to bolster the legitimacy of the decisions reached thanks to their consensus. In the meantime, whatever topic is being debated is likely to result in a superior product thanks to the collective minds teasing out every detail. Draai and Taylor (2009) elucidated that robust public participation mechanisms are essential components in the complicated machine of accountable governance, especially when considering local contexts. There are theoretical underpinnings on which public participation rests, with scholars such as Innes and Booher (2004) advocating for a reframing of traditional methods to align with contemporary democratic ideals. In modern contexts, this could mean a shift away from traditional town hall meetings where citizens go to voice their concerns in-person to participatory budgeting where citizens are involved with the budgeting or encouraging e-participation by building a virtual community process (Naranjo-Zolotov et al., 2019; Sintomer et al., 2008). To that point, digital tools and platforms offer new ways for citizens to engage with their localities, giving them avenues to deliberate via e-participation (UN, 2020). We will discuss more about these topics in later chapters.

Collaborative stakeholder engagement empowers all those involved to make contributions to the decisions-at-hand. Rather than focusing on formal procedures and legal requirements where stakeholders may be going through the motions that may be evident in traditional models, the end goals of public participation manage to be both genuine yet pragmatic by focusing on consensus-building. This approach, as exemplified by the work of Webler,

Tuler, and Krueger (2001), points to the diverse aspects of effective participation processes to be more inclusive to citizens. Aspects such as ensuring fairness, legitimacy, and enabling the exchange of differing ideological perspectives are all prioritized here. In practice, this may take the form of a participatory planning process where community members, local businesses, and government officials collaborate to develop urban development projects.

But public participation is not merely a pedant or theoretical conjecture, offering no tangible benefits to governments who try to implement it. McKenna (2011) underscores the promise for participation to act as a bridge between citizens and policymakers, thereby improving the outlook of local governance structures by improving the governance structures in terms of responsiveness and effectiveness. The strength of public participation lies in its ability to integrate diverse perspectives into government processes that would normally be off limits to the public. From these diverse perspectives comes collective intelligence, where group dynamics can enhance decision-making, which the government can harness to devise innovative solutions to complex challenges (Wolpert, 2003). Moreover, active engagement fosters a sense of ownership and accountability among citizens, bolstering trust in democratic institutions and mitigating the risk of disenchantment or apathy. Indeed, as the adage goes, "Many hands make light work," illustrating the transformative power of inclusive governance practices.

Internet Voting

Sometimes e-government provides new pathways for political action from citizens. In Estonia, internet voting has been permitted in local and parliamentary elections since 2005 (Vassil et al., 2016). The goal was to increase voter turnout and make the voting process more convenient (Vinkel, 2015). Consequently, Estonia pioneered the first internet voting operation at a national level, marking a significant step towards modern electoral participation (Alvarez et al., 2009; Ehin et al., 2022).

During the 2011 parliamentary elections, over 140,000 Estonian citizens voted online, representing 15.4% of total votes cast.[10] To protect the elections, the internet voting system allows citizens to cast ballots digitally

[10] https://www.osce.org/odihr/77557.

through a secure national ID system (Bochsler, 2009). Voters have the flexibility to modify their ballots multiple times as needed during the pre-voting period (Trechsel & Vassil, 2010).

E-government provides new ways for public managers to engage with their citizens, killing two birds with one stone. For one, it allows citizens to be more involved in the process of public administration and government policymaking. Additionally, it can make public managers' lives easier by giving them clear instruction on what they need to do. This is exactly what happened in Temse, Belgium, where the municipality launched its public participation program with one of its goals to be to incorporate the thoughts and viewpoints of its citizens.[11] Once the citizens input their ideas, the city was able to map out the concerns and allocate funds appropriately.[12] From a broader public innovation perspective, this strategy is a prominent display of how cities can use technology to transform their traditional methods of public administration into a more democratized decision-making process. This shift puts a greater emphasis on informed and equitable outcomes, empowering citizens to grab hold of their future and take the reins.

E-Petition

On the topic of democratized decision-making, petitions have been a way for citizens to voice their concerns. Over the past two decades, e-petitions, which allow proponents to directly policy ideas for consideration by governing bodies, have been a common form of e-participation. During this period, multifarious nations have instituted novel e-petition frameworks or adapted petition systems to e-government (Lindner & Reihm, 2009). As a mechanism enabling high-level public participation, petitions empower citizens to influence the policy agenda of official governing bodies (Oni et al., 2015).

Recent research using modern data analysis methods to uncover the complicated causal connections between e-participation and trust in public institutions sheds light on how people view the fairness of the process by which e-petitions are addressed in Parliament (Cruickshank & Smith, 2009; Leston-Bandeira, 2019; United Nations, 2020). Scrutinizing Twitter discourses circumscribing the UK e-petition process shows that public perception of Parliament may be shaped more by the downstream petition adjudication design rather than by case-specific determinations. Notably,

[11] https://www.citizenlab.co/blog/civic-engagement/offline-vs-online-mol-temse/.
[12] https://oecd-opsi.org/wp-content/uploads/2019/11/AI-Report-Online.pdf.

consequential issues include whether deliberations closely follow the initial petition, the adversarial nature of dialogues, and if there are adequate opportunities for all stakeholders to present their views (Asher et al., 2019; UN, 2020). Such revelations align with Rawls's (1999) theory of justice, which elevates the principle of fair process for adjudicating competing interests within governance. As e-petitions germinate novel channels for public participation, adherence to equitable processes that provide transparency and multivocal debate is indispensable for engendering institutional legitimacy.

From Civic Tech to Co-Production

To encourage social innovation through a novel avenue, the city of Boston has transformed the idea of innovation into an engaging experience. StreetCred is an app that Boston residents can use to collect information to address citizen-identified community problems through gamification. By incentivizing citizens to partake in municipal amelioration, whether by documenting potholes or showcasing betterments on social media, StreetCred aims to galvanize Bostonians through what Raphael et al. (2012) referred to as "civic game play"—using the concept of a game to make civic engagement more enjoyable and educational. Users can earn virtual coins by completing a series of tasks and then use these coins to cast their votes on real grants being awarded to community groups (Holden et al., 2017). This novel framework signifies that cities like Boston and the municipality of Temse are embracing "civic tech," initiatives that foster cutting-edge resolutions to enduring challenges via stimulating citizen–government collaboration (Lukensmeyer, 2017; Schrock, 2018). Here lies a compelling example of the co-production model's promise that we will discuss later in the book.

Drawing on the power of the crowd is a central tenet of public participation, and this concept of collective intelligence comes into play once again to address social problems (Wolpert, 2003). Over the past decade, challenge platforms have burgeoned as conduits for participatory governance, with Challenge.gov emerging as an illustrious exemplar (Draai & Taylor, 2009). Launched by the US General Services Administration in 2010 as a federal portal for crowd-based contests, Challenge.gov has hosted over 740 competitions across myriad agencies, tackling issues from curbing illicit robocalls to developing ultra-fuel-efficient vehicles. With over $250 million in prizes awarded and 5 million site visitors to date, Challenge.gov has become one of the most thriving realizations of the Motivator function in government—incentivizing and mobilizing civic problem-solving (Holden et al., 2017; Zhang & Guo, 2008).

Challenge.gov's success resonates with Ostrom's (1990) theory of collective action, whereby groups self-organize to produce public goods absent top-down control. By furnishing platforms for decentralized knowledge and steering prizes toward consequential, "wicked," issues, challenge models activate latent civic creativity and gumption. Much as polycentric systems avail flexibility across scales, multimedia channels like Challenge.gov fuse expertise across sectors (Germankos et al., 2005). As e-participation conduits widen, challenge platforms must ensure equitable access and inputs among populations. Integrating community perspectives into issue selection and adjudication is indispensable for just processes and outcomes. Inclusive design begets legitimacy.

For countries that have corruption problems, e-participation can also help bring justice to corruption that takes place in the government. Bogotá te escucha enables citizens to proffer petitions—from complaints to corruption allegations—to municipal authorities, embodying e-participation (Cruickshank & Smith, 2009; Leston-Bandeira, 2019). This system provides numerous avenues for public input on civic improvement, thereby amplifying diversity of views and increasing government accountability in line with Colebatch's (1998) theory that diffused participation plays a crucial role in oversight. Studies evince e-petition platforms correlate with mitigated corruption and boosted satisfaction when well-administered (Choi, 2014; Elbahnasawy, 2014; Zheng, 2016). Hence by investigating submissions and responding directly to filers, Bogotá te escucha mobilizes collective witness and administrative action around shared challenges. Still, equitable access to such participatory instruments remains imperative, as marginalized groups often lack digital fluency or time for engagement. Integrating community perspectives into platform design and resource allocation may ensure just processes and outcomes.

However, despite its undeniable strengths, public participation still encounters many challenges that plague public entrepreneurs. There are many obstacles that must be overcome, ranging from entrenched power dynamics, lack of stakeholder consensus, and the digital divide that plagues marginalized and rural communities. Additionally, public managers often face limited resources for which they are forced to compete with one another (Fraczkiewicz-Wronka & Szymaniec, 2013; Malatesta & Smith, 2014). Other times, there may be a lack of political sway within an organization to allow these programs to come into fruition. In instances like these, it can become even more difficult for successful public participation to occur (Isaksen, 2023; Van Bunderen et al., 2018). Nevertheless, although the path to public participation may have many obstacles along the way, the journey promises rich rewards that are commensurate with the effort invested.

Transparency

As mentioned before, another key benefit of e-government is the ability to provide greater transparency to the public. Government websites provide a great volume of information and data for citizens on policies, laws, regulations, government budgets, and more. This allows citizens to be better informed about government activities and facilitates transparency. It also helps the government to have timely analysis with public data. Citizens can easily search and find information instead of requesting it formally.

For instance, during public health crises, e-government provided the tools necessary to assist vital health organizations such as the World Health Organization and the Centers for Disease Control and Prevention in the US. Some of the tools included those that assisted with gathering real-time updates on the current state of the pandemic and disseminating the findings to the public via social media platforms. To make further use of these social media accounts, government agencies can share multimedia content, including images, videos and infographics, that help to deliver the messaging from the government and to provide transparency in regard to their activities and operations. Overall, the expansion of e-government has opened new avenues for communication, service delivery, and civic participation.

Government portals such as Data.gov in the US provide a wealth of data from federal datasets to the public for free. The advent of Data.gov in 2009 has significantly enhanced governmental transparency for the American public. This platform has published an extensive collection of over 200,000 datasets from across federal, state, and local agencies, providing open access to a wealth of what was previously obscured information. Making this data publicly accessible through Data.gov provides new levels of transparency and scrutiny into government spending and administration, providing taxpayers with a unique level of oversight and accountability. Both citizens and watchdog groups now have the necessary access to analyze the raw data to identify any inefficiencies, wastage, or fraudulent activities in government programs and spending. Moreover, Data.gov served as a catalyst of innovation—spurring the development of digital tools, applications, and visualizations that present governmental data in intuitive formats for the general public.

Similarly, Estonia's X-Road platform provides a mechanism for government departments to seamlessly share data with one another in a decentralized manner. Taking it a step further than Data.gov, X-Road facilitates connection and communication between the diverse public and private sector databases and systems across the nation. Upon consent from citizens, public and private organizations can pull together data sources and create complex queries through X-Road to deliver streamlined e-services.[13,14]

Importantly, X-Road also incorporates transparency mechanisms to prevent abuse of the system. Any time a data request is made, it is extensively logged into a public document repository. Because of these additional security measures, citizens have the ability to audit who accessed their information and when. Additionally, only data that has been explicitly designated as shareable data can be queried—the system does not allow mass surveillance. Through the strategic facilitation of data sharing across organizational silos, combined with robust consent mechanisms, security measures, and oversight solutions, X-Road fosters a culture of transparency and trust. Estonian citizens can reap the benefits of efficient digital public services, while retaining control over their data.

In Spain, Transparencia.gob serves as a lens into the inner workings of the government. It provides insight into the budget, contracts, and other government activities. It also allows citizens to request information through the country's Transparency Law and provides access to open government data.

Artificial Intelligence

Although hearing the term "artificial intelligence" or "AI" may conjure up images of human-like robots or computers that can think and act like people, AI is far more nuanced than sci-fi depictions. At its core, AI refers to any technology that enables computers to simulate elements of human cognition and behavior (Russell & Norvig, 2010). Whether it's detecting patterns,

[13] https://www.publictechnology.net/2023/12/20/society-and-welfare/estonia-how-the-x-road-paved-the-way-to-a-digital-society/.

[14] https://e-estonia.com/solutions/x-road-interoperability-services/x-road/.

understanding language, or making decisions, AI aims to perform mental tasks previously believed to be exclusively human.

AI as a field can be traced back to the 1950s when scientists started exploring if machines could be made to "think" (Nilsson, 2009). In the subsequent decades, AI capabilities have advanced tremendously. While the earliest AI programs were limited to specific tasks like playing chess, the field has evolved through advances in machine learning, deep learning, and transformer-based architectures, culminating in foundation models that demonstrate emergent capabilities, cross-domain generalization, and scalable intelligence. This progression has enabled more general-purpose AI systems that are able to be integrated across diverse sectors, from entertainment to government.

We're now seeing AI permeate virtually every industry and domain. In healthcare, AI is analyzing medical images to detect tumors with greater accuracy than doctors, and enabling robots to assist in surgeries (Topol, 2019). In transportation, self-driving car prototypes leverage AI to perceive their surroundings and navigate without human input (Paden et al., 2016). AI can also analyze previous natural trends and be able to predict weather and natural disasters such as hurricanes (Ajina et al., 2023). AI is even powering virtual assistants that many have come to rely on like Siri and Alexa to understand natural language requests.

In the public sector, a 2017 study conducted by Deloitte found that the US government could save between 96.7 million and 1.2 billion hours yearly by implementing automation (Eggers et al., 2017; OECD, 2019). For governments who have braved the frontier and attempted to implement AI, there have been significant gains in the quality of service and transparency for their citizens (Androniceanu, 2023). One example is the Govtech Chatbot in Singapore. The city-state suffered from the limitations of traditional customer service with long wait times and costly maintenance. With the rollout of several chatbots including Ask Jamie, HealthBuddy, and CPF Chatbot, the government was able to help resolve citizens' issues for a plethora of topics from housing to healthcare, resulting in a 50% reduction in call center workload and 80% faster response times.[15]

Across sectors, AI is improving workflows and helping organizations and individuals carry out tasks cheaper and more efficiently. But these gains have not been welcomed openly by everyone. Some fear AI may displace

[15] https://blog.govnet.co.uk/technology/ai-in-government-case-studies#singapore.

human jobs or be used in harmful ways if ethics and governance don't guide development (Agrawal et al., 2018). Others have highlighted biases that can emerge from flawed data and algorithms (Floridi et al., 2018). As with any powerful technology, it is clear that AI demands thoughtful oversight to direct its capabilities toward broadly benefiting society.

The future of AI is yet to be written. What we do know, however, is that it is one of the biggest technological breakthroughs that will shape the twenty-first century. So long as the guidance of AI remains moral and secure, we have the potential to harness the significant gains it can bring all the while providing better opportunities and solving complex problems for everyone.

AI in Government

Across the world, governments are witnessing the potential that AI possesses to drastically transform their operations and its ability to improve the decision-making processes across all of the workstreams they provide. Countries like China have pioneered the integration of AI into governance systems through initiatives such as the Social Credit System. This controversial system utilizes AI algorithms to monitor citizens' and organizations' behavior, affecting access to services and opportunities (Arsène, 2021; Lin & Milhaupt 2023; Sun et al., 2023).

Likewise, the United States has embraced AI in national security and defense, employing advanced algorithms for threat detection and cybersecurity. Additionally, the use of chat bots for agencies such as the IRS have begun to roll out as well to help alleviate the burden of government employees responsible for answering calls while providing potentially quicker service to citizens.[16] In Canada, the "bomb-in-a-box" initiative used AI to identify packages that were a potential security risk.[17]

At the local level, cities like Singapore have embarked on smart city initiatives, integrating AI for traffic management and waste disposal. Similarly, local governments in the United Kingdom have begun using AI chatbots to provide personalized support to residents, enhancing the efficiency of public services. However, the use of AI in areas like predictive policing has raised concerns about biases and privacy issues that require careful consideration.

[16] https://www.irs.gov/newsroom/irs-expands-use-of-chatbots-to-help-answer-questions-on-key-notices-expands-on-technology-thats-served-13-million-taxpayers.

[17] https://oecd-opsi.org/wp-content/uploads/2019/11/AI-Report-Online.pdf.

Challenges of AI in Government

The exponential uptake of artificial intelligence technologies and algorithmic systems by governmental agencies underscores the ethical imperative to implement such tools responsibly and humanely (Ferretti, 2022). Governments, even more so than private sector entities, have an enhanced duty of care to deploy AI in ways that minimize harm and advance the public good. Without proper oversight and governance frameworks, AI adoption in the public sector risks perpetuating and amplifying existing inequalities—a phenomenon known as the "Matthew effect" (Merton, 1968). There is legitimate concern that algorithmic tools could negatively impact already marginalized communities if biases, errors, or lack of transparency go unchecked. For instance, algorithmic risk assessment tools used in criminal justice contexts have demonstrated patterns of race and gender bias that deepen historic injustices (Angwin et al., 2016).

At its core, AI is driven by humans creating algorithms to help the machine find patterns, which is where much of the problem often lies. In Australia, the Robodebt scheme was an automated debt recovery system implemented by the Australian Department of Human Services between 2015 and 2019. It aimed to identify and recover overpaid welfare benefits by cross-referencing income data from the Australian Taxation Office with the information provided by welfare recipients. When disparities were detected, an automatic process initiated the generation of debt notices, which were then dispatched to individuals, demanding reimbursement for the purported debts. This system heavily relied on machine-learning algorithms to scrutinize and compare data, compute debt sums, and issue notices that were later discovered to be inaccurate (Kao, 2024). The flaws inherent in the Robodebt scheme triggered widespread criticism and public outrage, culminating in legal disputes and a class-action lawsuit filed against the Australian government. In November 2020, the government opted to settle, agreeing to a compensation package totaling $1.2 billion to approximately 400,000 affected individuals, recognizing the adverse impacts of the program.[18]

Governments' introduction of AI technologies into their operations and services also raises critical privacy issues that must be addressed through proper oversight and regulation. As government agencies collect more personal data and employ algorithmic systems to analyze it, there is heightened risk of "surveillance creep" if protections are inadequate (Pasquale, 2015).

[18] https://www.abc.net.au/news/2020-11-16/government-response-robodebt-class-action/12886784.

AI applications that spark privacy concerns include facial recognition for law enforcement, algorithmic prediction tools that rely on personal data, and "smart city" initiatives with ubiquitous monitoring (Ritchie et al., 2021). Once aggregated and processed through AI, data can reveal far more about individuals than the original collection intended (Barocas & Nissenbaum, 2014).

AI hallucination presents another big and common challenge. It happens when an AI model (usually a generative AI system based on large language modeling) produces nonexistent, false, misleading, or illogical information as if it was real. Limitations in training data, biases in algorithms, and misunderstandings of the contexts could all lead to the AI hallucination problem. The consequences of AI hallucinations could be quite significant if they took place in healthcare, potentially causing incorrect medical procedures, or in the field of media, possibly spreading misinformation.[19]

Comprehensive data governance frameworks are needed to ensure AI systems are designed and audited to minimize privacy risks. Transparency about if and how personal data is used for automated decisions is also essential, as opaque AI models inherently violate due process (Citron, 2008). Strict purpose limitations and mandatory ethics reviews for government AI projects would help maintain checks against privacy erosion. Overall, public trust and consent requires governmental AI to uphold privacy as a core tenet, not an afterthought. Failing to make privacy preservation central to AI implementation strategy may undermine the social legitimacy of such technologies (Stahl & Wright, 2018). With thoughtful regulation and democratic oversight, governments can harness the power of AI for public good while respecting constitutional privacy rights.

Despite the shortcomings and challenges of AI, most governments would agree that the benefits outweigh the risks and challenges. To that point, it is increasingly important that as AI becomes more integrated into our lives that we consider proper policies to protect us and maintain our privacy. Proactive policies that center transparency, due process, and human oversight will be critical to delivering on the promise of AI while safeguarding the public interest. Equally important as well is that we have a failsafe "stop" button to override the decisions of AI when necessary.

At the time of writing, not many countries have developed systematic AI policies. The new European Union's Artificial Intelligence Act (EU AI Act),

[19] https://builtin.com/artificial-intelligence/ai-hallucination.

therefore, stands as a pioneering piece of legislation, poised to become the world's first comprehensive regulatory framework for AI. This policy intends to strategically position Europe as a global leader in AI regulation balancing between innovation and protection of their citizens. The EU AI Act focuses on data transparency and requires that AI developers declare if contents are artificially generated and keep technical documentation and human oversight, all while carrying with it heavy penalties for noncompliance. Although it might be too early to know the efficacy of this policy, it certainly represents a significant shift in the AI landscape, potentially influencing global standards for AI governance and ethics.[20,21]

Blockchain Technology

Blockchain is another emerging technology that has received increased attention. While many may only link blockchain to financial applications such as Bitcoin and Ethereum, it has the potential to dramatically shift the public sector as well. Blockchain is "a distributed ledger of transactions that is shared and written by a group of non-trusting or trusting parties in a network, not controlled by a single central authority."[22] Blockchain provides a tamper-proof sharing of verified data transactions between multiple entities without central brokers. Data is held in encrypted distributed ledgers with copies maintained by all stakeholders. Shared recordings of each process update makes information immutable and transparent. As a result, some important affordances of blockchain include enhanced security, immutability, and disintermediation (Chen & Murtazashvili, 2023; Liu & Zheng, 2021).

In regions where trust in third parties is tenuous, particularly in areas plagued by historical corruption, blockchain technology could be a pivotal solution (Shabaab et al., 2020; Shang & Price, 2019). For one, thanks to its decentralized nature, blockchain technology disseminates information across multiple copies managed by independent nodes within a peer-to-peer network and validates every transaction. The blockchain ensures robust immutability and nonrepudiation, far surpassing the security and integrity

[20] https://artificialintelligenceact.eu/.
[21] https://www.ibm.com/topics/eu-ai-act.
[22] https://oecd-opsi.org/publications/blockchains-unchained/.

levels of centralized systems (Chen & Murtazashvili, 2023). This heightened security not only restores confidence in governmental processes and recordkeeping but also enhances the reliability and accountability of public and nonprofit sector entities responsible for managing funds and records (Chen & Murtazashvili, 2024). Additionally, it could potentially enhance the integrity of electoral processes and thus promote public participation in decision-making, fostering a sense of ownership and accountability (Buterin, 2014; Allen, 2017; Kotsialou & Riley, 2018). As a result, citizens are afforded greater agency in shaping the trajectory of their communities.

These affordances can work well with many functions of the public sector. For instance, blockchain can increase data security in the space of managing citizen health records. In addition, in terms of crisis and emergency management, it can balance information transparency and privacy, thus improving trust in government (Chen & Murtzashvili, 2023). Moreover, it can be leveraged to track student loans and grants or the collection of payroll tax.[23] As of January 2024, over 1,000 blockchain-related initiatives had been launched, thanks in large part to enthusiastic communities, technical enhancements, and broadly diverse use cases.[24] Additional use cases being explored include tracing contract deliveries, controlling border check-ins, monitoring construction permits, tracking taxes and digital citizen IDs that residents control. These are often completed through partnerships such as the UK's partnership with Credits that allows the government to theoretically provide blockchain-based solutions for their processes (Alketbi et al., 2018).[25] These initiatives encompass practical test runs as well as collaborative communities and partnerships aimed at exchanging insights and best practices across nations, regions, and sectors.

Blockchain and Voting

Voting is a crucial component to a functioning democracy. However, in instances where votes could be rigged or tampered with, either with paper ballots or electronic voting, the integrity of democracy is put at stake

[23] https://consensys.io/blockchain-use-cases/government-and-the-public-sector#loans.
[24] https://coinpaper.com/2977/how-many-blockchains-are-there-unveiling-the-ecosystem-s-diversity.
[25] http://www.cityam.com/246605/uk-government-now-has-its-first-official-blockchain.

(Springall et al., 2014). Blockchain's decentralized structure offers a potential solution. Some suggest that with this technology voters can cast votes on a peer-to-peer network, and results can be tallied transparently while preventing centralized manipulation (Zyskind et al., 2015). Voters validate their identity off-chain and cast blockchain-registered ballots anonymously using cryptographic keys. Encryption protects individual choices, but the public can verify totals (McCorry et al., 2017). Experiments are underway globally, like a 2018 municipal vote in the Swiss city of Zug using a blockchain-based eID system. The experiment claimed success in that it greatly increased voter participation while protecting their privacy.[26]

Despite the various benefits that the blockchain technology could potentially bring, analysts caution blockchain voting remains unproven at large scales (Jafar et al., 2021). Additionally, encrypting votes may raise concerns over verifying validity (Park et al., 2021). But under proper conditions, blockchain's resistance to tampering and its ability to link to one individual could enable votes that are private yet securely auditable.

Blockchain and Personal Identifiable Information Management

About 850 million people live today without having a legal identity.[27] In the meantime, in 2023, it was reported that over 70% of people have had some form of identity theft.[28] Blockchain technology could potentially help address both of these issues and aid governments in their efforts to stamp out identity theft by establishing secure digital identities for both citizens and businesses that can allow them to use that identity the same way they might use their driver's license or Employer Identification Number. Using blockchain technology, individuals have the ability to control and selectively share their personal identifying information, allowing them to choose which sensitive details, such as name, address, or phone number, are made available for specific purposes. Beyond serving as simply an application of blockchain, government-backed decentralized identity has the

[26] https://www.swissinfo.ch/eng/business/crypto-valley-_-switzerland-s-first-municipal-blockchain-vote-hailed-a-success/44230928.

[27] https://blogs.worldbank.org/digital-development/850-million-people-globally-dont-have-id-why-matters-and-what-we-can-do-about.

[28] https://www.usnews.com/360-reviews/privacy/identity-theft-protection/identity-theft-fraud-survey.

potential to revolutionize public service delivery by enabling features like electronic voting and secure access to public infrastructure.

The Swiss city of Zug made waves in 2017 when it became the first government to roll out digital IDs on the blockchain. Partnering with software company uPort, Zug issued residents virtual identity cards secured on the public Ethereum network. To participate, users downloaded the uPort app to create a self-managed identity tied to a unique cryptographic key. To get their digital Zug ID, residents would visit the city website, enter some personal details, and then head to the clerk's office to confirm their identity face-to-face. Once verified, the clerk approved a Zug ID credential that residents could access through their uPort app.

The virtual IDs let citizens sign documents, vote in polls, and access services online by flashing their Zug ID. The city got to meet know-your-customer requirements while residents enjoyed portable, self-controlled digital identities. Other cities are now looking to follow Zug's lead in giving residents their own virtual IDs (Salha et al., 2019).[29]

Blockchain and Asset Registries

Governments are exploring the potential of blockchain technology to strengthen the integrity and security of public asset registries against tampering or unauthorized alterations. Blockchain-based systems enable the creation of decentralized, distributed ledgers of asset ownership records that are cryptographically secured and immutable (Lemieux, 2016). Early initiatives in countries such as Sweden and the Republic of Georgia aim to migrate land registries to blockchain infrastructure to enhance the security of the data while providing a more efficient way to record land ownership. In 2016, the Swedish land registry piloted a blockchain solution for property transactions, with results indicating the technology could prevent record tampering and enhance trust (Lemieux, 2016). More ambitiously, Georgia partnered with blockchain company Bitfury in 2017 to transfer its entire land registry of over one million records to the Bitcoin blockchain, with assistance from the World Bank to ensure validity of data transferred (Qiuyn & Price, 2018). While official processes for information verification are still necessary prior to adding data to blockchain registries, their decentralized nature provides

[29] https://consensys.io/blockchain-use-cases/government-and-the-public-sector/zug.

greater resilience against falsification once records are codified. Therefore, blockchain demonstrates significant potential to securely extend asset ownership documentation in ways that can augment trust and accountability in government administrative systems.

Smart Cities

Over recent years, the concept of "smart cities" has become increasingly popular, especially in urban locations. Smart cities proport to have the ability to grapple with the challenges of rapid urbanization, population growth, resource constraints, and the increasing demand for better public services (Caragliu et al., 2011; Nam & Pardo, 2011). At its essence, a smart city embodies a community that adeptly utilizes ICTs, alongside cutting-edge tools and extensive data resources. These cities seek to devise innovative solutions that can enhance the well-being of their residents while also contributing to the efficiency and sustainability of urban services and infrastructure (Giffinger et al., 2007; Hollands, 2008; Schaffers et al., 2011). Moreover, a crucial element of smart cities lies in their capacity to nurture regional collaboration and inclusiveness. Serving as vibrant centers of innovation, they cultivate dynamic partnerships between public and private stakeholders, fostering the development of groundbreaking solutions (Anthopoulos & Fitsilis, 2010).

One of the technologies that smart cities have come to rely on is the Internet of Things (IoT). The proliferation of connected devices and sensors is quietly transforming urban landscapes. Estimates suggest over 11 billion internet-enabled smart objects now blanket our homes, workplaces, and public spaces, with projections that this figure could reach nearly 30 billion by 2030 as 5G technology continues to roll out.[30] Behind the numbers lies immense potential to reimagine cities as responsive, adaptive, and sustainable ecosystems.[31] The vision takes shape through countless incremental innovations. Smart parking systems dynamically adjust prices and direct drivers to open spots, smoothing traffic flow. Energy grids self-optimize based on usage patterns detected through advanced metering infrastructure. Responsive traffic signals harness real-time data to curtail congestion

[30] https://transformainsights.com/blog/top-10-reports-2022.
[31] https://www.oecd.org/cfe/cities/Smart-cities-measurement-framework-scoping.pdf.

and accidents. And the examples multiply—from AI-assisted public transit to crowdsourced pothole repair (Hollands, 2008). Underpinning these solutions are sophisticated sensor networks, data analytics platforms, and participatory governance models that enable real-time data collection and analysis to inform decision-making.[32]

Citizens largely welcome the shift, with surveys revealing widespread optimism that technology can make cities more livable and efficient.[33] Yet realizing the promise hinges on securing public trust. Thoughtful policies that safeguard transparency, accountability, and digital rights will be critical to fostering responsible smart cities that empower communities and uplift urban life.

Smart Sensors and Data Analytics

It has become a common understanding that it is imperative to rely on data to make informed decisions, whether determined by human or machine. However, for the data to be analyzed, it must first be collected and stored in a designated location. Smart cities make use of digital platforms and data-driven strategies to streamline the delivery of public services, promote citizen engagement, and uphold the general principles of transparency and accountability that are crucial for a civil society (Fox, 2007; Meijer & Bolivar, 2016). In an effort to deliver public services, Bogotá has harnessed its ICT infrastructure to regulate the city's traffic flow, bolster public safety measures, and improve the reliability of its public transportation network (Hollands, 2008).

Meanwhile, Singapore's Smart Nation Sensor Platform employs a comprehensive array of sensors, cameras, and other smart devices to furnish real-time insights into the functioning of urban systems.[34] Additionally, in Singapore, the innovative RATSENSE initiative utilizes infrared sensors and sophisticated data analytics to monitor rodent movements in real time, supplying local authorities with site-specific intelligence on infestation hotspots.

[32] https://legalinstruments.oecd.org/en/instruments/OECD-LEGAL-0464.

[33] https://itig-iraq.iq/wp-content/uploads/2019/12/Telecoms.com_Annual_Industry_Survey_FINAL.pdf.

[34] https://www.itf-oecd.org/sites/default/files/docs/data-human-centric-cities-mobility-g20.pdf.

Across the seas in Seoul, Korea, the Smart Station initiative heralds the future of urban subway systems. With a central control tower delivering commands across the city, this pioneering endeavor joins multiple technologies including IoT sensors, AI-powered image analysis, and deep learning technologies to streamline subway operations across all metro lines. Similarly, in Tokyo, Japan, the strategic installation of sensors on water pipelines has resulted in staggering water savings, exceeding 100 million liters annually, by curbing leaks.[35]

Tokyo and other leading cities have taken the forefront in installing sensor networks across key infrastructure elements like lighting, water, power, and waste systems. These networks enable continuous real-time monitoring and proactive maintenance, bolstering the city's autonomy and resilience. Additionally, cloud analytics are instrumental in optimizing energy usage, minimizing disruptions, and propelling sustainability efforts by finely adjusting the equilibrium between supply and demand. Meanwhile, Warsaw embarked on a groundbreaking initiative known as Virtual Warsaw to promote accessibility and inclusivity for the visually impaired. This smart city initiative deploys a vast network of beacon sensors with cutting-edge Bluetooth technology, empowering visually impaired residents to navigate the city independently all by using apps installed on their cell phones.[36]

In the US, many are concerned with basic information that pertains to their everyday lives. Boston's innovative CityScore dashboard meticulously tracks various livability metrics such as air quality and traffic patterns, enabling targeted interventions to enhance urban life. Moreover, harnessing the power of big data analysis enables cities to offer personalized services tailored to individual citizens' needs, thereby enhancing overall satisfaction and efficiency in service delivery.

Smart city initiatives also often provide digital services to their citizens. Singapore stands as a beacon of progress with its Smart Nation Initiative, boasting an impressive 99% digitization rate for government services. Emblematic of this initiative is the Moments of Life app, or LifeSG, designed to support families with young children by offering seamless access to essential services like birth registration and early childhood support.

[35] https://www.oecd.org/cfe/cities/OECD_Policy_Paper_Smart_Cities_and_Inclusive_Growth.pdf.

[36] https://www.oecd.org/gov/innovative-government/embracing-innovation-in-government-poland.pdf.

Despite the significant benefits afforded by smart sensors and extensive data analytics, concerns persist regarding issues such as privacy infringement, energy consumption, and data security (Cerrudo, 2015; Ismagilova et al., 2022). This apprehension is justified, as exemplified by the case of San Diego's smart streetlights, which, while intended for traffic data collection, have been utilized by law enforcement for surveillance purposes, sparking fears of unwarranted monitoring (Holder, 2020; Ziosi et al., 2024).

In Aizuwakamatsu, Japan, a distinctive opt-in approach to smart city initiatives has been adopted, granting residents the autonomy to decide whether to share personal information in exchange for digital services.[37] This departure from mandatory data collection practices observed in other smart cities reflects a commitment to data privacy. However, implementing such an approach with passive smart city elements not directly linked to specific residents poses logistical challenges.

Furthermore, cities around the world including Boston and Sydney are adopting an open-source communication standard that is meant to promote transparency and accountability for the government. The initiative called Digital Trust for Places and Routines has helped to promote secure digital interactions within urban environments, presenting promising prospects for widespread adoption.[38,39]

Smart Mobility

One crucial area that every city must consider is in the realm of mobility. When it comes to smart cities, we have briefly discussed how smart cities can leverage new digital sensors to transmit the necessary information for machines to exchange transportation data such as in Seoul and Tokyo. To that point, urban planners around the world are exploring innovative ways to enhance mobility and connectivity through smart technology. Intelligent transportation systems that analyze real-time data can help optimize traffic flow, provide commuters with updates, and promote sustainability by guiding people to public transit or bikeshare stations. One compelling example is in Tallinn, Estonia's pioneering use of augmented reality in their

[37] https://www.jlgc.org.uk/en/news_letter/japans-super-city-plans.

[38] https://www.boston.gov/departments/new-urban-mechanics/digital-trust-places-and-routines.

[39] https://dtpr.io/.

app called Avalinn AR to engage residents in transportation planning. The city called on citizens to provide ideas for their Pollinator Highway—a new linear park and green corridor meant to better link neighborhoods. Using the app, locals can view and interact with different proposals for the route, from flower-filled medians to bike paths to playgrounds.[40,41]

By blending the digital and physical, platforms like Avalinn AR enable cities to tap the collective imagination of residents. This helps urban spaces evolve into communities shaped not just for people, but by them as well. Smart mobility is not just about easing traffic; it's about empowering people to co-create solutions that meet their needs and dreams.

Smart Economy

Another important aspect of a smart city is the development of a smart economy. This involves fostering innovation and entrepreneurship, attracting knowledge-based industries, and promoting digital transformation in traditional sectors (Ionescu et al., 2023). For instance, smart cities often support the growth of startups and provide a conducive environment for research and development activities (Ionescu et al., 2023).

A smart economy goes hand-in-hand with the smart city movement. This smart economy differentiates itself from other traditional economies through its promotion and use of technology, innovation, and collaboration to boost efficiency, and to ultimately provide smart jobs. Detroit's story illustrates just how a smart economy can be incorporated effectively.

After emerging from bankruptcy years before, Detroit aimed to diversify its economy beyond automaking. Detroit's meteoric rise as a hub of mobility innovation through the Planet M initiative defies urban decay tropes. As the motor city sputtered economically in the twenty-first century, losing near 850,000 with over half being in the manufacturing industry between 2000 and 2010,[42] Detroit envisioned a future beyond automation and offshoring (Gallagher, 2010). Planet M emerged in 2016 as a public–private consortium among government, industry partners like Ford and GM, and academia to establish Detroit as a global center of research and development

[40] https://www.tallinn.ee/en/tallinnovatsioon/pollinator-highway.
[41] https://oecd-opsi.org/publications/trends-2023/.
[42] https://www.mlive.com/news/2010/12/looking_back_at_michigan_2000-.html.

around transportation technologies including self-driving cars and clean energy vehicles.[43]

Aligning with Hall & Hubbard's (1996) and Jessop's (1998) theorization of the entrepreneurial city model, Detroit sought to resuscitate its fortunes not through smokestacks and factories of yore, but by placing greater emphasis on its people's brainpower and creativity. One prominent example of this was Planet M, which achieved significant progress in its urban transformation efforts by strategically partnering with key institutions, aligning diverse stakeholders, and rapidly testing innovative solutions that ultimately accelerated the pace of meaningful change (Almirall et al., 2016; Cantwell & Janne, 1999; Lorentzen, 2008).

With over $740 million invested into a Ford campus[44] and the development of the 500+ acre American Center for Mobility,[45] the initiative ricocheted Detroit's economic trajectory toward tech-fueled inclusive growth. A major takeaway here is that collaboration is key: the auto giants provide expertise, universities offer talent, and the city cultivates an innovation ecosystem (Hollands, 2008, Xie & Wang, 2020). Here we can see that Detroit leveraged its unique strengths to establish itself as a leading global center for mobility innovation.

Smart Contracts

As aforementioned, the implementation of distributed ledgers and smart contracts has the potential to curb discretionary power and corruption (Parenti et al., 2022; Sanka & Cheung, 2019). Conversely, in well-governed societies characterized by robust governance structures and checks and balances, blockchain's benefits manifest through innovative approaches to public service delivery and interaction models (Ølnes et al., 2017). These approaches streamline public–private information exchanges, reducing costs, time, and complexity. For example, smart contracts can automate the determination and governance of social and humanitarian aid distribution, setting clear eligibility criteria and conditions for continuation

[43] https://www.detroitnews.com/story/business/autos/2016/06/01/planet-mobility-campaign/85254058/.

[44] https://www.michiganbusinessnetwork.com/blog/planet-m-mobility-report-mid-july-2020.

[45] https://acmwillowrun.org/about-us/#mission.

(Adediran et al., 2024; Coppi & Fast, 2019). Such streamlined, personalized citizen–state interactions yield efficiency gains and economic benefits for citizens. Additionally, many smart cities have adopted smart contracts to automatically manage parking space, track and reward individuals for segregating waste, and collect public transportation fares.[46]

Moreover, decentralized information technology solutions have arisen as a more efficient means of improving various collaborations and optimizing operational workflows both within and between government agencies. Governments can utilize blockchain technology for swift and dependable exchange of information between various government bodies. The architecture of blockchain aligns well with the "once-only principle," the notion that one only needs to provide their data once and it can be reused and can significantly boost operational efficiency by breaking down organizational IT barriers among public agencies (Allessie et al., 2019). The concept revolves around establishing a Government Service Blockchain, fostering data sharing in a secure and adaptable manner without imposing uniform processes and technologies on all participating entities. This goal can be achieved through decentralizing services and employing smart contracts, effectively utilizing the blockchain as a sort of "asynchronous communication bus" (Marchionni, 2018). Therefore, many cities, such as Dubai, Dallas, Shanghai, and Singapore, have all pledged to implement smart blockchain-based contracts to make their urban areas smarter.

To conclude, the past twenty years have seen an explosion of new approaches and tools that have greatly altered the work life of public managers. At the heart of many of these developments has been the progression of industry and technology to provide new opportunities, expanding the horizons of cities who perhaps were defined one way before but are seeking to reinvent themselves like Detroit in the US. Learning how to wield each one effectively will be the determining factor between those cities able to harness the opportunities afforded from the new technology compared to their counterparts succumbing as victims to a rapidly changing technological landscape. Without the proper knowledge, strategy, and guardrails, these changes could prove to only be costly mistakes, leaving the public entrepreneur wishing they had devised a proper plan beforehand. As the saying goes, "Fortune favors the prepared."

[46] https://smacite.eu/index.php/en/dissemination/posts/102-smart-contracts-making-cities-smarter.

Chapter 4
Three-Legged Stool
Coproduced Public Innovation

An ancient Chinese saying goes, "Don't learn from spiders to weave nets individually, but learn from bees to work collaboratively." Similar reasoning is applicable to institutions as well. Multiple collaborations between the public sector and other industries have been recorded in history. About 2,000 years ago, Romans built an outstanding highway transportation system that originated in Rome while spanning to the far reaches of its empire to Britain, Spain, Greece, and northern Africa to move their military forces with ease from one border to the next. To accompany the vast expansion of all these new roads, the Roman legions created a network of postal stations to not only facilitate the transport of troops and goods, but also information. Instead of being managed by the government, these postal stations were built and managed by a private business. With the help of these businesses, a collaborative information-sharing ecosystem emerged, connecting government, businesses, and the public regardless of where they were within the empire. However, these postal services would not have been possible had it not been for the Roman government's foresight and vision to build the road network and in turn the partnership that was forged as a result (Dalgaard et al., 2022; Ramsay, 1920; Ramsay, 1925).

Outside of road development, back in eighteenth-century Massachusetts in the US, the two towns of Boston and Charleston relied on Harvard College to transport people across the Charles River for over 100 years. As the population grew, the local government then partnered with the Charles River Bridge Company to span the Charles River, connecting the two cities via the newly created Charles River Bridge. Due to the large demand from the public, the bridge was a huge success in the area and collected close to one million dollars in toll fares within the first forty years.[1]

[1] https://www.encyclopedia.com/social-sciences-and-law/law/court-cases/charles-river-bridge-case.

Innovation and Entrepreneurship in the Public Sector. Wendy D. Chen and David B. Audretsch, Oxford University Press. DOI: 10.1093/9780197679470.003.0004

As the nation exploded into the nineteenth century, the billowing smoke from the engines of railways reshaped society as we knew it (Fogel, 1964). America continued to grow, and the dream of linking coast-to-coast ignited the imaginations of numerous American companies (White, 2011). This Transcontinental Railroad would become the embodiment of the ambitious endeavors and fierce competition among railroad companies vying to etch their name in history as the pioneers of westward expansion. Nonetheless, a sense of caution prevailed among these enterprises, reluctant to embark on the venture alone and seeking assurance amidst the risks (Borneman, 2010).

In a defining moment in 1862, the US Congress responded with the Pacific Railway Act, a legislative maneuver that set the stage for a transformative journey.[2] The selected route, known as the 32nd parallel, witnessed the government's provision of support via bonds, facilitating the construction of railway and telegraph lines along its path.[3] Stretching from the Missouri River to the Pacific Ocean, the prospective railroad was riddled with logistical puzzles aplenty.[4] With a boost from governmental backing, the Union Pacific and Central Pacific railway companies gained the nod to embark on the ambitious task of laying down the tracks. The railroad would go on to become known as the Transcontinental Railroad.

The culmination in 1869 marked a watershed moment, opening new avenues for commerce and beckoning the westward migration of an aspiring nation eager to seize opportunities (Duran, 2013; Wang & Latham, 2001). This monumental effort exemplified the intricate dance between government support, private enterprise, and the evolution of a nation during this transformative era (Duran, 2013).

Now the world is more connected than ever, and governments across the world constantly face challenges, are presented with new needs, and must identify new tools to address these public problems. Despite having resources, government alone cannot fully address public health or fight against terrorism, for example. It is common among public administration, political science, and management domains to refer to business, government, and civic society as a "three-legged stool." By mobilizing resources and

[2] https://www.archives.gov/milestone-documents/pacific-railway-act.

[3] https://www.loc.gov/collections/railroad-maps-1828-to-1900/articles-and-essays/history-of-railroads-and-maps/the-transcontinental-railroad/.

[4] https://www.brainerddispatch.com/news/local/construction-of-northern-pacific-railroad-faced-challenges.

taking risks together, institutions can achieve the same goal more efficiently and innovatively, especially when governments collaborate with others who seek to address the same specific issues, be it environmental science, food science, health science, and more.

Collaborative Governance

Before we dive into each of the ways governments facilitate collaboration, however, we would first like to discuss the taxonomy of the roles that the government plays. Many have probably heard of some of these specific methods such as public–private partnerships (PPPs), but the parent category is often referred to as "collaborative governance." Collaborative governance has proliferated as an antidote to polarized politics, harnessing networks beyond insular institutions to tackle complex public challenges (Ansell & Gash, 2018). This multistakeholder model convenes cross-sector stakeholders—government, business, nonprofits, and community—in consensus-oriented decision-making processes aimed at shared goals (Emerson & Nabatchi, 2015).

Operationalizing Innes and Booher's (2010) communicative planning theory, collaborative governance is predicated on reciprocity—exchanging views, co-producing knowledge, and recognizing interdependence. While time-intensive, the process can build relational capital and more holistic, actionable decisions compared to conventional insular policymaking (Sager, 2009). Successful examples like Cuyahoga Valley's collaborative park planning and the Sustainable Groundwater Management Act in California illustrate that equitable representation and skilled facilitation are integral to meaningful participation and just outcomes (Dobbin & Lubell, 2021; Worley & Parker, 2011). With wicked problems impervious to unilateral approaches, collaborative governance offers an adaptive method that is capable of translation to multiple settings, blending diverse insights into solutions. Yet lasting transformative change requires transferring collaborative capacity to communities themselves as opposed to an overreliance on government oversight.

Within the framework of collaborative governance, three principal methodologies emerge through which governments foster and facilitate collaboration: cross-sector collaboration, coproduction, and public–private partnerships. While these terms overlap in some regards and can sometimes be conflated, there are a few differences we will discuss.

Cross-Sector Collaboration

Cross-sector collaboration refers to stakeholders from disparate spheres including government, private business, or nonprofits joining forces to address a common challenge. The rationale for this joint force is due to the complex nature of societal challenges, which frequently require a multipronged approach to tackle (Austin & Seitanidi, 2012; Kania & Kramer, 2013). The stakeholders in these arrangements can play different roles as facilitators, catalysts, or primary actors who are on the frontlines of these challenges. Rather than dealing with organizations independently, it is better to join forces and to allow each side to contribute the portion for which they have the most expertise. Put differently, there is a multiplier effect when these forces come together to tackle social challenges and are more likely to address systemic root causes of problems rather than the symptoms.

Governments play a pivotal role in bringing about cross-sector collaborations to address complex policy challenges. As Kania and Kramer (2011) elucidate, modern problems are intricately interwoven, necessitating collective efforts. Governments' unique position allows them to play an important role in facilitating these alliances between stakeholders (Bryson et al., 2015). When these stakeholders and their respective interests coalesce around shared societal goals, innovation is a natural byproduct thanks to this synergistic commitment (Kania & Kramer, 2011; Porter & Kramer, 2011). The scholarly discourse illuminates the complexities and rewards of cross-sector partnerships, with governments as catalysts harnessing collective prowess to engender transcendent solutions.

Co-Production

Closely interlinked with cross-sector collaboration is the notion of co-production. Co-production theory reimagines the roles of state, market and citizens in public service delivery as active co-creators (Ostrom, 1996; Pestoff, 2006). Moving beyond hierarchical models, it advocates collaborative partnerships leveraging stakeholders' unique knowledge and resources for more effective solutions (Brandsen & Honingh, 2018). Citizens aren't passive recipients but engaged participants co-designing, co-managing, and co-evaluating policies and programs (Bovaird, 2007). This participatory ethos fosters ownership and social capital (Nabatchi et al., 2017). Potential benefits include enhanced service quality, public trust, and contextualized innovations from diverse perspectives (Ostrom, 1996). Implementation challenges like power imbalances exist (Brandsen & Honingh, 2018). However, the transformative vision of coproduction shifts relationships away from traditional hierarchies and toward shared responsibility, fostering a more collaborative and equal partnership among all involved parties. Cooperative production models redefine the relationship between citizens and the state by fostering more collaborative and participatory forms of governance, leading to increased inclusivity, responsiveness, and tangible positive change (Pestoff, 2012; Nabatchi et al., 2017). This paradigm shift holds promise for revitalizing public services via participation.

Public–Private Partnership

Public–private partnership (PPP) is a more specific type of cross-sector collaboration, taking the form of a cooperative venture between government entities and private organizations to deliver public services or infrastructure (Vries & Yehouse, 2013). Typically, in PPPs, there are formal agreements or contracts shared between the entities involved. Often, the goals for PPP are to deliver public services or develop some form of infrastructure. While safeguarding autonomy, strategic partnerships harmonize complementary strengths by amalgamating frontline acumen within policy overhauls (Kania & Kramer, 2011). The goal is to allow both sides to leverage their respective strengths to tackle complex and costly projects. When hazards are equitably counterbalanced and incentives coalesce societal and civic value, collaborative endeavors catalyze shared novelties, precipitating systemic metamorphosis (Osborne, 2000; Bryson et al., 2015).

Governments worldwide have established dedicated innovation units in recognition of PPPs as pivotal mechanisms for societal advancement. Acting as facilitators, these units create environments conducive to innovation by fostering collaborations between the public and private sectors. Via these partnerships, governmental initiatives seamlessly integrate cutting-edge technologies and solutions from the private sector. Denmark's GovTech program and Germany's Research Campus Program, for example, embody the collaborative research and development (R&D) efforts of public and private entities. Similarly, the New Zealand Callaghan Innovation Agency aids Kiwi businesses and the Center for the Biomedical Advanced Research and Development Authority, which operates within the US Department of Health and Human Services focuses on accelerating progress and availability of medical countermeasures.[5,6] These organizations concentrate on diverse yet interconnected spheres: supporting businesses in their R&D endeavors or facilitating commercialization respectively. Worldwide—over 125 government innovation labs have been established—signifying the escalating importance PPP holds in the propulsion of innovation in tackling intricate societal challenges. These labs provide an entrepreneurial environment to promote experimentation, collaboration, and the exploration of innovative ideas and solutions.

Take the US Interstate Highway System as an example. Initiated in 1956 via the Federal Highway Act, this ambitious project aimed to connect the country through a vast network of highways, allowing for many citizens who had found themselves confined to their location a newfound freedom. The federal government provided funding and oversight for the construction. Meanwhile, the individual states and private contractors were responsible for the carrying out of the projects. In this partnership, the government looked to the private sector for expertise and resources in the ways of road building, laying the foundations on which America furthered its growth thanks to its newfound transportation infrastructure. As a result, there was a surge in economic prosperity, as millions of Americans were now able to mobilize. Here, the PPP arrangement allowed for the government to address complex infrastructure challenges through the collaboration between private sector entities, and federal and state agencies (Levitt et al., 2019).

Comparison Between Concepts

There are several elements that distinguish each of these types of collaboration. First, in cross-sector collaboration, there is a larger societal issue that each stakeholder is working toward. The collaboration is often looking to leverage the expertise, resources, or points of view from the stakeholders as opposed to producing a tangible good or service. An example might be the Sustainable Apparel Coalition, which brings together apparel and footwear companies with nonprofits, academics, and government agencies to work toward solving sustainability issues.[7]

[5] https://www.callaghaninnovation.govt.nz/about-us/.
[6] https://aspr.hhs.gov/AboutASPR/ProgramOffices/BARDA/Pages/default.aspx.
[7] https://apparelcoalition.org/.

In the co-production model, the entities generally work toward producing a tangible good or service. However, one key difference here as well is that the service users are one of the key stakeholders involved. An example here could be the FixMyStreet platform in the UK.[8] Developed by nonprofit mySociety, the platform allows citizens to report issues witnessed such as potholes, graffiti, or public vandalism.

Finally, PPPs are similar to cross-sector collaboration in some ways but form more binding bonds between the public and private entities involved in the shared goal. Often there are contractual agreements signed between parties that all must abide by. Additionally, PPPs involve a level of shared risk between the partners. An example could be Global Alliance for Vaccines and Immunization (GAVI). This international PPP brings together public and private sector organizations, to collaborate on making vaccines more accessible to low-income countries and improving global immunization coverage. Different from cross-sector collaborations, GAVI has clear roles and responsibilities in their agreed upon partnerships including funding commitments, vaccine supply agreements, and country engagement frameworks.[9]

State and Local Collaborations

The collaboration between the public and private sectors is not limited to only federal partnerships in the US. Since 1989, when the State of California became the first state to enact laws specifically laid out for collaborations between the government and private sector, an increasing number of states in the US have followed suit to encourage public–private partnerships. The Congressional Budget Office estimates that each year Public Private Partnerships expenditures range between $4.4—$13.2 billion for highway, transit, or water infrastructure.[10] Meanwhile, Canada has partnered with businesses for over $139 billion in PPP projects over the past thirty years.[11] In other words, in recent decades, public–private partnerships have been established worldwide for all projects ranging from social services, waste management, and economic infrastructure to modern military technology (Siemiatycki, 2012; Wang et al., 2018).

A similar local state level cross-sector collaboration is also found in rural New Hampshire in the US. Even today, internet access in the US can still be

[8] https://www.fixmystreet.com/.
[9] https://www.gavi.org/.
[10] https://www.cbo.gov/publication/56044.
[11] https://www.pppcouncil.ca/.

a challenge, especially in rural communities. According to the Department of Agriculture and Federal Communications Commission, "22.3% of Americans in rural areas and 27.7% of Americans in Tribal lands lack coverage from fixed terrestrial 25/3 Mbps broadband, as compared to only 1.5% of Americans in urban areas."[12]

It is known that wiring rural America is costly given the long distances. Many modern aspects of life rely on stable internet connections, including commerce, bill payments, and even aspects of school. Without a stable internet connection, the daily lives of residents would be negatively impacted. Furthermore, lack of reliable infrastructure, including high-speed internet, deters new businesses from entering or expanding into a region. The town of Chesterfield in the State of New Hampshire in the US recently partnered with Consolidated Communications, a broadband company, to provide every home in town with access to high-speed internet. The partnership was enabled by Senate Bill 170, which allows municipal governments to issue bonds to fund broadband infrastructure in disadvantaged areas.[13] Voters approved a $1.8 million bond with the company for twenty years.[14] Because of this partnership, local residents have avoided paying additional taxes for their internet access. Instead, they pay a small subscription fee to the company. This arrangement became especially valuable to the town during the pandemic as it allowed local students to access online education programs to continue their schooling.[15]

Benefits of Government Collaboration with Other Sectors

Government collaboration with the private sector is beneficial in several ways. For one, collaboration leads to knowledge sharing and innovation. An innovative government embraces the entrepreneurial mindset through data-driven strategies and keeping its eye on the horizon. Entrepreneurs, even public ones, are on the lookout for emerging products and technologies that may aid their business. Employing robust data collection mechanisms in addition to monitoring the ever-changing landscape of

[12] https://www.usda.gov/broadband.

[13] https://www.consolidated.com/about-us/news/article-detail/id/659/consolidated-communications-partners-with-rural-new-hampshire-town-to-build-fiber-to-the-premises-broadband-network-for-residents-and-businesses.

[14] https://communitynets.org/content/new-hampshire-towns-join-chesterfield-partner-consolidated-communications-fiber-builds.

[15] https://www.consolidated.com/about-us/news/article-detail/id/738/consolidated-communications-helps-schools-and-students-connect-and-learn-remotely-during-covid-19-crisis.

their business allows governments to devise holistic interventions catalyzing entrepreneurial growth while addressing societal challenges.

Government agencies store a large amount of data, including environmental data and educational data. However, they do not always have the capability to analyze and utilize data. As a result, governments invite private businesses that have dedicated resources and talent to collaborate with and to share collective knowledge. For instance, US federal research labs partner with businesses to share equipment in many types of joint research projects. The government grants companies access to their data and facilities. Such collaborations often lead to mutually beneficial results. The government distributes the research results to a greater scientific community for future research innovation. Meanwhile, private businesses often turn those results into products, such as new medicines or technical devices and sell them to provide more jobs and bring in strong earnings for positive stock performances.

Another example is the collaboration between the US Census Bureau and companies to create federal statistical research data centers across the country so that researchers who are not associated with governments can have equal and secure access to restricted government data. Here, academics, data hobbyists, companies, and others who could benefit from access to this data are able to provide new insights into the data. Consequently, these data centers can help researchers to identify new problems, solutions, and new innovations.

Governments frequently partner with businesses to increase community consciousness around social and environmental issues. In other words, the partnership between the public sector and startups amplifies governmental administrative efforts through broadened dissemination while simultaneously elevating its reputation. With these synergistic relationships comes the opportunity to further promulgate government policies, which in turn could inspire future innovation. West Hartford, a town in Connecticut, is an example. West Hartford was once referred to as "dumps."[16] To educate local residents on how to recycle plastics, the town partners with a land management business. The business set up bins around town to encourage people to drop off plastics.[17] The recyclable plastics collected by the town residents will then be given to another manufacturer business to produce wood-alternative

[16] https://patch.com/connecticut/westhartford/west-hartford-recycling-center-project-clears-hurdle.

[17] https://www.westhartfordct.gov/town-departments/public-works/curbside-collection-recycling.

products. Through partnerships with various local businesses, the town government has amplified its efforts to promote sustainability, providing residents with actionable steps and clear messaging on how to contribute to a more environmentally conscious community. Analysis of public commentary regarding the new recycling initiative on various social media platforms reveals that numerous community members perceive the partnerships as highly effective, with many reporting a significant improvement in local cleanliness.

Government's Role in Collaboration

Many people know that the government works with various organizations to achieve its goals. Consulting firms such as McKinsey, KPMG, Accenture, IBM, Booz Allen, Deloitte, and CGI Federal that use tools such as ServiceNow, Salesforce, Pega, Jira, and other custom-developed software have all been heavily involved with the shaping of the government as we know it today. Similarly, nonprofit organizations have supported the public sector to address a wide range of societal issues including disaster relief, public safety, and human rights. However, what remains less clear is the exact manner in which government collaborates. A careful examination of cross-sector collaboration demonstrates that government plays at least four key roles in cross-sector collaboration including as a resource provider, coordinator, advocate, and learner (Figure 4.1). In other words, government serves a visible hand deliberately and actively engaging in cross-sector collaborations.

Government as a Resource Provider

In collaborative governance, providing public funding is one of the primary services from the government to support innovation and economic growth. Scholars have argued that companies such as Apple would have never achieved their success had it not been for the supportive role government played in assisting the company with the development of its products (Mazzucato, 2015).

Providing public funding may take various forms such as contracts and grants. To give an indicator of the scale of contractor involvement, the US government spent $665 billion in Fiscal Year 2020 alone on government

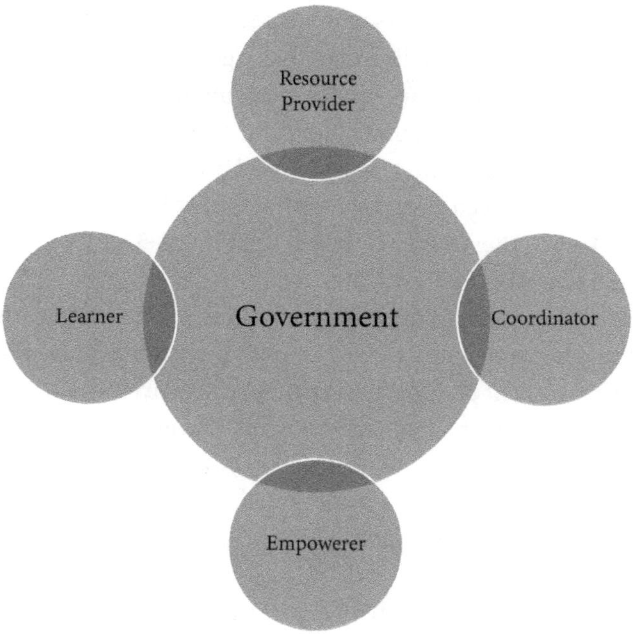

Figure 4.1 Government's role in collaborative governance

contracts.[18] To put this number in perspective, the total spending in 2020 was $1.6 trillion,[19] meaning that over 41% of the spending went to contractors. These contracts span all departments of government and offer varying levels of support, including developing new technical tools to assist the government, providing managerial advice, and hiring workers to complete the day-to-day operations of the agency.

One example of these contracts is the US Department of Defense's contracts with aerospace and other defense contracting companies such as Lockheed Martin, Boeing, and Raytheon. During World War II, the exigencies of the conflict precipitated the imperative for the United States to bolster its aircraft innovation, despite the incipient state of aviation technology and the attendant risks associated with manufacturing jet engines. One prime challenge lay in the enormous R&D costs, but the government stepped up and made tremendous investments with the National Advisory Committee on Aeronautics and National Aeronautics and Space Administration.[20]

[18] https://www.gao.gov/blog/snapshot-government-wide-contracting-fy-2020-infographic.
[19] https://www.cbo.gov/publication/57172.
[20] https://insight.ieeeusa.org/articles/a-brief-history-of-the-u-s-federal-government-and-innovation-part-iii-1945-and-beyond/.

Interestingly, it was contractors who helped win World War II. The world-famous P-51 Mustang, a small aircraft that is generally believed to be the best all-around fighter for the war was designed and developed by North American Aviation. Originally manufactured for the British Royal Air Force, it later became a staple in the US Army Air Forces as well. While the Allies air superiority had been faltering, the tide of battle dramatically shifted in March 1944 when the Americans began bombing Berlin, thanks in no small part to the success of the P-51.[21,22]

In addition to investing in the aircraft industry, the US government also funded the development of electronic digital computers and semiconductors. The government played a particularly supportive role during the initial high-risk phase, where nascent inventions faced a greater risk of failure. Similarly, the Department of Defense (DOD) in the US also spent nearly $20 billion to develop the Global Positioning System (i.e., GPS) and now estimates place that there would be $96 billion in damages each year should the system go down.[23]

Additionally, the US government heavily invests in federal labs. Those labs are "any laboratory, and federally funded research and development center (FFRDC), or any center that is owned, leaser, or otherwise used by a Federal agency and funded by the Federal Government, whether operated by the Government or by a contractor."[24] Organizations like the Rand Corporation, MIT Lincoln Laboratory, the National Renewable Energy Laboratory, and MITRE are some examples of FFRDC.[25] Prior to World War II, almost all of America's research took place in universities and industry. During the war, the increased demand for new technological innovations led to an increasing number of scientists and engineers who joined the war effort.[26] The US military and many government-sponsored labs that are free of organizational conflicts of interest without any civil service restrictions also started to conduct research and development with a goal of advancing technology for the purpose of war such as building computers and radar, and a famous one was the Manhattan Project developing nuclear weapons (Price & Siegel, 2019). Following the war, the government expanded its support for research at these laboratories, and some estimate that over one-third of the federal

[21] https://palmspringsairmuseum.org/p-51-mustang/.

[22] https://www.nationalww2museum.org/visit/museum-campus/us-freedom-pavilion/warbirds/north-american-p-51-mustang.

[23] https://odimpact.org/files/case-studies-gps.pdf.

[24] https://www.ncbi.nlm.nih.gov/books/NBK568354/.

[25] https://www.nsf.gov/statistics/ffrdclist/.

[26] https://www.princeton.edu/~ota/disk1/1995/9501/950105.PDF.

R&D dollars are invested in federal labs.[27] They served as a bridge between the public and private sectors, combining the academic rigor of universities with the market-driven approaches of industry, thereby complementing the innovative efforts of both.[28] Other federal labs, such as Sandia National Laboratories, Defense Advanced Research Projects Agency (DARPA), and more also played a crucial role in advancing semiconductor technology. Sandia's Center for Microelectronics Technologies worked closely with SEMATECH and industry partners to develop innovative semiconductor manufacturing technologies, including the use of projection X-ray lithography and projection electron beam lithography. Meanwhile, DARPA helped oversee SEMATECH on behalf of the DOD paid $100 million per year over a five-year period to help spur the growth of the consortium. This collaborative effort enabled US manufacturers to maintain their global dominance in the sector.[29,30]

Government-funded institutions like Research Triangle Park (RTP) in North Carolina and University of Virginia Research Parks in Virginia in the US were created to foster knowledge spillovers from local universities (Audretsch & Link, 2012; Díez-Vial & Fernández-Olmos, 2015). RTP's history traces back to the late 1950s when advocates from North Carolina State University, Duke University, the University of North Carolina at Chapel Hill, business leaders, and government officials brainstormed on a collaborative ecosystem that fostered scientific research and technology development. One of the key drivers of this ecosystem was the North Carolina General Assembly, who along with legislative support also provided financial incentives to attract companies and foster research activities. Alongside the North Carolina General Assembly was the federal government who infused the project with federal funding to construct the requisite infrastructure and to promote new research initiatives in the fields of pharmaceuticals, biotechnology, environmental sciences, and more. As time went on, RTP has evolved to embody a healthy ecosystem that draws stakeholders from universities, government agencies, and research institutions, as well as businesses. Using this cross-disciplinary method has accelerated a valuable exchange of knowledge and promoted high-skilled entrepreneurial activities (Armanios et al., 2017).

[27] https://www.ncbi.nlm.nih.gov/books/NBK568354/.
[28] https://insight.ieeeusa.org/articles/a-brief-history-of-the-u-s-federal-government-and-innovation-part-iii-1945-and-beyond/.
[29] https://www.gao.gov/assets/rced-92-283.pdf.
[30] https://www.sandia.gov/media/old_factsheets/facts19.htm.

Meanwhile, North Carolina's neighbor also had a similar effort with its creation of the University of Virginia Research Park (UVRP). University of Virginia purchased the land back in the 1980s[31] and established the research park to promote innovation and commercialization of scientific research.[32] Through this park, now named North Fork,[33] technology transfer could occur while boosting the local economy and providing hands-on learning opportunities for students. North Fork's tenants include government agencies, nonprofits, academic institutions, startups, and more.[34] To help with the development of the park, North Fork has received $3 million in grants to help attract additional businesses.[35] The presence of the park has created an ecosystem between the university, government, and private sector companies. Just as with RTP, UVRP exemplifies the power of partnerships among universities, government, and industry to drive scientific advancement and entrepreneurship (Audretsch & Link, 2012; D'Este Cukierman & Fontana, 2008).

Notably, government involvement as a resource provider could be a double-edged sword. Many scientific breakthroughs and other innovations, as mentioned earlier, are funded by the public sector. However, critics argue that when programs are funded and decided by unelected bureaucrats, there is a risk that taxpayer money may be allocated to initiatives that do not necessarily align with the public's interests or reflect the will of the people.[36] Therefore, "pay for success" serves as a new government financing approach. This approach is also known as performance-based budgeting. In such arrangements, the government only allocates funding should projects achieve the predetermined goals, signaling a potential for radical change that could permeate throughout the government (Costa & Shah, 2013; Greenblatt & Donovan, 2013). According to the US Government Accountability Office, the State of Utah used the method to fund a preschool program for at-risk children and New York adopted the pay-for-success approach to reduce recidivism rates and increase employment rates of high-risk individuals.[37]

[31] https://www.cbs19news.com/story/43248073/uva-rebrands-research-park-near-airport-road.
[32] https://www.discovernorthfork.com/.
[33] https://news.virginia.edu/content/newly-renamed-north-fork-discovery-park-opens-doors-innovation-collaboration.
[34] Ibid.
[35] https://dailyprogress.com/news/uva-research-park-gets-3m-grant-to-help-attract-businesses/article_f45bc51e-9cea-11ed-bc37-db617e2a482e.html.
[36] https://issues.org/has-nih-lost-its-halo/.
[37] https://www.gao.gov/assets/680/672446.pdf.

Some also worry that government funding could influence research and innovation agendas and priorities in addition to its effectiveness.[38,39] Although there is some debate surrounding the exact extent to which we can attribute the government's support contributing to progress,[40] it is still a significant contributor to the survival of many different health organizations. In sum, when the public sector acts as a resource provider, it should balance between leveraging government resources to drive innovation and ensuring transparency and accountability in how these resources are deployed. This balance is key to maintaining public trust and contributing to public innovation and entrepreneurship.

Government as a Coordinator

The traditional public management landscape is being transformed by the need for collaborative endeavors that transcend conventional boundaries (Ansell & Gash, 2008; Emerson & Nabatchi, 2015). As governments navigate contemporary challenges, they are increasingly recognizing the importance of cross-sector partnerships to devise holistic solutions. However, organizational silos often hinder the exchange of ideas and resources, making it challenging to overcome these obstacles. To address this issue, many governments have served as vital coordinators and matchmakers, connecting organizations in different sectors, identifying and fostering opportunities where organizational resources align harmoniously (Boadway, 2001). Through strategic orchestration, governments can unlock untapped potential and drive meaningful impact across sectors, ultimately fostering more innovative approaches to collective problem-solving.

The National Institutes of Health (NIH) Collaboratory, a trailblazing US government initiative in medical research coordination, embodies a transformative paradigm to large-scale clinical investigations that can be readily applied to real-world healthcare ecosystems. Informed by collaborative governance and network theory, this initiative engages a diverse body of stakeholders, fostering an environment conducive to innovation and discovery (NIH Collaboratory, 2020, 2021, 2022). Emphasizing pragmatic studies

[38] https://www.washingtonexaminer.com/news/2871014/three-shocking-taxpayer-funded-scientific-experiments-on-animals.

[39] https://www.yahoo.com/news/nih-closes-experimentation-labs-accused-023439626.html.

[40] https://www.wsj.com/articles/dont-thank-big-government-for-medical-breakthroughs-1483660786.

like comparative effectiveness and patient-centered outcomes, it aligns with pragmatic trial design principles and implementation science (Zwarenstein et al., 2008).

The Collaboratory harnesses the power of interdisciplinary collaboration, partnering with academic institutions, healthcare organizations, and patient advocacy groups to accelerate the transfer of research insights into practical, evidence-based healthcare innovations (NIH Collaboratory, 2020). This collaborative, evidence-based approach, resonating with scholarly discourse on stakeholder engagement and knowledge translation (Greenhalgh et al., 2016), positions the NIH Collaboratory as a positive change maker for better health outcomes (NIH Collaboratory, 2021).

The Israel Innovation Authority (IIA), recognized for its pioneering initiatives, orchestrates a network of cross-disciplinary centers strategically aligned with the nation's public innovation and technology priorities (IIA Annual Report, 2022)[41]. These dynamic centers serve as vibrant focal points where entrepreneurial creativity intersects with strategic objectives, catalyzing innovative solutions to urgent national issues. Through collaborative collaboration and multidisciplinary partnerships, these centers leverage the collective knowledge of varied stakeholders, including startups, educational institutions, and government bodies (IIA Strategy and Policy, 2023)[42].

In 2020, Queensland Australia's health department launched Bridge Labs, a pioneering government-university partnership in the health domain amplifying clinical innovation capacity on the frontline. This program, recognized with prestigious awards, has evolved into a vibrant ecosystem uniting clinicians, consumers, and academic experts, driving diverse service transformations replicated across local health services statewide.[43]

Another Australia's program is Jobs and Skills Australia (JSA), a dynamic workforce initiative that ingeniously orchestrates the pairing of individuals with employment opportunities. Founded on a robust framework, JSA harmonizes job seekers with prospective employers through targeted matchmaking strategies.[44] This avant-garde approach involves a meticulous assessment of candidates' skills and aspirations, creating bespoke pairings that transcend conventional employment paradigms. Transitionally, JSA

[41] https://innovationisrael.org.il/files-en/Annual%20Innovation%20Report%20-%20State%20of%20High-Tech%202022.pdf.
[42] https://innovationisrael.org.il/en/strategy-and-policy/.
[43] https://oecd-opsi.org/innovations/queensland-bridge-labs/.
[44] https://www.jobsandskills.gov.au/.

navigates the intricate landscape of contemporary job markets with an astute understanding of evolving skill demands.[45] The JSA program effectively bridges the gap between an individual's aspirations and available job opportunities, serving as a key driver of personal career development and contributing to Australia's broader goal of strengthening its workforce.

Collaborative efforts among diverse stakeholders are essential for driving innovation and tackling pressing societal issues, as exemplified by these examples. Effective collaboration relies on strategic pairings between organizations, cultivating synergistic relationships grounded in shared interests and mutual capacity development (Austin & Seitanidi, 2012). This convergence of expertise enables more effective identification and addressing complex problems, ultimately leading to lasting positive change. As trust and cohesion are fostered over time, these partnerships can drive transformative changes, enabling governments to tackle complex challenges with greater efficacy and coherence (Bryson et al., 2015).

In Greater Jakarta, grappling with regular flooding, PetaBencana.id emerges as an answer that has plagued the region for much of its region through collaboration between academia, NGOs like PetaBencana.id, and the government. The Jakarta branch of the National Disaster Management Agency supported the project from inception, ensuring alignment with operational needs. PetaBencana.id, led by MIT's Urban Risk Lab, revolutionizes flood mapping with real-time data gathered from social media, significantly enhancing service quality and accessibility for both government and the public.[46,47]

The public sector also plays a critical role in coordinating tech transfer efforts. For instance, federal labs, composed of "a heterogeneous group of organizations with differences in their types of operators; their missions; and their size, scale, and geography," are quite essential to the US economy.[48] As the pressure of international competition of technology and innovation grew, especially in terms of new development of products, the US government enacted legislation, and agencies like the National Institute

[45] https://www.jobsandskills.gov.au/publications/towards-national-jobs-and-skills-roadmap-summary/context.

[46] https://www.oecd.org/gov/innovative-government/embracing-innovation-in-government.pdf.

[47] Chen, W.D. (2025). Crowdsourcing resilience: Boosting response to megacity flood events with social media data, In "Drought, deluge, and data" report, IBM Institute for Business Value. https://www.businessofgovernment.org/sites/default/files/Drought%2C%20deluge%2C%20and%20data%20report_0.pdf.

[48] https://www.ncbi.nlm.nih.gov/books/NBK568354/.

of Standards and Technology play a pivotal role in coordinating technology transfer efforts across federal labs within the federal government.[49] This coordination is crucial for ensuring that federally funded inventions are effectively commercialized and utilized in real-world applications.

These examples demonstrate that the public sector can serve as an impartial mediator or a broker in forging connections among diverse elements. In this capacity, governments initiate collaborative engagements between stakeholders, which has been compared to adept conductors orchestrating a symphony of interests. Scholars suggest that this metaphor illustrates the dynamic nature of governmental involvement, highlighting the necessity for agility and adaptability in navigating societal complexities (Bingham et., 2005). Moreover, governments, acting as central nodes, cultivate an environment conducive to collaboration rather than imposing unilateral directives. They delicately weave the aspirations of diverse institutions, fostering an atmosphere of shared objectives and mutual understanding (Wondolleck & Yaffee, 2000). Such craftsmanship demands diplomatic finesse to maintain the delicate balance of interests (Peters, 1998). This notion captures the government's unique position as a coordinator, akin to a skilled conductor harmonizing the varied voices of society (Ansell & Gash, 2008).

Government as an Advocate

Small enterprises and startups stand as the heartbeat of our economy, propelling job creation and breathing life into burgeoning businesses and services. In the United States, nearly half of the population finds employment within these small businesses—a statistic that balloons to a staggering 90% when considered on a global scale.[50,51] In essence, the impact of small businesses reverberates profoundly throughout the economy.

Moreover, these enterprises are not merely economic contributors but pioneers of innovation and breakthroughs. Throughout history, the forefront of transformative ideas and superior products has been commandeered by small businesses and startups. Witnessing the ripple effect of

[49] Ibid.
[50] https://www.forbes.com/advisor/business/small-business-statistics.
[51] https://www.worldbank.org/en/topic/smefinance.

these innovative endeavors, we have observed how they have fundamentally reshaped and revolutionized our world.

However, in the dynamic economic landscape, startups encounter numerous obstacles that may never have confronted established businesses (Chen, 2023). These barriers, whether financial, related to human resources, or stemming from regulations and competition with larger counterparts, impede their progress. Consequently, startup survival rates across all sectors remain alarmingly low. Small businesses require support to navigate these initial challenges and to stand on equal footing in the market. This is where government can play a role.

The National Science Foundation's Small Business Innovation Research (SBIR) and Small Business Technology Transfer (STTR) programs in the US are designed to provide unique grant opportunities for small businesses, facilitating as much as $4.4 billion per year for R&D.[52] Seven years after renowned chemist and entrepreneur Arthur Obermayer testified before Congress on the importance of small business, the SBIR program was founded in 1977 to help small, high-tech businesses with the commercialization of their products. Senator Edward Kennedy was one of the early supporters of the program, advocating for increased small business participation in government R&D. Alongside Arthur and his wife Judith Obermayer, Kennedy called on federal agencies with budgets in excess of $100 million research and development dollars to set up their own programs. Then, after staunch resistance from the academic community, the SBIR government wide program was signed by President Reagan in 1982, cementing a strong ally for small tech businesses looking for assistance with their innovations.[53]

Both SBIR and STTR programs include specific efforts to support small businesses owned by members of underprivileged communities. These programs are designed to aid startups from ideas to commercialization. Projects are evaluated based on their commercial potential and the prospective performance of the awardee. The programs occur in three phases, with each building upon the last until the eventual commercialization of the project in phase 3. Notably, STTR also require participants to collaborate with nonprofit research institutions including universities and federal labs.[54,55]

[52] https://www.sbir.gov/analytics-dashboard.
[53] https://www.sbir.gov/birth-and-history-of-the-sbir-program.
[54] https://www.sbir.gov/about.
[55] https://ras.mit.edu/document/sbirsttr-overview-and-best-practices.

More new initiatives have surfaced as well, including the NIH's Small Business Program, which allocates over $1.3 billion annually[56] for scientific endeavors like medical technologies, and ARPA-E's entrepreneurial projects, supporting innovations in energy.[57] The NIH program extends funding to small businesses undertaking high-risk research ventures with potential commercialization prospects. Its aim is to convert scientific findings into marketable offerings that tackle unmet medical requirements. This is a prominent example of how public–private collaborations help overcome barriers and challenges commonly faced by resource-constrained startups in high-cost industries, thereby enabling the successful launch and development of innovative ideas that may have otherwise remained unexplored.

In addition, the US government also offers startups expert advisory and infrastructure resources. For example, the National Laboratories offer various programs that enable partnerships with startups, which can then pay the labs for services that may aid them in their scientific development efforts.[58] Seventeen labs are currently scattered throughout the country, each focusing on a different area of research including aerospace, climate change, and health. These resources include lab or office space to carry out their experiments, relevant data sources, lab equipment, and staff to counsel the startups.[59] These labs help startups from the beginning, including validation for their technologies, providing licensing, and pivoting, to enhance their R&D efforts. As a result, startups that work with the labs enjoy a much higher success rate in securing additional venture capital and filing more patents.[60] Moreover, access to startup lab staff provides valuable insights into government needs and enables startups to tailor their products to increase their chances of winning government contracts (Kramer, 2016). This could be a significant benefit for startups looking to register and compete for government contracts.

Israel, a country that is also known as a "startup nation," has produced an enormous number of ground-breaking technology startups, largely due to

[56] https://seed.nih.gov/small-business-funding.
[57] https://arpa-e.energy.gov/.
[58] https://www.energy.gov/eere/wind/how-partner-national-labs.
[59] https://www.usa.gov/agencies/national-laboratories.
[60] https://www.nrel.gov/news/features/2024/how-nrel-helps-startups-from-the-beginning.

government's support.[61] Since late 1980s, the Israeli government has started the Yozma Program, which offers vast tax incentives for foreign venture capitalists to invest in their startup businesses.[62] As a result, Israel has seen a solid upward funding trend from foreign investors. Israeli startups raised $230 million in 2018 and $768 million in funding in 2020.[63] The Israeli government is especially supportive of its high-tech industry. Recently, it has launched a new funding program to encourage other institutional entities to invest their own venture capital funds by kickstarting the program with 4 billion shekels ($1.1 billion) over a five-year period.[64]

Mentorship is another invaluable aspect that the government can aid startups. A prime example of such support is Innovation Norway, where each startup is assigned an account manager offering tailored advice and insights into potential benefits and partnerships. Navigating the early stages of a business can be daunting, particularly concerning regulatory compliance, taxes, and other governmental requirements necessary for operation (Corthay, 2009).

Increasingly, governments go beyond just attempting to help startups, focusing instead on enabling the founders of the companies. A substantial body of literature highlights the disproportionate obstacles confronting minority and women entrepreneurs, hindering their ability to catalyze economic and social advancement (Fairlie & Robb, 2008; Brush et al., 2018). Empirical studies consistently demonstrate their restricted access to affordable capital, experiences with discrimination, and comparatively limited business networks in relation to their nonminority male counterparts (Bates & Robb, 2016; Eddleston et al., 2016).

Meanwhile, entrepreneurs operating in rural contexts face a distinct constellation of challenges, including deficient infrastructure, dwindling populations, and geographic remoteness from major commercial hubs (Pato & Teixeira, 2016). Concurrently, there is a growing recognition among policymakers that fostering entrepreneurship within underrepresented groups unlocks invaluable innovation by amplifying the perspectives of underserved communities (Brush et al., 2019). The unique lived experiences and

[61] https://techcrunch.com/2021/01/21/israels-startup-ecosystem-powers-ahead-amid-a-year-of-change/.

[62] https://apolitical.co/solution-articles/en/government-venture-capital-fund-boosted-israels-start-economy.

[63] https://techcrunch.com/2021/01/21/israels-startup-ecosystem-powers-ahead-amid-a-year-of-change/.

[64] https://innovationisrael.org.il/en/press_release/stimulus-to-boost-israeli-high-tech/.

vantage points of minority, female, and rural business owners position them to identify unmet needs and develop tailored solutions for their communities (Zelekha et al., 2014). Nonetheless, surmounting systemic impediments, such as insufficient startup capital, gender-based biases, and the challenge of geographic isolation, remain an uphill battle (Coleman et al., 2016; Marlow & Martinez Dy., 2018). Prioritizing the cultivation of inclusive entrepreneurial ecosystems that dismantle barriers is imperative to enabling the full entrepreneurial potential of marginalized groups, thereby catalyzing economic growth and driving societal progress (Feld, 2012; Motoyama & Knowlton, 2017).

In the United States, federal agencies dedicate substantial budgetary allocations exclusively for minority and women-owned enterprises through programs like the Small Business Administration's (SBA) 8(a) Business Development initiative (Dilger, 2018). This flagship program nurtures firms owned by socially and economically disadvantaged individuals, with 5% of all federal spending reserved for 8(a) firms.[65] More recently, cross-agency collaborations have germinated to holistically empower underrepresented entrepreneurs.

The SBA's Veterans Business Outreach Center in the United States exemplifies this synergistic approach, syncing veteran-owned startups with experts who can help them draft a business plan, conduct feasibility analysis, and provide additional counseling to help them launch their business while they transition into civilian life.[66] Another multistakeholder alliance, NSF INCLUDES, orchestrates a national network advancing inclusive STEM ecosystems (Howley et al., 2022). Research-intensive universities forge partnerships with minority-serving community colleges and industry, forging pathways for underrepresented groups into the STEM workforce and entrepreneurship pipeline.

These targeted initiatives signify growing acknowledgment that unleashing America's fullest innovative capacity necessitates democratizing opportunity across demographic strata. Programs such as 8(a) help to level the playing field by reducing barriers to entry, thereby challenging and mitigating the historical exclusion of marginalized communities from

[65] https://warrenaverett.com/insights/sba-8a-program/.
[66] https://www.sba.gov/local-assistance/resource-partners/veterans-business-outreach-center-vboc-program.

entrepreneurship opportunities (Dilger, 2018). In concert, ecosystem-building coalitions strive to nurture environments where the ingenuity and talent of all Americans can thrive, regardless of background.

Outside the US, the Specialized Training and Employment Programme (STEP) provides targeted sector-specific support to help Vulnerable Persons and Vulnerable Children's Resettlement Scheme participants navigate the workforce entry process, reflecting evidence-based integration strategies that prioritize early economic stability as a key factor in promoting the overall welfare and resilience of forcibly displaced populations.

These types of programs are not always limited to economic programs for individuals. Horizon Europe stands as the European Union's primary funding program for research and innovation.[67] The initiative is another example that plays a crucial facilitator role in addressing pressing global issues, such as climate change, and contributes to the realization of the UN's Sustainable Development Goals.[68] The program fosters cooperation that amplifies the influence of research and technological progress on shaping and applying EU policies. Additionally, the program nurtures the creation and broader distribution of outstanding knowledge and solutions. The combined efforts aim to strengthen the impact of scientific work and innovation for policymaking and global problem-solving.[69]

Connecting underrepresented innovators to established resource streams constitutes a core thrust. Alongside financial capital, know-how, networks, and credibility accrue through curated engagement with academic, public, and private sector stakeholders (Rossi et al., 2017). Collectively, the federal landscape reveals a multipronged strategy for democratizing innovation by dismantling structural barriers impeding entrepreneurial human potential.

The Israeli government follows a similar philosophy as well, in that it does not just help tech startups, it especially tries to help marginalized communities. For example, Arab Israelis are extremely underrepresented in the high-tech sector although its population accounts for 20% of Israel's total population. The Ministry of Economy and Industry launched the Hybrid Program to encourage and nurture Arab startups. Despite previous government funding to help Arab startups, those businesses often cannot get to

[67] https://research-and-innovation.ec.europa.eu/funding/funding-opportunities/funding-programmes-and-open-calls/horizon-europe_en.

[68] https://commission.europa.eu/funding-tenders/find-funding/eu-funding-programmes/horizon-europe_en.

[69] Ibid.

the next stage. For this reason, the government created and subsidized the Nazareth Business Incubator Center to help them grow their businesses.[70,71]

Pioneering South African initiatives catalyzes inclusive technological and economic growth. Nationally, the Technology Innovation Agency (TIA) nurtures black-owned tech clusters through a multipronged strategy—combining university R&D funding, accelerators, and corporate venture capital across provinces like Gauteng and Western Cape.[72] Concurrently, SHE Trades Africa orchestrates multistakeholder hubs, galvanizing women agro-processors by applying innovations to female-led farming cooperatives' needs.[73] In KwaZulu-Natal, Tongaat forges symbiotic partnerships mobilizing commercialization support for rural food ventures, catalyzing integration with global supply chains.[74]

South Africa's multifaceted efforts to catalyze entrepreneurship across demographics powerfully demonstrate a commitment to inclusive innovation (Lose, 2021). Through high-tech hubs embracing diversity and initiatives cultivating marginalized communities' agribusiness acumen, a holistic democratization of economic opportunity is unfolding (Manikas et al., 2019; Odame et al., 2020).

This aligns with Acemoglu and Robinson's (2012) theory of inclusive institutions, whereby representative governments seeking broad-based prosperity must actively remedy exclusionary practices. By strategically directing resources and forging partnerships with small and diverse-led enterprises, South Africa's state-led ecosystem-building dismantles systemic impediments to participation like inadequate financing, networks, and role models for underrepresented founders (Lose, 2021; Odame et al., 2020).

Moreover, as Goldstein (2012) and Thompson and Lopez Barrera (2019) pointed out, such collaborations can catalyze community resilience by uplifting diverse voices and hyperlocal solutions. Platforms amplifying marginalized innovators redress overlooked challenges and accelerate localized renewal. Ultimately, by rectifying inequities and energizing latent human capital across all communities, South Africa's multipronged approach portends an entrepreneurial renaissance buoyed by the nation's

[70] https://www.timesofisrael.com/arab-entrepreneurs-get-a-tech-boost-from-idf-veterans/.

[71] https://finder.startupnationcentral.org/program_page/nazareth-business-incubator-center.

[72] https://www.tia.org.za/core/uploads/2022/11/TIA-Annual-Report-2021_2022.pdf.

[73] SHE Trades. (2022). *Key Trends & Insights: SheTrades Outlook 2022.* International Trade Centre. https://outlook.shetrades.com/admin/upload/publications/documents/SheTrades%20Outlook_Key%20Trends%20&%20Insights_2022.pdf.

[74] https://www.tongaat.com/stakeholder-value-creation/supporting-our-farmers/.

full diversity and dynamism. With inclusive innovation, maximizing quality of life and competitiveness, realizing entrepreneurship's democratizing potential is imperative for governments in the innovation era.

These public–private efforts highlight South Africa's holistic vision to help establish new pathways for entrepreneurial pursuits to all people across the demographic spectrum. From energizing high-tech clusters reflecting diversity to catalyzing agribusiness ecosystems enriching marginalized communities, a multipronged democratization of opportunity is crystallizing. As innovators neglected by society ascend, the entrepreneurial frontiers of South Africa are slowly but surely being redrawn.

Additionally, multibenefit partnerships are underpinned by the fundamental concept of joint value creation, as articulated by Le Ber and Branzei (2010) and later elaborated on by Bridoux and Stoelhorst (2022). At its core, these partnerships unite two or more parties over shared objectives, seeking to find an elusive equilibrium between risks and rewards. This balance is meticulously recalibrated as parties work together, navigating endeavors side by side. Through collaborative partnerships, diverse stakeholders pool their expertise, resources, and capabilities to create a cohesive force that leverages shared incentives and aligned interests to drive coordinated achievement of mutual objectives.

This collaboration not only amplifies the overall impact of initiatives but also serves to mitigate the inherent weaknesses or vulnerabilities that come with isolated endeavors (Hadaya & Cassivi, 2012). Thanks to the seamless integration of complementary capabilities and resources, multibenefit partnerships are able to transcend the normal limitations of operating independently, bringing about great levels of innovation while promoting sustainable change. Collective problem-solving and opportunity-seizing lay the groundwork for a more resilient and equitable future.

Government as a Learner and Coproducer

In our prior discussions on governmental partnerships with other sectors, governments in general have taken a top-down method and played a leading role. They have provided financial and other critical resources to private businesses, universities, and other entities to produce innovation. They have also tried to lift disadvantaged organizations up with various approaches to be able to compete with larger and more established organizations. In addition, they are also a matchmaker to connect organizations across different sectors and industries to collaborate together.

However, there is something to be said about the importance of government breaking out of its traditional role of only being the deliverer of policies and instead being adaptable and open to learning (Leeuw, 2020). To that point, there are instances where the government receives advice and learns from organizations from both for-profits and nonprofit organizations; by leveraging frontline expertise, it can strategically pivot policymaking on innovation frameworks. Those organizations usually have a good grasp of what the most needed service is as well as more cutting-edge technology.

For example, the Israel Innovation Authority, an independent nongovernmental entity, advises the government and Parliament committees regarding innovation policy. It designs a variety of important programs under divisions including the Startup Division, Growth Division, Technological Infrastructure Division, Advanced Manufacturing Division, International Collaboration Division, and Societal Challenges Division to facilitate innovation at various stages and promote important initiatives.[75]

In the US, focusing just on technology innovation alone, at least twenty organizations such as the Pew Research Center, Internet & Technology, the Center for Technology Innovation at Brookings, the Center for Democracy and Technology, and the Center for AI and Digital Policy all advocate for innovation while advising the government on technology policies that would create a more informed, sustainable, and equitable society.[76]

In the United Kingdom, the Industrial Strategy Challenge Fund (ISCF) serves as a dynamic nexus, fostering collaborative synergies among government, businesses, and nonprofits. Departing from traditional funding mechanisms, the ISCF solicits ingenious solutions from diverse sectors by channeling resources into strategic challenges or missions. This participatory model marks a departure from top-down frameworks, with organizations actively contributing their expertise rather than being mere recipients. The ISCF embodies a shift toward collaborative governance and participatory policymaking, where government actively seeks answers from external entities. This interactive approach redefines innovation and policy implementation, emphasizing the value of diverse perspectives and collaborative

[75] https://innovationisrael.org.il.

[76] https://alltechishuman.org/all-tech-is-human-blog/20-organizations-talking-about-tech-policy.

endeavors in addressing societal challenges. Through the ISCF, the UK government cultivates an ecosystem where stakeholders come together to develop solutions and drive meaningful progress in tackling complex issues.

Nesta's Innovation Growth Lab, another organization in the UK, also has its own initiatives to help support technology and innovation. It was created in 2012 to help encourage innovation domestically and internationally with a focus on catalyzing economic growth through its commitment to experimentation and utilizes science to encourage evidence-based policymaking. It has collaborated with over thirty-five government agencies across five continents, helping them adopt more experimental and innovative thinking approaches. This collaboration identifies effective policies and interventions conducive to promoting innovation-centric growth.[77] The organization uses various evaluation methodologies to inform policymaking and public innovation.

In addition, rather than traditional rigid public procurement with established businesses and other organizations, collaborations with startups provide unique opportunities for shared value creation in which both the government and startups can learn from one another while reducing transaction costs as compared to larger businesses (Bryson et al., 2015; Hawkins et al., 2018). Through this collaboration, governments can learn about new products, technologies, or methodologies, while the startups can learn how to adjust their products or services for their customers and even make improvements to their own business processes. One study shows that by partnering with government, startups increase their patenting activities by 74%.[78]

However, these innovative solutions are not invariably constrained within the realms of technology and economics. In the realm of governmental collaboration with the arts, a tangible instance can be found with the Arts Council England's strategic consultation for cultural policy development. As a non-departmental public body championing arts and culture in England, Arts Council England actively seeks insights from a spectrum of stakeholders. The diverse group of stakeholders includes arts organizations, artists, and various contributors, all becoming integral to navigating the Council's strategic path and financial allocations.

[77] https://www.innovationgrowthlab.org/innovation-growth-lab.

[78] https://itif.org/publications/2020/08/24/collaboration-between-start-ups-and-federal-agencies-surprising-solution/.

For instance, in 2020, Arts Council England spearheaded a comprehensive consultation endeavor to glean perspectives on its decade-long arts strategy, aptly named Let's Create.[79] In this undertaking, the organization dynamically engaged with its diverse body of stakeholders grasping multifaceted insights into the future of the arts in England. The insights derived from this consultation proved instrumental in sculpting Arts Council England's strategic objectives and funding allocations. This exemplifies the government's steadfast dedication to actively seeking counsel from the arts sector, underlining its commitment to informed policymaking and targeted investments in cultural ventures.

These examples show that government can both speak and listen. It can help drive progress across multiple domains and solicit the input of external organizations to shape its strategic future. Employing these learning techniques, governments help to promote a coproduction ecosystem that takes all of its stakeholders into consideration.

Throughout this chapter, we have seen the multiple roles government plays and how the various approaches they take in collaborating. At times they are the purse, providing necessary funds to further innovation and social causes. Other times they play the role of the matchmaker, bringing parties together to work toward a common goal. Yet other times they will be down in the front lines, rolling up their sleeves alongside the citizens to co-produce valuable services. In all these cases, however, it is clear that the government has experimented with many different ways to provide services and to tackle gargantuan social causes that alone it would struggle to face. These experiments, we argue, are all examples of innovation, and innovation that spurs innovation in others.

[79] https://www.artscouncil.org.uk/lets-create/strategy-2020-2030.

Chapter 5
We the People
Democratized Public Innovation

> Ask not what your country can do for you—ask what you can do for your country.
>
> —John F. Kennedy

Cadillac Ranch is a common art display destination along the historic Route 66 on the outskirts of Amarillo, TX in the US. Created in 1974 as a quirky display of Cadillacs stuck headfirst in the ground to display the evolution of the Cadillac tailfin, the art display quickly became a fun place for visitors to go take a can of spray paint and sign their names on the cars. The tradition began as a way for visitors to leave their literal mark on something significant and to have a sense of shared belonging. Just like that Cadillac Ranch, we now have the tools to allow literally everyone to participate in civil discourse and to have their voices heard.

Throughout human history, when citizens were not satisfied with their governments, they opted for revolution over oppression. Following the government's imposition of the unpopular poll tax in England back in 1380, the peasants revolted against King Richard II. Ralph atte Wode grabbed a stack of documents from the local official and stuck them on his pitchfork, carrying the documents as a sign of rebellion against the king.[1] Rebels marched to London, even damaging the University of Cambridge in the process, and the government was forced to negotiate.[2,3]

This same revolutionary spirit of course also crossed the Atlantic with the founding of the United States. In the eighteenth century, "no taxation without representation" was the rallying cry of colonists in North America

[1] https://brewminate.com/charters-pitchforks-and-green-seals-text-and-materiality-in-late-medieval-revolts/.
[2] https://www.britannica.com/event/Peasants-Revolt.
[3] https://www.publicbooks.org/rereading-the-revolt/.

Innovation and Entrepreneurship in the Public Sector. Wendy D. Chen and David B. Audretsch, Oxford University Press. © Oxford University Press (2025). DOI: 10.1093/9780197679470.003.0005

against the British government's taxes, including the ones on the importation of tea. Little did the British know that their actions had lit the powder keg, marking the beginning of the American Revolution. Having felt their wishes fall on deaf ears in the chambers of King George III, the colonists had little choice but to rise up and create a new system unlike the world had ever seen.[4]

These acts of violence were unfortunately the only means people felt they had to draw attention to their grievances and demand for change. For most of human history, as civilizations rose, power tended to be concentrated in tight-knit circles of aristocrats who had helped the winning ruler come to power. But since the advent of the American system of representative republic, that power balance began to shift toward the people. When Alexis de Tocqueville famously came to the US to observe the prison system in 1831 sent by the French government, he saw a democratic America with a limited government. Amazed by the tight-knit community and the inner workings of democracy, he wrote about the America he saw in his book *Democracy in America.*

Over time, governments around the world have expanded both in their overall size and scope of services provided. In contrast, public trust in government has been following an opposite trend. Using the US as an example, when the National Election Study started surveying individuals' trust in government at the end of 1950s, nearly 75% of Americans believed that the federal government represents them well and that the government does the right thing for them. Today, trust in the government barely exceeds 20%.[5] In other words, people are dissatisfied and feel that their voices are being heard. While we may not necessarily be quick to grab our pitchforks, we still harbor much of that same raw human emotion of our ancestors wanting equal representation and fairness.

In 1989, the government of Prime Minister Margaret Thatcher implemented a controversial local taxation policy, the poll tax, which imposed a flat rate tax on all adults in the UK regardless of income or assets owned (Butler et al., 1994). This new system contrasted with the previous rating system that was based on property values. As a result, the public felt unfairness and led to massive protests across Britain.[6]

[4] https://www.loc.gov/classroom-materials/united-states-history-primary-source-timeline/american-revolution-1763-1783/colonies-rebellion-1773-1774/.

[5] Pew Research Center, 2024. "Public Trust in Government: 1958-2024". https://www.pewresearch.org/politics/2024/06/24/public-trust-in-government-1958-2024/.

[6] https://www.huckmag.com/article/the-history-of-the-poll-tax-and-the-power-of-direct-action.

At the time of writing, Dutch farmers are protesting their government's policy to limit the use of nitrogen and ammonia emissions by up to 95%.[7] In protest, the farmers have blocked traffic with their tractors, which in some cases has resulted in having their vehicles shot at by police.[8] These types of situations are common occurrences when democracies fail to listen to the voices of the people or to take other points of view into consideration when drafting policies.

In the private sector, we are all familiar with entrepreneurs and the entrepreneurial mindset that seeks to make radical changes and to disrupt innovations since as you could probably guess, corporations are always looking for ways to stay competitive and to reduce risk. That entrepreneurial mindset has led to drastic shifts and new industries being born, from Henry Ford's assembly line bringing the automobile to the masses to the latest app that allows you to have pizza delivered to your door with the click of a button. Typically, however, this mindset is applied to smaller organizations who operate in an agile environment.

Far from being agile, governments are large organizations with vast resources yet tend to be bogged down by bureaucracy. They largely employ a conventional top-down governance model that limits innovation due to its structure limiting individuals' chances to voice or express their own ideas. The decision-making largely only happens at the top of the organizational structures, leading to the same problem that has been occurring everywhere at large. Despite the introduction of New Public Management in many countries in the 1980s to solve this issue that gave managers more power to enhance innovation, the results have still not seemed to address the problem (Theodoulou et al., 2016). Governments must be able to pivot and adapt in response to the evolving needs and expectations of their constituents if they wish to retain legitimacy and remain in power. However, implementing such changes is rarely straightforward.

Bottom-Up innovation

Bottom-up corporate entrepreneurship, often known as intrapreneurship, encourages innovation and entrepreneurial thinking from employees at all levels of the organization, not just top management. In other words,

[7] https://www.msn.com/en-gb/news/world/farmers-e2-80-98freedom-convoy-e2-80-99-takes-aim-at-strict-dutch-net-zero-regulations/ar-AAZoEnU.

[8] https://www.agriland.ie/farming-news/video-dutch-police-fire-shots-during-farmer-tractor-protest/.

everyone within the organization is engaged in the innovation process. Companies including IBM, Motorola, and Cargill have embraced this approach witnessing the benefits of involving people from all levels to bring up the needs and wants from the customers.[9]

Bottom-up solutions have been proven to work in many scenarios exactly as intended. For instance, Staples Inc., a leading office supplies company in the US, has an open call to invite the general public to submit their business or product ideas to the company.[10] The selected ones are then commercialized by the company, allowing the winner to see their idea put in place and have a sense of pride knowing that their idea is special. Because these commoners are also the users and customers of the company, this strategy allows the company to significantly increase its accuracy in identifying what the market wants. Similarly, the consulting firm Accenture invited employees to propose a new name for their company, switching their name from Anderson Consulting.[11] The company has kept that name since 2001 when it provided its initial public offering to the public.

It may be easy to wonder at this point what this has to do with government soliciting input from all its employees as these scenarios identified above had little to no similarity to the service delivery of a government agency. One lesson we can still learn from these private sector scenarios is the strength of collective intelligence and how it can help arrive at a better idea than if the process relied on any one individual (Wolpert, 2003). Furthermore, a significant challenge arises when decision-makers at the top of organizations are often far removed from the people experiencing the effects or feedback of the product or service. This separation can create a disconnect between leadership and those affected by policies, services, or products. Without direct exposure to the everyday realities of users or frontline staff, leaders may base their choices on abstract information or second-hand reports, which can result in decisions that overlook important nuances or fail to meet actual needs.

Using a parks and recreation department as an example, a park ranger or visitor's center employee or park visitors may have more insight into what new services are needed or complaints the people are having. If those people are empowered to be able to make recommendations or decisions, it is more

[9] https://sloanreview.mit.edu/article/the-four-models-of-corporate-entrepreneurship/?switch_view=PDF.

[10] https://www.staples.com/sbd/cre/tech-services/explore-tips-and-advice/tech-articles/make-your-idea-happen-retail-business.html.

[11] https://newsroom.accenture.com/news/2000/andersen-consulting-announces-new-name-accenture-effective-010101.

likely to reflect the wishes of the customers, or citizens in the case of a democracy. These bottom-up innovators provide invaluable answers to complex problems. Due to their direct and active involvement with the product or service they offer, their knowledge and passion for the *right* solution drive them strongly, perhaps even more so than those who sit at the top removed from the situation.[12,13]

When the bottom-up innovation approach (also known as citizen-centered innovation) is applied to government services, it promotes citizen participation and engagement as opposed to government authority (Bason, 2010). Bottom-up solutions truly seek to allow more voices to be heard, and to provide the best possible solutions. Because citizens may be thought of as customers of public services including health, education, transportation, the postal service, and the Internal Revenue Service, public policies directly impact them. They therefore know well what services they need, the drawbacks of the existing ones, and the possible solutions to these problems.

Although governments are often too big to adapt or innovate, many governments are brave and entrepreneurial enough to experiment with new methods to collaborate with their employees and citizens by using the bottom-up solution. Enabled by superior modern technology, these governments have set up various digital platforms for their citizens to report problems, participate, and get involved with policymaking. They invite citizens including children to participate in government budgeting with e-democracy. In addition, they use digital crowdfunding platforms to ask individuals for their solutions to local problems and give them matching funds. Moreover, some governments have tried to experiment applying the new blockchain technology to their governance.

Government as a Platform

Historically, the ancient Greek government, the ancestor of our modern democracy, gave people an opportunity to participate in government and to directly contribute to the community. However, as time passed, governments across the globe began to expand and people's participation and involvement in governmental affairs have been limited. Today, few people

[12] https://www.sciencedirect.com/science/article/pii/S0048733315000670.

[13] https://www.dau.edu/library/defense-atl/blog/A-Bottom-Up,-Innovative-Approach-for-Delivering—What-We-Need-Now.

attend town hall meetings in cities, and modern governments are not communicating with their citizens. As a result, citizens' trust in the public sector has been on a drastic decline.[14]

Governments are often slow to change, constrained by politics, bureaucracy, and risk aversion. According to the World Government Summit report in 2019, as many as 80% of major change initiatives in government fail to meet their objectives.[15] Failure can be for any number of reasons including incorrect expectations of correlation between policy and results and a lack of cooperation, to a lack of experts in the expert community (Polterovich, 2014; Rezende, 2002).However, entrepreneurial governments dare to challenge these conventions by embracing risks and championing new ideas, aiming not just for efficiency but for societal progress. They prioritize agility, adaptability, experimentation, prototyping, collaboration, technology integration, and continuous learning.

Many governments are embracing new technology and innovation. At varying levels of government, they have adopted a new "government as a platform" role by leveraging modern digital platform technologies (O'Reilly, 2011). This decentralized and democratic approach affords citizens a viable channel to exchange information with the government and provides the government with a chance to increase transparency in their initiatives. In other words, these governments provide digital platforms to enable and empower citizens to collaboratively address local problems. Thomas Jefferson and many of the other Founding Fathers had envisioned a democracy in which people and government have the freedom to organize with one another to form a more perfect union.[16] This new method can help increase civic engagement, allowing people to feel a sense of belonging to the country in which they live and to have a sense of contribution to their local communities.

Governments develop online platforms to seek solutions from the public, also known as crowdsourcing. Crowdsourcing seeks the promise of collective intelligence and the belief that it can exceed individual capabilities under certain conditions (Estellés-Arolas & González-Ladrón-de-Guevara, 2012; Surowiecki, 2004). It highlights user engagement and represents emerging phenomena whereby large groups of individuals can join forces online to

[14] https://hub.beesmart.city/en/strategy/how-smart-cities-boost-citizen-engagement.
[15] https://www.worldgovernmentsummit.org/observer/reports/2019/detail/reframe-to-reform.
[16] https://www.monticello.org/research-education/thomas-jefferson-encyclopedia/thomas-jefferson-and-religious-freedom/.

work toward shared goals (Stiver et al., 2015). Wikipedia and open-source software development are prominent examples of crowdsourcing. Many governments have taken this new approach to gather feedback, data, or ideas from a wide array of people to impact products or services through digital platforms.

Some governments harness the power of digital technology to facilitate two-way conversations with citizens, fostering open communication and participation in policymaking and public management that were previously limited by geographical and administrative constraints. For instance, the City of Boston developed multiple new phone apps such as Bos: 311, also known as Citizens Connect, to invite residents and visitors to participate in city management by reporting issues like potholes and graffiti.[17] The reports are then automatically received by the government system that can then assign service teams. Similarly, in New York, the city government created a NYC311 platform where the government updates information on different public programs and services such as the SNAP program, while encouraging citizens to connect with city agencies to file complaints and make suggestions through convenient phone calls to increase city government transparency and efficiency.[18]

Montevideo, the capital city of Uruguay, launched Montevideo Decide, a digital platform designed to foster greater citizen engagement with the municipal government. Through this platform, registered users can actively partake in a variety of crowdsourced governance activities, such as online discussions, polls, and forums that allow them to voice their opinions on local issues. Additionally, citizens have the opportunity to propose new initiatives aimed at improving life in the city. Admirably, Montevideo Decide goes beyond traditional civic engagement by allowing citizens to interact directly with local officials. They can interview the mayor and other municipal leaders, offering them a unique opportunity to ask questions, raise concerns, and play an important role in local policymaking.[19]

Better Reikjavik is another notable online civic engagement platform used by the City of Reikjavik in Iceland.[20] In the wake of the financial crisis of Iceland in 2008, the Icelandic government collapsed the following year, triggering massive public outrage and a deep erosion of trust in government.

[17] https://www.boston.gov/departments/boston-311.
[18] https://portal.311.nyc.gov/.
[19] https://oidp.net/distinction/en/candidacy.php?id=1218.
[20] https://thegovlab.org/static/files/better-reykjavik.pdf.

Citizens demanded greater transparency, accountability, and involvement in decision-making processes. This online platform gives their government a second chance to bridge the gap between residents and their local government. It also helps to regain the trust of their people by creating an opportunity for residents to propose ideas to address municipal issues online such as urban planning and social services. Interestingly, the platform also has a feature to allow citizens to debate these ideas with one another and to vote on the best ideas. The most popular ideas are reviewed monthly by Reykjavík City Council, ensuring that citizen input plays a direct role in shaping local policy. By facilitating open dialogue and participatory governance, Better Reykjavík serves as a valuable tool for rebuilding trust between citizens and their government, turning civic frustration into constructive engagement.[21]

Another noteworthy model that some governments have explored combines the expertise of innovation professionals across sectors with citizens' active input. Amsterdam InChange, also known as Amsterdam Smart City, is an open innovation platform serving the Amsterdam region and beyond.[22] While it draws on the knowledge and experience of professionals to develop smart solutions for a more livable urban future, it also invites all changemakers to join force. The platform is an open and safe space for cooperation and innovation. The platform offers a meeting place where individuals from diverse backgrounds come together with a shared goal to make better streets, neighborhoods, and cities. for informing citizens and inviting them to brainstorm, some online platforms run by the public sector also enable citizens to collaborate on ideas to innovate the city together. So far, over 8,000 innovators have joined this platform to create solutions to improve the quality of life in the city.[23]

Participatory Budgeting

Models of participatory governance aim to promote greater citizen involvement, openness, and cooperative efforts between members of the public and government in deciding on policies and programs. "It recognizes that

[21] https://thegovlab.org/static/files/better-reykjavik.pdf.
[22] https://amsterdamsmartcity.com.
[23] https://amsterdamsmartcity.com/about.

the best ideas may not come from within government and that governments can learn from the diverse perspectives of their people."[24] By enabling transparency around decision-making and giving residents opportunities to contribute their input and ideas, these approaches seek to enhance the quality of public service delivery and to allows a diversity of voices and perspectives to be heard so that solutions have broader buy-in and better reflect the needs and priorities of those impacted. When citizens feel their concerns and feedback are being considered, it can build trust in institutions and result in outcomes viewed as fair by the public.

Participatory budgeting has emerged as a prominent example of participatory governance and democratic innovation enabling citizens to directly influence allocation of public funds (Cabannes & Lipietz, 2018; Denhardt & Denhardt, 2015; Gilman, 2016). Participatory budgeting aligns with participatory democratic principles granting citizens decision-making authority over spending priorities, rather than concentrating budget control exclusively among elected officials and administrators (Cohen, 1989; Pateman, 1970). Through participatory budgeting, citizens are given the opportunity to decide how and where public resources should be allocated (Cabannes, 2004; Sintomer et al., 2008).

It aims to prioritize spending commitments in a way that better addresses the needs of the local population. Incorporating public input through participatory budgeting helps to enhance government transparency and legitimacy, as well as promote a more inclusive and representative form of democracy that empowers community members to shape the allocation of resources and priorities (Cabannes, 2004). Citizens also gain enhanced understanding of government finances by grappling with budgetary decisions, enabling them to better evaluate officials' performance and advocate informed priorities (Utzig, 2002).

Additionally, participatory budgeting employs open, inclusive, and deliberate meetings and presentations to collaboratively determine spending priorities. It emphasizes collective reasoned discourse to reach consensus on public policy, contrasting limitations of traditional voting (Chambers, 2003; Saari, 2003). Through dialogue, negotiation, and consensus-building, participants are encouraged to weigh priorities, consider trade-offs, and propose solutions that reflect the collective needs of the community. As a

[24] https://www.oecd.org/gov/innovative-government/embracing-innovation-in-government.pdf.

result, participatory budgeting also fosters a greater sense of community, civic responsibility, and empowerment (Cabannes, 2004).

In 2011, the Open Government Partnership (OGP) was established to create a collaborative platform where government leaders and civil society organizations from around the world could come together to promote transparency, accountability, and civic participation.[25] Recognizing that traditional governance mechanisms often left citizens feeling disconnected from decision-making, the OGP placed a strong emphasis on leveraging technology to bridge the gap and to engage citizens further. One such initiative is the development of electronic participatory budgeting process. which provides another opportunity for citizens to control the government's purse strings, thus leading to a greater shared sense of democracy.

The city of Tartu in Estonia serves as a prime example, widely recognized as the country's intellectual capital.The city government started to invite citizens to participate in the city's budgeting process back in 2013. All citizens can present their proposals on how the city should spend 140,000 euros on the city government website or email to the City Public Relations Department.[26] The ideas are then filtered down by a group of experts. To date, sixteen ideas that target public safety, health, community development, and the like have been implemented with Tartu's participatory budget. Some of the projects included the lowering of sidewalk curbs, building a new walking trail, and reconstruction of a historic site.[27] What's more innovative about Tartu's participatory budgeting process is that the city also created an Idea Collection Map tool to streamline the idea submission process by only requiring citizens to enter a few lines of description of a project, which also links to the specific geographic location where the initiative will take place.[28]

In the US, the City of Boston was the first one to create a participatory budgeting process called Youth Lead the Change to train young people to become change makers. The city government intends to use this initiative to engage citizen participation in government starting from an early age and to ensure that all voices are heard. Through the online platform, twelve- to

[25] https://www.opengovpartnership.org/about/.
[26] https://www.tartu.ee/et?page_id=24758&lang_id=2&menu_id=13.
[27] https://news.err.ee/1608586219/55-ideas-submitted-to-tartu-s-participatory-budget-program.
[28] https://participedia.net/case/7795.

twenty-five-year-old Bostonians make decisions on how to spend one million dollars of the City's budget. The platform is run by the Mayor's Youth Council comprised of youth delegates appointed by the mayor. The platform asks young people across the city to suggest ideas to spend that amount of capital to make improvements to areas including education, parks and recreation, and the environment. City staff, participatory budgeting project staff, and area experts then help them develop proposals. The projects must create public value, cost at least $2,500, and expect to last for more than five years. Based on these criteria, young people throughout Boston vote on the projects that should be prioritized for government funding.[29]

Meanwhile, South America has experimented with participatory budgeting as well. In Porto Alegre, Brazil, the city's entrepreneurial seminal experiment of participatory budgeting represents a noteworthy attempt at striving toward democratic governance. Initiated under Workers' Party leadership in 1989, it enabled citizens to directly shape municipal spending priorities (Baierle, 2003). This contrasted sharply with traditional budgeting concentrated in bureaucratic and political elites who were previously the ones in control of budget decisions. Porto Alegre thus provided an early model of participatory budgeting that inspired replication worldwide (Avritzer, 2006). With that said, scholars highlight both significant benefits and limitations of its model.

The process included successive stages of citizen involvement (Marquetti et al., 2012). Neighborhood assemblies identified local needs, which fed into thematic assemblies on citywide priorities. A Budget Council of elected delegates then developed an integrated budget for approval. Through this process, citizen voices became institutionalized as their priorities could be reflected in budgeting decisions (Baierle, 2003).

The implementation received acknowledgment from the world over, with proponents praising participatory budgeting's democratic deepening by incorporating marginalized groups often excluded from governance (Piper, 2014). Involving citizens fosters a more engaged public and budgets reflecting broader needs, despite some scholarship questioning representativeness (Avritzer, 2006; Marquetti et al., 2012). Participants also gain empowerment through budgetary control and oversight (Piper, 2014).

[29] https://www.bu.edu/ioc/files/2017/01/Youth-Lead-the-Change_Report.pdf.

Crowd-Based Financing Innovation

Travel back in history and we can find Mozart's concertos and the Statue of Liberty were both the beneficiaries of crowdfunding. When the French government tried to give the Statue of Liberty to the US as a gift to celebrate the Franco-American Union, they found they were unable to fully finance the project. In order to complete the statue, both governments campaigned to the public to fund it. The campaigns were successful with the US raising $100,000 and the French raising 250,000 francs.[30] Using private donations avoids potential taxpayer objections and congressional disagreements.

Crowdfunding refers to raising funds from the crowd to finance various projects and initiatives (Chen, 2023; Ordanini et al., 2011). The main way that crowdfunding operates is by receiving relatively small amounts of funding from many individuals (Chen, 2022, Mollick, 2014). It provides individual funders with autonomy to use their own discretions to choose which ones to support and determines contribution amounts, thus broadening access to financing in a more democratic manner than traditional capital sources which utilize centralized decision-making processes (Gerber & Hui, 2013).

Crowdfunding has emerged as a prominent alternative funding source to grants, bank loans, and so on over recent years when digital technology enables convenient crowdfunding through online channels (Chen, 2023; Clarkin, 2014; Manzoor, 2020). A growing number of organizations and individuals have taken advantage of digital crowdfunding to get their projects funded by the public. Interestingly, the concept of crowdfunding has been extended to public governance. Governments are largely reliant on tax collections and public finances, which may be constrained by economic conditions outside their control. Raising taxes is often politically challenging due to concerns about overtaxing citizens and businesses, which could discourage economic activity. Crowd-based collaboration serves as a new type of financing innovation that shifts traditional boundaries between organizations and their external environments. For example, civic crowdfunding is an emerging technological development to connect citizens with their communities and the government online. The decentralized nature of crowdfunding and crowdsourcing promotes an inclusive process to engage

[30] https://medium.com/jsc-powershare-foundation-portfolio/psychology-behind-crowdfunding-a1def0fb30f.

both government and citizens. Through civic crowdfunding, individuals can propose new ideas for their local communities such as the fixing of old bridges or even organizing citizen-managed libraries since they know how to best serve the community. In turn, the government will be able to fund more targeted projects within its budget without raising additional taxes. In this way, the government is no longer just a gatekeeper or decision-maker who is likely to overlook areas that have been prioritized by its citizens.

In the United Kingdom, the City of Plymouth has launched crowdfunding campaigns on a popular reward-based crowdfunding platform Crowdfunder. This is the city's new initiative to reach their citizens, to invite them to propose new projects to support the city, and to raise extra funding for those projects. When a citizen's proposal is promising, both the city and the public contribute funds to the projects. "For every £1 spent by the city, residents have donated more than double for an additional £1 million in support for communities."[31] In the first five years, the city pledged £475,010 to ninety-three projects including startup businesses, charities and social enterprises, and other community groups. After those projects get funded by city residents, they are eligible to receive additional funding opportunities from the city government to increase their chances of being successful.

In other words, the City of Plymouth has adopted a civic crowdfunding platform that enables residents to play a direct role in shaping the city's development. Through this platform, citizens are encouraged to participate in campaigns to propose innovative ideas for the city. Once a proposed idea demonstrates strong public backing shown from their crowdfunding success, the city government steps in to provide additional resources, guidance, or funding to help bring the project to fruition. This citizen-led innovation approach not only empowers individuals to take initiative but also fosters a stronger partnership between the government and the community. In recognition of these efforts, the City of Plymouth was honored with the Engaged City Award, highlighting its commitment to democratic innovation and citizen engagement.[32]

In other scenarios, the government uses existing crowdfunding platforms to raise funds for their local government projects. While crowdfunding platforms such as Kickstarter are almost exclusively for businesses, IndieGoGo is a platform that is open to many different types of projects including

[31] https://www.crowdfunder.co.uk/crowdfund-plymouth.
[32] https://pressreleases.responsesource.com/news/98635/plymouth-crowd-helps-city-win-international-prize.

businesses, artists, nonprofits, and even local governments. For example, Blacksburg, Virginia, in the US used crowdfunding to help fund a series of bike trails for a park. In a collaboration between the town of Blacksburg and the nonprofit the Friends of the Huckleberry Trail, the two joined forces to attempt to build a mountain biking park.[33] Similarly, another project started by the National Trust for Historic Preservation and Heineken USA set out to restore the Miami Marine stadium, raising over $100,000.[34] Campaigns like these demonstrate a strong sense of togetherness as government, non-profits, business, and citizens all join together to attempt to enhance their communities.

Blockchain Technology

As aforementioned, over recent decades, public trust in governments around the world has plummeted. One of the primary reasons for this decline is due to governments' lack of transparency and their failure to protect citizens' personal data.[35] In the UK, a large national survey conducted by the Information Commissioner's Office in 2017 revealed that only 49% of citizens trusted how the government departments store their data.[36] Similar findings were found in Australia and the US. One in two Australians expect that the government would compromise their data at some point because their government had a poor track record of data breaches.[37] In the US, 80% of adults are concerned about the government collecting their private data from the internet without their consent and 93% would prefer to have control over their own information.[38,39] Different from our expectations of large organizations, we place our trust in governments to provide transparency and accountability to the public. While these governments have been grappling with these challenges, blockchain has been evolving over time with promising applications that may have the answer to these wearisome woes.

[33] https://www.indiegogo.com/projects/blacksburg-mountain-biking-skills-park#/.
[34] https://www.indiegogo.com/projects/restore-miami-marine-stadium#/.
[35] https://www.pewresearch.org/internet/2017/01/26/americans-and-cybersecurity/.
[36] http://yourrates.co.uk/uk-trust-organisations-data-ico-survey.
[37] https://www.afr.com/markets/equity-markets/australians-dont-trust-government-or-telcos-to-protect-their-data-survey-20150701-gi2arn.
[38] https://www.pewresearch.org/internet/2014/11/12/public-privacy-perceptions/.
[39] https://www.pewresearch.org/internet/2015/05/20/americans-attitudes-about-privacy-security-and-surveillance/.

Blockchain is a distributed ledger technology that records data in a secure, immutable, and distributed fashion. "Blockchain has disruptive potential across many industries and areas of society. This innovation allows for decentralized networks where transactions can take place directly among individuals and organizations without the need for intermediaries" (Chen & Murtazashvili, 2024). Although it has been typically associated with finance technology thanks to the rise of the (in)famous bitcoin, its applications have begun being applied for other use cases as well in the energy, healthcare, and supply chain domains (Chen & Murtazashvili, 2023; Chen & Murtazashvili, 2024).

Experts around the world have demonstrated that blockchain technology should be incorporated into governance and governments on all levels to offer citizens new safeguards on their data while also increasing transparency and trust with their populace. For instance, government agencies can use the technology to scan a citizen's ID to confirm the individual's identity. Although many governments are hesitant to implement, as the old saying goes, fortune favors the bold.

In 2019, Sierra Leone became the first country to hold an election on a blockchain.[40] Using the Agora blockchain, Sierra Leone wanted to make sure the election was transparent and to instill trust in their government. All of this is thanks to the fact that votes can take place anonymously while remaining immutable thanks to the blockchain technology. Republic of Georgia saw a different way to put blockchain technology to use. Leveraging the security and reliable ledger that blockchain produces, Georgia saw an opportunity to use the technology to allow its citizens to register land titles. At the time of writing 1.5 million registered land titles have been able to be registered successfully, which has allowed for the transferring of land to not only be secure but also reduce the transaction to a mere minute.[41]

Back in the US, the city of Reno in Nevada made a groundbreaking move in 2022, making it the first city in the country to use blockchain technology to manage city data. Known as the "Biggest Little Blockchain," this innovative city-run and resident-focused blockchain platform was designed with

[40] https://www.blockchain-council.org/blockchain/top-countries-that-conducted-elections-on-the-blockchain/.

[41] https://www.oecd.org/corruption/integrity-forum/academicpapers/Georg%20Eder-%20Blockchain%20-%20Ghana_verified.pdf.

a focus on residents and transparency.[42] One of the first major uses of the technology is for Reno's historic building registry. Since 1993, the city has been documenting all the historic buildings that hold cultural significance, with the goal of preserving the city's heritage for future generations. This registry, which plays a crucial role in maintaining the city's character, now benefits from the security and transparency offered by blockchain technology. The Biggest Little Blockchain platform enables residents to easily access and monitor the status of changes to historic buildings.[43] This transparency ensures that community members are informed and involved in the preservation process, fostering a sense of shared responsibility for the city's cultural landmarks. Reno's forward-thinking approach to blockchain adoption positions it as a leader in utilizing technology for civic engagement and urban management. Looking to the future, the city of Reno is exploring further applications of blockchain technology.

Blockchain can also serve as a powerful tool for governments to improve public services for citizens. In Denmark, the government created the Vehicle Wallet with blockchain. In the modern world, it is difficult to imagine what life would be like without the car. Often, when a buyer purchases a used car from a seller, both parties have very limited information about each other. To increase information transparency and protection for the car exchange market, the Danish Tax Administration created Vehicle Wallet.[44,45] Here, all the important information about the car is recorded including the sale of the car, insurance information, repairs, and accidents. Vehicle Wallet utilizes blockchain technologies so that all data associated with a car's life cycle—from the moment of import right through to decommissioning—are documented and saved in a shared ledger where both the buyer and seller can see the same information and thus not only increase transparency but also efficiency. Another interesting case is that in the so-called City of Gold, Dubai. Viewed as a global innovation hub, the city is experimenting with the implementation of blockchain technology in governance. Dubai's ambitious vision for blockchain implementation is outlined in the 2016 Dubai Blockchain Strategy, a document brimming with aspirations.[46] This

[42] https://www.themunicipal.com/2023/01/reno-launches-biggest-little-blockchain-to-test-new-record-keeping-method/.

[43] https://cities-today.com/reno-pilots-blockchain-for-building-records/.

[44] https://www.hashcashconsultants.com/pdf/government-denmark.pdf.

[45] https://www.nets.eu/perspectives/Pages/Blockchain-technology-could-add-transparency-to-buying-and-selling-a-car.aspx.

[46] https://www.digitaldubai.ae/initiatives/blockchain.

strategy aimed to take a sizeable portion of government transactions onto the blockchain platform, streamlining processes, increasing security, and enhancing efficiency.

One area where blockchain is making waves is in its ability to expedite property transactions. The Dubai Land Department utilizes blockchain to track land ownership records, significantly reducing the risk of fraud and ensuring clear and secure ownership trails, as documented by Baroudi and Benghida (2022).[47] This not only benefits the government but also streamlines the process for citizens, eliminating unnecessary bureaucratic hurdles.

Another area of Dubai's success lies in their use case of simplifying business registrations. The Department of Economic Development leverages blockchain to enhance the user experience for business owners, creating a more business-friendly environment by offering a seamless and efficient registration process, as highlighted in Khan et al.'s (2019) study on the Dubai Economic Department.[48] This eliminates unnecessary paperwork and expedites the process for businesses to establish themselves in Dubai. Dubai's innovative efforts in integrating blockchain technology into the public sector are setting a global precedent. The city is well on its way to becoming a model for successful blockchain adoption, paving the way for a more efficient, transparent, and secure future for its citizens and businesses. This commitment to innovation fosters a thriving ecosystem that positions Dubai as a leader in the digital transformation landscape, driving its reputation as a forward-thinking and visionary global destination.

As we discussed earlier, a widespread lack of trust in government is a sentiment shared by many people today, reflecting growing concerns about transparency, accountability, and responsiveness in public institutions. This standpoint of believing in blockchains as a more trustworthy alternative to government has been gaining momentum and interestingly is even being promoted by government officials, such as the Miami mayor Francis Suarez. Stating that he believes cities need to be knowledge-based economies, Suarez has expressed his vision of positioning Miami as a crypto hub to attract more tech companies to the city. He even announced that he would take his salary payment in bitcoin.[49] Similarly, New York City's mayor Eric Adams

[47] https://www.springeropen.com/collections/bccc.
[48] https://blockchain.ieee.org/.
[49] https://www.bloomberg.com/news/articles/2021-12-03/miami-mayor-seeks-wider-crypto-use-after-taking-pay-in-bitcoin.

also received his first three paychecks in bitcoin.[50] Just like Suarez, Adams hopes to turn New York into the crypto capital of the world. Although cryptocurrency is yet to find its place and proper levels of regulation in today's world, the decentralized blockchain technology has been and will be used by more governments to increase data security and information transparency.

In sum, Tocqueville noted in *Democracy in America* that civic engagement and trust in government often reinforce each other. When the government allows citizens to participate in democratic decision-making, it is more likely to unite people with diverse backgrounds and interests toward a common good. Elinor Ostrom, Nobel Laureate in Economics, was also an advocate of using a bottom-up approach to address public issues (Ostrom, 1990). The digital age brought to us monumental advancements in technology that have given governments around the world new opportunities to innovate. Building online platforms to seek solutions from ordinary citizens instead of maintaining the traditional top-down governance approach, inviting citizens to participate in government budgeting, engaging them and raising public funds through civic crowdfunding, and the exploration of new blockchain technology in governance are all signs of government entrepreneurship and innovation.

[50] https://www.nytimes.com/2022/01/20/nyregion/eric-adams-bitcoin-cryptocurrency.html.

Chapter 6
Candy and Ice Cream
Is Public Innovation and Entrepreneurship Always a Good Thing?

Most of the previous chapters have focused on the wonderful advancements that have come about as a result of public innovation. We have witnessed the evolution of public innovation starting from its humble beginnings focusing on efficiency and basic service delivery to where we are today with governments around the world adopting emerging technologies like AI, blockchain, and IoT to build smarter, more responsive cities.

But is government-led innovation always a good thing? Are there ever any drawbacks that we should consider? What happens when innovation takes a negative turn? After all, it's not as though *all* innovation in other domains has been *all* good. So too is the case for government innovation. Like any other entity, the public sector is also susceptible to mistakes, uninformed decisions, or even corruption, which can occasionally lead to adverse effects and potentially even hurt its citizens. The impact of these instances can be far-reaching, affecting the well-being and trust of the population, and ultimately the health of society. This is the central topic that we are exploring in this chapter.

Government Interest ≠ Public Interest

The foundation of democracy rests on a simple relationship between the government and the governed. The governed elect individuals to public positions who they believe are best fit to represent their rights. In exchange for this power, the elected officials carry out the wishes of the governed. In the case of public innovation, this would theoretically entail the pursuit of advances in the causes or missions that are believed in by the majority. For example, there are often areas that garner overwhelming support, such as

Innovation and Entrepreneurship in the Public Sector. Wendy D. Chen and David B. Audretsch, Oxford University Press. © Oxford University Press (2025). DOI: 10.1093/9780197679470.003.0006

medicine and other scientific advancements for which the government are the patrons.

However, as is often the case in a democracy, what benefits one group may not necessarily be good for another, which can potentially lead to civil unrest among those who may be on the receiving end of negative public innovation. There are often opportunities for misalignment between the objectives of public innovation and the broader public interest. Innovation driven by political motivations alone rather than sound policy or technical expertise can lead to ineffective solutions, outright waste, or even harm to certain segments of the population. In some cases, this misalignment can give rise to corruption and result in a misallocation of resources that could have been put to better use for other priorities. Public innovation is unfortunately not always straightforward, and even when the motives are pure, can be found straddling the divide between global, national, and local interests, the haves and the have-nots, and various subgroups of a population.

In the Netherlands, for example, the government has outlined goals to reduce their greenhouse gases by 49% by 2030. Similar to what was witnessed around the world in regard to climate change, new policy innovations were put into place to help achieve this goal. Drawing on the current state of environmental science and its accompanying recommendations, one measure the Dutch government took was to reduce the amount of nitrogen in the soil and water.

If you have ever tried to tend to your own garden, you probably know that there is a delicate balance that must be achieved in the soil for successful crops, and one such ingredient that must be balanced is nitrogen, which is typically delivered through fertilizer. Consequently, Dutch farmers who relied on this fertilizer for their crops staged protests against the government's mandates to eliminate nitrogen due to climate change concerns.[1] The plan from the Dutch government was to potentially shutdown thousands of farms, leading to many concerns around food security for the Dutch people. Naturally, farmers were concerned about their livelihood and those of others. Additionally, many members of the public who were not farmers also joined the cause to protest over fear of food security.[2]

[1] https://dutchreview.com/news/outraged-dutch-farmers-block-supermarket-distribution-centres-in-protest.

[2] https://www.theguardian.com/environment/2022/jul/21/emotion-and-pain-as-dutch-farmers-fight-back-against-huge-cuts-to-livestock.

What these protests demonstrate is a misalignment of priorities between the public and the government. In these cases, the government acts unilaterally in their pushing public innovation rather than democratically cooperating with the governed. The main problem here, however, is not merely the effort to reduce nitrogen in the atmosphere. Rather, the government chose not to consult with the public to reach an agreement on how to move forward. For an analogy, it's like trying to tear down a house because it had a hole in the wall without even having the blueprints for the next one. This type of behavior is the unfortunate result of poor government innovation.

Unintended Consequences

When new public innovation is successful, it can bring about positive changes that improve the lives of many people. However, sometimes even in those successful cases, unintended consequences can arise that call into question whether a new public policy or initiative should truly be considered a success.

Dating back to 1906 under the Wiley Act during Theodore Roosevelt's presidency, the US Food and Drug Administration (FDA) was created to protect consumers from food and drug products that misrepresented or adulterated their ingredients. Beginning as a chemist at the USDA, a chemist by the name of Harvey Washington Wiley pioneered food safety standards, laying the foundation for the eventual creation of the FDA to regulate and ensure the quality of food and drugs.[3,4] While the FDA represents a major public innovation in health and safety regulation, it has also produced unintended consequences. For new drugs and medical devices to get approved, companies can expect the process to take an average of ten years and hundreds of millions of dollars to obtain approval.[5] A prominent example of this was the Sapien Transcatheter Heart Valve, which was approved in the US in November of 2013 while Europe had been using the device since 2007, allowing Europeans an additional six years to save lives. There are ways to help expedite the process including developing alternatives to clinical trials and finding creative solutions to answer benefit-and-risk questions without the need for human studies (Von Eschenbach & Hall, 2013), but these would

[3] https://www.sciencehistory.org/education/scientific-biographies/harvey-washington-wiley/.
[4] https://www.fda.gov/about-fda/fda-history.
[5] https://www.nationwidechildrens.org/family-resources-education/700childrens/2018/03/what-does-it-take-to-get-a-drug-approved-through-the-fda.

require changes to the current FDA approval process and thus go through their own internal review processes. It is essential to critically assess government policies aimed at enhancing public welfare and safety, particularly when the potential for unforeseen repercussions exists. These unintended consequences may adversely affect numerous individuals—a significant population whose lives might be endangered as a result of well-meaning yet misguided initiatives.

The government's pursuit of clean energy is a powerful example of public innovation to reduce pollution and improve the environment. Through policy tools such as grants, tax incentives, and regulatory frameworks, governments are helping to expand opportunities for clean energy development and make technologies like solar power more affordable for everyday people. As a result, countless new clean energy businesses and jobs have emerged, and many individuals have switched to solar power for their homes. However, these developments have also brought some unintended consequences.

The Three Gorges Dam in China, the world's largest hydroelectric project, was conceived as a monumental step toward clean energy and flood control. It has generated immense benefits in flood control, power generation, water regulation, and economy. As of 2024, it "had generated a total of 1.66 trillion kWh of electricity, equivalent to saving 528 million tonnes of standard coal and reducing carbon dioxide emissions by 1.43 billion tonnes."[6] It has also helped reduce over 400 million tons of carbon emissions. Improvements to navigation along the Yangtze River have transformed it into a "golden waterway", benefiting both commercial shipping and tourism.[7] Nevertheless, it remains controversial whether its implementation has led to some unintended environmental and social consequences. Some believe it may have impacted local biodiversity, and there are also concerns that the reservoir's flooding could affect historical sites and lead to the loss of cultural heritage (Berkman, 1998; López-Pujol & Ren, 2009).

Similarly, the Dhauliganga Dam in India was constructed with the primary objective of generating hydroelectric power to meet the region's growing energy demands. However, the dam's construction and operation have altered the natural flow of the Dhauliganga River. Additionally, the relocation of local communities has also led to the loss of agricultural land.[8]

[6] https://www.ctg.com.cn/ctgenglish/news_media/news37/20250126131808I4119/index.html.
[7] https://www.stdaily.com/web/English/2023-05/11/content_1922443.html.
[8] https://www.spotlightnepal.com/2013/06/21/india-refuted-the-charges-of-opening-dhauliganga-dam/.

But these unintended consequences are not limited to clean energy alone. Another area that has had tragic consequences is the area of humanitarian food aid that is sent to developing countries. It is a relatively new concept that the government would provide food for other countries. For the US, the practice of sending food started after World War I. It was during this time that Congress pushed a massive government-led program to provide food to Eastern and Central Europe to contain the spread of Bolshevism. However, the practice of food aid drastically accelerated after World War II, as US agriculture became involved with the United Nations Relief and Rehabilitation Administration and the UN Food and Agricultural Organization to help alleviate food shortages around the world.[9]

Despite the noble intentions, these innovative solutions have often led to more harm than good. In the aftermath of the 2010 earthquake, Haiti has received over $13 billion in aid over the last decade to assist with food and nation building. Local farmers and merchants complained that the influx of food had created unstable markets, resulting in many feeling they could not compete against the free food being provided from US Agency for International Development and UN World Food Program. Further, this aid has led to increased instability that has resulted in civil unrest.[10,11]

Picking Winners and Losers

While government innovation can sometimes have unexpected consequences, in other cases those negative consequences are knowingly baked into the cake. The government's picking of winners and losers has been witnessed throughout history. In ancient Rome, politicians often engaged in a system of patronage where wealthy elites, known as patrons, would provide financial support to political candidates in exchange for favors once they were in office. When this occurs, policies and initiatives are formed that monetarily favor one group and hurt their competitors. Another word for this behavior is "cronyism," or the appointment of friends or other relatives to positions of power with disregard for merits.

[9] https://20092017.state.gov/p/eur/ci/it/milanexpo2015/c67068.htm.
[10] https://publicintegrity.org/accountability/haitian-farmers-undermined-by-food-aid.
[11] https://www.voanews.com/a/food-aid-hurts-haitis-farmers--92405389/116708.html.

Impact on the Tech Industry

Often, cronyism is influenced by lobbyists. In the US, K Street has become symbolic of the close relationships between lobbyists and politicians, where influence is exerted through high-end dinners and other forms of quid pro quo deals aimed at mutual gains.[12] To be fair, there is nothing inherently wrong with having lobbyist groups. Thanks to lobbying, government innovations can be proposed and help guide the government in a specific path. Lobbying is just one way for the will of the governed to reach the governing body. After all, many nonprofits are lobbyists who have advocated for individual liberty and the protection of citizens' rights. Even corporate lobbyists supported initiatives intended to help create jobs and make other positive social changes.

But of course, this does not mean that lobbying is all *good* either. When powerful industries with a plethora of resources at their fingertips can buy the ear of an open-minded politician, new policies that are not necessarily good for the people can be passed and repackaged in a way that sounds like it is good for everyone instead of an unfair rent-seeking opportunity to oust their market competition.

A prominent example of this was the role of the US in fostering the growth of Silicon Valley and the tech industry. While many may see Silicon Valley as a modern hub thriving on innovative and cutting-edge technology, its roots actually trace back much further. Starting in the late 1950s, the US government started having more interest in science and technology and thus began investing in areas such as computer science, semiconductors, and other emerging technologies. This support came primarily through federal grants, tax incentives, and subsidies provided to universities, private companies, and individual researchers.

One pivotal moment came from the establishment of the Advanced Research Projects Agency (ARPA) in 1958. ARPA, later known as DARPA (Defense Advanced Research Projects Agency), was tasked with funding cutting-edge research and technology development that had the potential to deliver an edge to the US military and civilians. One of its most notable projects developed during this time was the ARPANET, which would later go on to serve as the foundation for the modern internet.

[12] https://www.washingtonpost.com/politics/2022/01/12/social-lobbying-legislators-influence.

Another critical ingredient in the success of Silicon Valley was the presence of venture capital firms, which provided seed funding for many startups looking to develop new products and break into new markets. During this period the US government, through various programs and initiatives, played a significant role in developing these venture capital firms into how we know them today. For instance, the Small Business Administration spearheaded a new program in 1958 to aid these venture capital firms, which in turn helped create and finance over 300 venture capital funds between 1962 and 1972.

The government's support for this industry paid off handsomely. The tech industry grew exponentially, and Silicon Valley became a global hub for innovation and entrepreneurship. Companies like Apple, Intel, Hewlett-Packard, and Google emerged during this period, revolutionizing industries and creating new markets. All this painted a picture of Silicon Valley as the forward-thinking and trendy place it has become known for today.

On the other hand, this unequal distribution of resources did not come without bearing consequences. Industries that did not receive similar support or investment opportunities faced challenges in competing in the marketplace. For example, the US textile industry saw significant decline during this period as technological advancements, automation, and consolidated capital led to a decrease in demand for labor-intensive production methods. Although this time period has been called the US Textile Renaissance, it did not feel like one to the thousands of workers who had mills closed with little concern from the government.

Thus, while government intervention in picking winners and losers can lead to notable success stories, it also carries risks of creating disparities between industries and potentially hindering the growth of others that do not receive similar support. It is crucial for governments to carefully evaluate the potential benefits and drawbacks of such policies to ensure a balanced and equitable economic landscape.

The Energy Independence and Security Act "mandated that renewable fuels be mixed into America's gasoline supply, primarily by using corn-based ethanol."[13] However, there were some clear winners and losers as a result of the policy. The soybean farmers and corn farmers who are responsible for providing the raw ingredients for ethanol found a new income stream. Energy companies including biofuels, gasoline, and electric were happy to have a new fuel that could be purchased cheaper and added to

[13] https://fee.org/articles/8-big-government-policies-that-hurt-the-poor/.

their products. Not surprisingly, big energy companies, automakers, and even Monsanto, one of the world's largest providers of seeds and pesticides, were behind the bill.

With the increased demand for this new bio-gasoline product, the government has shifted the market in favor of these particular products. Meanwhile, consumers have ultimately paid the biggest price in terms of food prices and gas prices. Farmers who rely on feedstock have also suffered from these policies as these grains have been shifted away from animal feed.[14]

Impact on Public Health

Another unique area of government innovation has been the government's involvement with people's diets. The control of diets all began back in 1789 with tariffs being passed on sugar imports, although this was primarily a tax policy rather than a health policy. Later, in 1980, the US government introduced official nutritional guidelines, which evolved into the food pyramid we've all seen in the 1990s. As new policies have been created to promote healthy diets, there have been clear winners and losers along the way.

One such program is the Federal Sugar Program that was created under the Farm Security and Rural Investment Act of 2002. The Program allows for government intervention in the prices of sugar by limiting the amount of sugar allowed to be produced domestically while simultaneously acting as a trade barrier for imports via price supports. While the program does help the sugar industry, the program is estimated to cost Americans over $3.7 billion a year and has resulted in the loss of jobs for many confectionary workers. What's worse, the program has had a significant negative impact on the poor, who according to USDA spend roughly 30% of their household income on food by raising the prices of groceries.[15]

Impact on Economic Development

A significant portion of government funding programs has been created to support companies expected to innovate and contribute to the

[14] https://fee.org/articles/8-big-government-policies-that-hurt-the-poor/.

[15] https://theconversation.com/swelling-grocery-bills-are-pummeling-the-poorest-who-spend-over-a-quarter-of-their-incomes-on-food-186980.

broader economy. The US Small Business Innovation Research (SBIR) and Small Business Technology Transfer (STTR) programs are administered by the Small Business Administration. Both programs provide funding to support innovative small businesses in bringing high-risk technologies to market, while also promoting collaboration between small firms and research institutions to facilitate technology transfer. Widely recognized as successful federal initiatives, they have played a significant role in the growth of numerous high-impact companies across various industries.

When any sort of competition occurs, certain criteria must be agreed upon and evaluated in order to determine a winner. In evolutionary theory, this is referred to as the selection mechanism. Survivors are selected, while others are left to their dismal fate. In the event that public funding is to be given out for loans or grants, a review team will typically evaluate the project proposals that have been prepared by the competing companies. The proposal will usually include the scope of the project, the greater impact (social benefits), budget, and team.

However, it is unclear where the reviewers are always the most qualified to judge the projects. We also do not know if nepotism is at play—for example, when a Principal Investigator (PI) selects certain subcontractors. A 2023 GAO report *Small Business Research Programs: Information Regarding Subaward Use and Data Quality* found that about 70% of SBIR/STTR award recipients used subcontractors or consultants, yet only about 10% of these subawards were reported on USAspending.gov. This lack of transparency in reporting subawards could obscure potential conflicts of interest or favoritism in the allocation of subcontracted work.

In addition, historical data shows a geographic concentration of SBIR awards. For instance, between 1992 and 2005, companies in these two states received over 35% of the Phase II awards nationally. This concentration raises concerns about equitable distribution and whether certain regions are disproportionately favored in the award process.[16] Unlike in the private sector, when a government-funded project fails, there is often no way to recover the lost funds. Instead, taxpayers are left to absorb the losses from investments they had little or no say in approving.

[16] National Academies Press (2008). Chapter 3 "Statistics of SBIR Awards" in *An Assessment of the SBIR Program.*

Impact on Academic Research Agendas

To understand how the public sector influences academic research agendas, one must first grasp the intricacies of research conduct and funding. At its core, academic disciplines like biology, chemistry, and history operate within distinct research paradigms. Researchers affiliated with universities or nongovernmental organizations must undertake rigorous studies to advance their respective agendas. However, most research comes with substantial costs. Hard sciences such as chemistry and biology often require lab fees, material expenses, and compensation for test subjects, whereas social sciences like sociology and anthropology may involve costs for large data collections.

Institutions sometimes provide partial or full funding for these expenses, but external financing is often necessary. This is where the government plays a role, offering grants that align with specific research topics, such as those from the National Institutes of Health (NIH) or US Department of Health and Human Services. Assuming equal opportunities, researchers can secure grants to support their work, thereby obtaining funding to conduct their studies and contribute to innovations.

While this system has fostered groundbreaking discoveries, it has also created an uneven playing field in research and influences the broader academic landscape. Let's consider a scenario where we are a biologist at a prominent university with a highly ambitious research agenda. Imagine that we are on the cusp of cracking the code to eradicate the flu virus, which could potentially lead to its global eradication.

Initially, we identified two major hurdles: securing funding and transitioning out of teaching responsibilities at our universities for two years. To achieve these goals, we estimated that we needed a team of volunteers, new lab equipment, and approximately $500,000 in funding. We began our search for government grants to support our research, scouring online databases for matching opportunities. After several days of researching, however, it became clear that no government agency had posted a grant program that aligned with our objectives. Perhaps the closest we could find was a grant program for B virus, an area that does not fit our expertise and a virus that is much rarer. With the need for funding driving our agenda, our research focus shifted dramatically as we set out to secure funding for a topic outside of our original scope, and perhaps even needing to change our entire research agenda altogether.

Now let's assume we are humanities researchers. Just like our scenario with the biologist earlier, we too need to secure funding to carry out our research project, but we will only need $50,000 to cover fieldwork, surveys, and transcription services. However, unlike hard science, there are even fewer opportunities in our domain. Grant-making government agencies allocate significantly fewer resources to the humanities and social sciences. In the end, despite the intellectual value of our proposed work, it might be entirely possible that our research could go unfunded for years.

One of the most striking instances of inequity lies in the government's favoritism toward certain disciplines, leaving others to struggle. There is often an overemphasis placed on STEM fields for research, which can overshadow the value of studies in other disciplines. According to the National Science Foundation's (NSF) 2022 data, federal obligations for research were distributed as follows: life sciences received $41.6 billion, engineering $15.5 billion, and physical sciences $12.1 billion. In stark contrast, the social sciences were allocated only $1.9 billion, accounting for less than 2.5% of total federal research funding.[17] This disparity reflects longstanding funding priorities that emphasize fields perceived to have direct economic or technological benefits.

Granted, STEM fields are important for any society as everyone wants advancements in medicine, science, and to have the best defense possible. It is also true that STEM fields do carry with them significant costs. However, we must ask ourselves: What does that say about us as a society that we show such blatant disregard for other fields of study? Is a political scientist's research uncovering why people who feel disenfranchised by political institutions not important? Should a sociologist call it quits who wants to understand how remote work has reshaped social relationships? Or what about research exploring how early-stage startups leverage news tools like AI to gain competitive advantage and the barriers they face? All of these are pressing issues of our time, but chances are that little governmental funding would support these research agendas.

Even within the domain of STEM fields, over the recent decades, advocacy by disease-specific groups has increasingly influenced funding priorities for biomedical research, including rare diseases, and this shift reflects a broader trend in how scientific opportunity, public health need, and advocaty efforts shape government funding (Dresser, 2009; Hegde & Sampat, 2015). Concerns about the allocation of resources by NIH have been

[17] https://ncses.nsf.gov/pubs/nsf24322.

raised by many scientists and researchers. Gillum et al. (2011) highlighted significant discrepancies between NIH funding levels and the burden of disease. The authors noted that public spending for AIDS research was disproportionately high, even when considering worldwide and projected burden, and suggested that strong political influences may play a role in maintaining high levels of funding in the US. Hegde and Sampat (2015) found that lobbying by disease advocacy groups is associated with increased political support, including Congressional "soft earmarks" for the diseases they represent. Scholars have also observed that the prioritization process can sometimes appear opaque (Dresser, 2009). All this raises an important question: What underlying criteria do public grant-making organizations use to inform their funding decisions, and how can these be clearly communicated to researchers, institutions, and stakeholders?

Data Breach and Privacy Violation

As discussed in the previous chapters, governments across the globe have been implementing internet, technology, and big data in various areas ranging from smart city buildings, smart street lighting, and smart trash cans to smart water management, to smart parking, and beyond.[18] While all of these smart tools help make cities more efficient, manage pollution, and provide an overall healthier environment, these technologies often track individual behavior and collect data from them. However, the public sector may not be able to protect people's data, and governments have experienced repetitive cyberattacks, which have caused massive data breaches for individuals.[19] Back in 2015, the Office of Personnel Management in the US was hacked exposing the personal information of over 21 million people. In 2017, the hack of the Swedish government led to the loss of massive driver's license data, and in 2018 Indian government's database was hacked, which exposed government employees' Aadhar numbers (confidential numbers assigned to Indian citizens, similar to Social Security number in the US).[20] Between 2014 and 2023, the US government suffered from over 1,000 data breaches,

[18] https://itif.org/publications/2023/03/06/balancing-privacy-and-innovation-in-smart-cities-and-communities/.
[19] https://www.cnn.com/2023/06/16/politics/cyberattack-us-government/index.html.
[20] https://www.executech.com/insights/the-5-scariest-data-breaches-in-government/.

and it is estimated that these breaches have cost the government over $30 million.[21]

Data security and individual privacy are closely linked. The public sector that stores citizens' personal data is also responsible for protecting people's privacy. Nevertheless, areas using smart technologies are especially vulnerable to data breach and privacy violation, and governments often fail to safeguard our data. Local governments in particular prioritize less on cybersecurity.[22] In addition, as previously mentioned, many public innovations are the result of governmental coproduction with the private sector. Innovations like smart cities usually have partnerships with private companies that provide certain technologies, and typically those companies receive access to public data that local governments collect.[23]

The public is concerned with data breach and violation of privacy. According to a recent poll in the US, over 90% of the population would delete an app if they found out that it sells their information. More than two-thirds of Americans are concerned with facial-recognition technology.[24] This growing public apprehension underscores the urgent need for the public sector to prioritize data protection as a fundamental component of technological innovation. Therefore, it is important for the public sector to make data protection a top priority while innovating, ensuring that governments also balance data privacy and public safety to maximize the effective use of technologies.

Violation of Human Ethics

While a public innovation maybe helpful, it can be at the expense of human ethics. The famous Manhattan Project is an example. Initiated in 1939, the US government along with a group of world-renowned scientists developed the first atomic bomb during World War II. The Manhattan Project was undoubtedly a groundbreaking scientific and technological achievement of harnessing nuclear technology for weapons that forever changed the world.

[21] https://www.comparitech.com/blog/vpn-privacy/us-government-breaches/.
[22] https://itif.org/publications/2023/03/06/balancing-privacy-and-innovation-in-smart-cities-and-communities/.
[23] Ibid.
[24] https://www.digitaltrends.com/news/smart-cities-privacy-security/.

However, the invention of the atomic bomb has also raised serious concerns and debates over its impact on human ethics. It is estimated that the bombing claimed between 110,000 to 210,000 lives, most of whom being civilians, and the long-time aftermath radiation continued to affect human life (Hersey, 1989; Selden & Selden, 1989). Moreover, the secrecy of the Manhattan Project violated the ethical norms of scientific research since many people who were involved with the project were not aware of its lethal impact (Rhodes, 1986).

Another scientific innovation led by the US government that has been widely condemned is the Guatemalan STD Study. In the late 1940s, the US Public Health Service and the Pan American Sanitation Bureau conducted research in Guatemala that included purposely exposing marginalized populations to sexually transmitted diseases without getting their informed consent.[25] The experiment intentionally infected Guatemalan prisoners, psychiatric hospital patients, soldiers, and sex workers with syphilis and other STDs. They were then given antibiotics as a treatment to observe how the diseases progressed. The key point here is that the subjects involved in the research were intentionally not told about the full details of the study protocols, with researchers using misleading information and pressure to gain compliance. The lack of transparency in the research involving vulnerable populations left them uninformed about the potential risks and consequences, thereby denying them a fundamental right to make informed decisions about their own health and well-being (Rodriguez & García, 2013).

Corruption

Previously we noted that public–private partnerships, such as public procurement or external contracting, provide an effective way to facilitate government innovation. Public procurement and contracting refers to the government agencies' necessary purchases of goods and services from the other sectors and external contractors to perform social innovations and improve public services. Large infrastructure, defense, and healthcare projects often involve external contracting and procurement. Overall, public procurement makes up around 13% to 20% of a country's gross domestic product on average, and the amount spent worldwide on procurement is

[25] https://matthewolapade.medium.com/the-dark-side-of-innovation-where-does-technology-stop-38b78a71b281.

approximated to be around 9.5 trillion US dollars.[26] However, public procurement and government contracting are often found to breed corruption as the process is often opaque and lacks transparency. Government officials have been known to abuse their authority and roles to grant contracts to family members and friends or cronies, ignoring the tenets of competition and merit. It is now estimated that anywhere from 10% to 25% of a public contract's total value may be lost due to corruption.[27,28]

Corruption in public procurement can occur in various forms, such as bribery, extortion, and kickbacks (Mizoguchi & Van Quyen, 2014; Sharma et al., 2019). It is estimated that the amount paid in bribes is between 8% and 25% of the total value of the goods, services, or construction projects that were obtained through the procurement process.[29] The practice of government officials taking jobs in the private sector after leaving public office, and then using their connections to direct government contracts to their new employers is another common form of public procurement corruption.

The effects of corruption in public procurement and government contracting are significant. To begin with, corruption diverts public resources away from their intended uses. Money that should be allocated to healthcare, education, infrastructure, or other social innovations is instead misused, wasted, or even stolen by dishonest officials. This damages the credibility of government institutions and erodes public confidence and trust in the public sector. Corruption in public procurement also discourages competition and innovation. Suppliers who are willing to engage in bribery or other unlawful acts frequently are more likely to be chosen than qualified competitors. As a result, the public is not able to have access to the finest public goods and services and public innovation stifles.

Waste of Public Funds

Waste in government expenditures is not a new topic. Rather, it is a long-standing challenge confronting the public sector globally. "Rajiv Gandhi was Prime Minister of India, he famously remarked that for every one rupee spent on poverty alleviation programs in India only 15 paise (i.e., 15%)

[26] https://www.worldbank.org/en/news/feature/2020/03/23/global-public-procurement-database-share-compare-improve.

[27] https://images.transparencycdn.org/images/2010_5_TI_CorruptionandPublicProcurement_EN.pdf.

[28] https://www.worldbank.org/en/news/feature/2020/03/23/global-public-procurement-database-share-compare-improve.

[29] https://blogs.worldbank.org/developmenttalk/reducing-corruption-public-procurement.

reached the intended beneficiary."[30] Multiple government reports in the West have suggested that public spending has not been effective as well. The Sir Philip Green Report on the UK government showed government waste in office supplies.[31] The 2010 Government Accountability Office (GAO) Report of the US Government estimated that improper payment amounts were about $125.4 billion in total for fiscal year 2010.[32]

In an effort to promote public sector innovation, governments often set up multiple initiatives and various programs working toward shared objectives while lacking sufficient coordination. This strategy consequently leads to the duplication of efforts, unnecessary overlap, and the squandering of public financial resources. It also causes the expansion of government and increasing financial burden by creating redundant departments and infrastructures.

Take the examples of the Department of Energy and the Department of Labor in the US. Both departments offer various grant programs to support educational initiatives and workforce development including those from underserved populations. However, their responsibilities for these programs overlap, resulting in possible duplication of efforts and resources. Along the same line, the US Department of Agriculture and Department of Energy have programs aimed at promoting energy efficiency in agriculture, so their efforts often overlap. For example, the USDA's Rural Energy for America Program provides funding opportunities in the form of loans and grants to agricultural producers and small rural businesses who focus on renewable energy and energy efficiency projects.[33] The Department of Energy offers similar incentives through its various initiatives. Streamlining government programs through consolidation can help alleviate fiscal pressures while also simplifying bureaucratic processes, ultimately allowing for more efficient allocation of resources and reduced administrative costs.

Yet another example of waste through redundancy can be found with NASA and the Central Intelligence Agency (CIA). While NASA is primarily known for space exploration for civilians and astrological research, the CIA has a space program as well that is utilized to support its intelligence-gathering missions. However, both agencies have spent significant resources on developing these space programs, including the development of their

[30] https://blogs.worldbank.org/en/governance/waste-in-government-expenditures.
[31] https://assets.publishing.service.gov.uk/media/5a78f0be40f0b62b22cbe018/sirphilipgreenreview.pdf.
[32] https://www.gao.gov/assets/gao-11-363t.pdf.
[33] https://www.rd.usda.gov/inflation-reduction-act/rural-energy-america-program-reap.

own satellite capabilities for data collection and their corresponding infrastructure, leading to redundancy and inefficiencies.[34] In some cases, collaboration or consolidation of efforts could lead to cost savings and improved outcomes.

In addition, the pursuit of public innovation across various sectors including but not limited to transportation, social welfare, healthcare, and education, poses significant challenges. As they strive to push forward with public innovation initiatives, competing priorities emerge, placing strain on the allocation of public resources. This can lead to an uneven distribution of resources and give rise to extensive waste of public resources. A GAO report from 2017 recommended merging or eliminating some programs to reduce redundancy among different departments.[35]

The unpredictability of the actual return on investment and potential payoffs also renders government innovation using public funds a risky endeavor. Sometimes public innovation projects fail to deliver on their original promise, which could be due to not having the right people or strategies to accomplish the original goals. If so, the expenditure on those projects is wasted (Jordan, 2014; Meijer & Thaens, 2020). The realization of public innovation is also subjected to the impact of external factors such as changes in social dynamics, economic conditions, public policies, and technological advancements. Due to the unpredictability of these factors, government innovation by spending public funds can be a risky task. The long-term effects of government initiatives are often hard to measure in the short run because the benefits may not be realized until years later, making it difficult to accurately gauge the return on investment. As a result, Osborne and Brown (2005) argued that public sector innovation usually spends more than needed or was intended.

At the state and local government level, the Big Dig Project in Boston, managed by the Massachusetts Turnpike Authority in the US, was a massive urban construction undertaken with the goal of enhancing transportation framework within and surrounding the city by constructing a core tunnel network underneath Boston. The project started in 1991 and was planned to be completed in 2004. It was championed to be "the largest, most complex and technologically challenging highway project ever attempted in American history."[36] Though originally budgeted at $2.5 billion, the project wound

[34] https://www.nytimes.com/1986/04/23/us/nasa-wasted-billions-federal-audits-disclose.html.
[35] https://www.gao.gov/assets/gao-17-491sp.pdf.
[36] https://www.nytimes.com/2008/07/18/us/18brfs-BIGGERPRICEF_BRF.html.

up costing more than $14 billion and did not complete until 2007, as a result of inadequate planning, severe design flaws, and poor administration. In 2014, the *Boston Globe* estimated that "by the time state and federal taxpayers finish paying for the Big Dig sometime around 2032, with interest, it will have cost a stunning $24.3 billion."[37] It is also estimated that the project will not be paid off until 2038.[38]

Another prominent example of this waste of public funds can be found with Gravina Island Bridge project in Alaska. Dubbed as the "bridge to nowhere," this proposed engineering marvel aimed to connect the tiny island of Gravina to the mainland via a highway and ferry terminal. The intent behind this audacious project was to open up greater transportation access for the residents of the remote community who previously had only relied on ferry access, allowing for easier travel, commerce, and emergency response services.[39]

However, as funding requests reached Congress during the early 2000s, controversy brewed beneath the surface. Alaska's Representative Don Young championed the project by introducing a bill to raise the necessary funds by incorporating it into the Transportation Equity Act: A Legacy for Users in 2005. The legislation allocated a whopping $450 million for the bridge, but the sticker shock and questionable necessity raised eyebrows among taxpayers and lawmakers alike.[40]

As news of the story spread, public outrage grew, with the questions largely remaining unanswered. Opponents argued that the funds allocated to this remote project would be better spent on other pressing infrastructure needs across the country. The controversy reached a fever pitch, with critics demanding more from the government, namely transparency and accountability in government spending.[41,42]

Despite these growing concerns, Alaska's congressional delegation remained steadfast in its pursuit of the bridge, insisting that it would accrue significant economic benefits to the region and improve accessibility for the residents on Gravina Island. Yet the tide began to turn against them

[37] https://www.necn.com/news/local/_necn__big_dig_cost_climbs_to_24_3_billion_necn/1918218/.

[38] https://www.nytimes.com/2008/07/18/us/18brfs-BIGGERPRICEF_BRF.html.

[39] https://web.archive.org/web/20100305091126/http://dot.alaska.gov/stwdplng/projectinfo/ser/Gravina/assetts/ROD/Final_GAP_ROD.pdf.

[40] https://www.adn.com/alaska-news/article/how-bridge-nowhere-became-road-nowhere/2015/11/17/.

[41] https://www.heritage.org/budget-and-spending/report/the-bridge-nowhere-national-embarrassment.

[42] https://www.cagw.org/thewastewatcher/bridge-nowhere-update.

as public pressure mounted, and the project faced increasing scrutiny from both within and outside Congress.

In a dramatic twist, the very people whose voices had been raised in opposition to the bridge ultimately were the ones to bring about positive change in the name of the people. The controversy surrounding the Gravina Island Bridge served as a stark reminder of the importance of transparency and accountability in government spending, forcing the cancellation of the project and resulting in the funds being redirected toward other transportation projects across the country where they could be put to better use.

Social Cost-Benefit Framework for Public Innovation

Public innovation aims to drive growth, improve competitiveness, and promote economic development. However, these efforts can also have unintended consequences, such as increased social costs and negative externalities. In recent years there has been growing recognition of the need to carefully consider the potential social impacts of public innovation, and to ensure that they are designed and implemented in a way that balances competing interests and promotes sustainable growth.

While the benefits of public innovation are undeniable, it is essential to acknowledge and address the potential downsides. Here we present the social cost-benefit framework for public innovation (Figure 6.1),

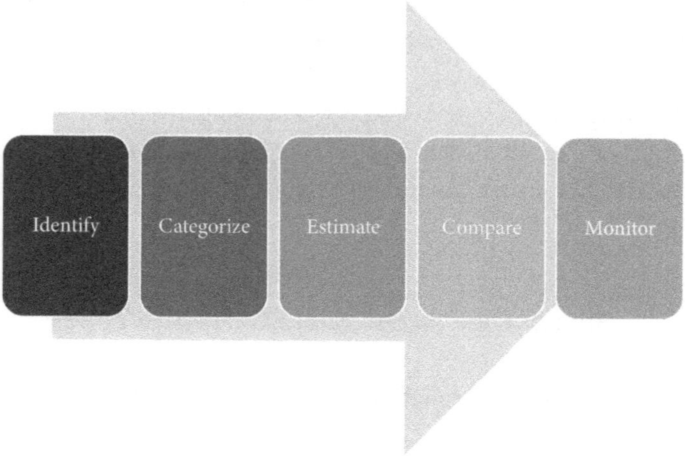

Figure 6.1 Social Cost-Benefit Framework for Public Innovation

which provides a comprehensive strategy for identifying, analyzing, and managing these risks. Using a systematic approach, public innovators can make more informed decisions that balance the need for progress while not losing sight of social responsibility.

Step 1: Identify Potential Social Costs and Benefits

Conducting thorough risk-benefit assessments is crucial when evaluating public innovation policies that may impact various groups, including those who may be negatively affected by these changes. To do this effectively, we must analyze the potential benefits of public innovation policies against their potential drawbacks, such as job displacement, impacts on individuals' freedoms or privacy, or increased energy consumption.

Consider the economic, social, environmental, and human dimensions of these potential impacts, and identify areas where policy interventions or alterations can mitigate negative effects and enhance positive outcomes. For instance, a new policy aimed at reducing carbon emissions might have benefits for the environment, but also pose financial costs to businesses that rely on fossil fuels. There can be many different competing interests to be weighed, but it is crucial to have a holistic understanding of them so we can create a more comprehensive understanding of the change being proposed.

When in doubt, it is a good idea to bring in additional stakeholders to help identify these costs. For example, if there was a new library program to help children learn to read, one might assume that the only stakeholders involved would be the library. But it could also be beneficial to bring in other stakeholders, including the parents who might identify other concerns such as not having adequate transit to take their child to the library or the hours might not work with parents' work schedules.

Step 2: Categorize Social Costs into Types

To systematically work through the financial costs associated with a policy or program, it is essential to consider the perspective of both government and the public. Implementing a classification system that categorizes social costs into distinct types can help identify areas where interventions may be needed most.

One effective approach is to develop a comprehensive framework that acknowledges the diverse and often competing interests at play. This framework should distinguish between different types of costs to capture a holistic understanding of impacts. For instance, direct costs might include financial burdens on organizations, such as increased taxes or regulatory compliance costs. At the same time, these costs can also have a ripple effect on the broader community, manifesting as indirect costs like social isolation or decreased community cohesion.

Externalities offer another layer of complexity, representing unintended consequences that transcend both organizational and societal boundaries. These might include environmental impacts, such as climate change, or market distortions, like reduced competition. By recognizing these interconnections, policymakers can better understand the far-reaching implications of their decisions and craft more effective solutions.

This consideration highlights the importance of involving diverse stakeholders in the classification process. Government agencies, community groups, and advocacy organizations each bring unique perspectives to the table, shaped by their respective interests, values, and experiences.

Step 3: Estimate Social Costs

Unlike Step 2, here we must attempt to estimate social costs, which may be harder to quantify. However, the magnitude and frequency of each type of social costs may be estimated using economic models, surveys, or other methods. This will provide a comprehensive understanding of the scope and nature of social costs. It is a good practice to consider factors such as population growth, technological advancements, and demographic changes that may impact social costs.

Some questions might be helpful to ask include: Who is intended to benefit from the policy, and who may ultimately lose resources or opportunities as a result? Furthermore, how do we measure the success of our program? If we deliver exceptional service but compromise other critical aspects of our organization, can it still be considered a success? These analyses can significantly influence the development of effective and equitable policies.

Step 4: Compare Benefits against Social Costs

Once the social costs are estimated, it's essential to compare them against the potential benefits of public innovation policies. This involves using decision-making frameworks such as cost-benefit analysis (CBA) or multicriteria decision analysis (MCDA). CBA helps to weigh the expected monetary value of benefits against the expected monetary value of costs, while MCDA considers multiple stakeholders' interests and prioritizes policy decisions based on their relative importance.

Step 5: Monitor and Adapt the Framework

Finally, regularly review and update the framework to reflect changing circumstances and new information. Government agencies should continuously assess the effectiveness of public innovation policies in mitigating social costs and promoting benefits, and refine the approach as needed. This involves tracking policy outcomes, monitoring social cost trends, and adjusting the framework accordingly to ensure that it remains relevant and effective over time.

Through this iterative process, policymakers can develop a more nuanced understanding of the complex interplay between public innovation policies and their social impacts. This deeper insight enables more informed and adaptive decisions about how to shape these policies for maximum public benefit.

As we have seen covered in this book, public innovation can be a great boon for society. It has been used to help tackle wicked problems. In most regards, public innovation attempts to have people's best interest in mind and are well-intended efforts. However, it does not come without its drawbacks and challenges. At times there can be a misalignment between the public interest and public innovation in which the government essentially works separately and sometimes even against the will of the public with new initiatives and developments. This is why it is crucial for governments to employ a feedback loop from the public to keep a pulse on the will of the people and what policies they would like to see. If there are policies that adversely affect certain groups of people, governments should meet with those groups to try to come to a consensus on how to accommodate both sides.

Other times, there can be unintended consequences that must be evaluated and mitigated as a result of public innovation such as the case for the FDA approval process. In these situations, downstream impacts of decisions need to be assessed by the government and to do various forms of risk-benefit assessments. Similar to the previous suggestion as well, governments should seek to speak to all stakeholders for decisions including the citizens who are likely to be impacted by decisions, good or bad.

Meanwhile, we have also seen the government picking winners and losers and having an exceptionally large impact on entire industries. The textile example is not too different from today's focus on artificial intelligence (AI) and how it is poised to phase out different jobs while receiving at least moderate levels of support from the government. This time around, however, it would behoove the government to learn the lessons from before and should limit their favoritism in markets. Instead, they should seek to be on guard against the fallout from volatile markets and have backup plans for workers in industries that do not receive favor from the market or government. This could be for example providing worker training programs with job placement for workers who were displaced due to technological shifts.

For all the drawbacks of public innovation, the larger lesson is to always take a holistic view of the innovation being proposed and how it may adversely impact groups. Sometimes those groups are not immediately apparent, while other times they may be the other side of the same coin of innovation. That is why it is crucial to have mitigation strategies in place to limit the negative impact of any change.

Chapter 7

Simple Ingredients, Better Cake

Building a Public Innovation and Entrepreneurial Ecosystem for Good

In ecology, an ecosystem refers to a system or environment where dynamic exchanges and interactions take place among all organisms (Agren & Bosatta, 1998). Extending this to the organization level, we can extrapolate that an entrepreneurial ecosystem includes a variety of independent actors, including government, educational and other forms of institutions, capital opportunities, and other various social factors that operate in a location (Isenberg, 2010; Stam, 2015). Regions that have well-established, supportive ecosystems have a higher propensity to produce more high-growth startups and attract entrepreneurs from other regions or countries (Acs et al., 2017). The importance of this supportive entrepreneurial ecosystem has been of growing importance to countries and cities as they strive to create an environment conducive to revolutionary unicorns that can drive economic growth and create a culture of vibrant innovation.

One prominent example of a pioneering ecosystem is Silicon Valley that has served as a spawning ground for many global tech giants and startups. The support from the government, easy access to risk capital, connectivity with local universities, and an entrepreneur-friendly culture enabled the success of Silicon Valley (Kenney, 2000). Tel Aviv in Israel is another major entrepreneurial ecosystem exemplified by its close collaboration among different stakeholders including government, industry, and investors (Avnimelech & Teubal, 2004). Bangalore in India has become the world's fastest-growing tech hub benefiting from a large talent pool of 1.5 million engineers developing advanced technologies like IT and machine learning.[1] Further east, China has given rise to ecosystems in large urban cities, such as Beijing,

[1] https://thescalers.com/bangalore.

Innovation and Entrepreneurship in the Public Sector. Wendy D. Chen and David B. Audretsch, Oxford University Press. © Oxford University Press (2025). DOI: 10.1093/9780197679470.003.0007

Shanghai, and Shenzhen, by leveraging government incentives and unicorn enterprises to drive innovation at scale.[2]

An insight the public sector should grasp from these examples is the importance of building public innovation and entrepreneurial ecosystems to generate new ideas, develop new technologies, and innovative management tools to significantly improve public program performance and delivery. In this chapter, inspired by the successful entrepreneurial ecosystems for the private sector, we develop a model of public innovation and entrepreneurial ecosystem that consists of human capital, entrepreneurial culture, cross-sector collaboration, supporting resources, public policy, and new management and leadership (Figure 7.1).

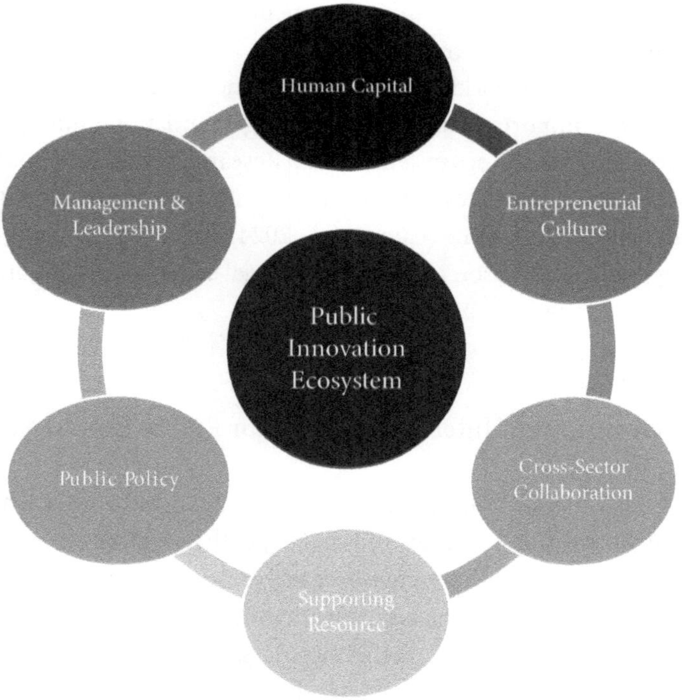

Figure 7.1 Public innovation ecosystem

[2] https://eqvista.com/startup-fundraising/startup-ecosystem-china/.

Human Capital

When all of the fancy technology and fancy buzzwords are stripped away, the soul of innovation is people. Organizations with highly skilled individuals are usually better positioned to identify opportunities, research new ideas and develop more advanced technologies. Put differently, human capital is key to public innovation. Interestingly, the public sector faces a catch-22: It seeks top-tier, inventive minds to propel governmental progress, yet without fostering an environment conducive to innovation, it risks repelling those very individuals who harbor the drive to pioneer transformative solutions.[3]

To tackle this conundrum, instead of waiting on highly skilled and entrepreneurial individuals to enter the public sector, governments should take "the two birds, one stone" strategy by training current government employees to be innovative and entrepreneurial while preparing individuals to be future public entrepreneurs.

In order to have a workforce ready to be innovative and entrepreneurial, however, it is important to establish strong foundations through proper education and strong ecosystems early. Research has found that having access to proper resources early in life is critical to someone developing entrepreneurial aspirations (Chen et al., 2024). To that point, developing a thriving public innovation and entrepreneurial ecosystem is not only based on space, but is also temporal.

Government Internal Training for Public Employees

As we learned earlier, entrepreneurship is a long, drawn-out learning process, fraught with opportunities and challenges that must be overcome by the entrepreneur. Many of the same issues are present in public entrepreneurship as well. The entrepreneurial process is not undertaken in isolation. To truly be successful with this metamorphic shift, the existing government workforce must be engaged at every level. To that point, government leaders and managers should play the role of cultivators, providing the opportunity for employees to receive routine training sessions and programs tailored

[3] https://www2.deloitte.com/ie/en/pages/public-sector/articles/govlab-blog/why-should-gov-public-service-innovate.html.

to elevate employees' skills in the fertile fields of public sector innovation including areas like data-driven decision-making, the Internet of Things, artificial intelligence, and blockchain.

We can see hints of this growth in São Paulo, Brazil. Placing an emphasis on creating a highly engaged civil society, the Agents of Open Government initiative was created as a peer-to-peer learning platform to provide a way for citizens with special skills to develop curriculum for government workers. This dynamic program not only disseminates cutting-edge methodologies to public servants but also bridges the gap between government and citizens. Through this transformative model, civil servants gain access to a diverse arsenal, including the dynamic agility of open-source software development, the navigational precision of community mapping, and the amplifying reach of social media. Concurrently, they interact with a spectrum of stakeholders from private enterprises, academia, and civil society, sparking a surge of curiosity and establishing connections with their constituents.[4]

Government External Training and Selection for Future Public Entrepreneurs

It is crucial to build a future public innovation force within the public sector. Just as those high-impact startup ventures are often found to be within close geographic proximity to universities, governments can also leverage human capital from higher education and nurture public entrepreneurship in the university and college settings. Most universities and colleges have programs and courses related to public administration. Governments on different levels may collaborate with local higher education institutions to develop tailored initiatives and specializations in areas including health, environment, public policy, and urban planning that can equip students with the ability to identify opportunities for innovation and enhance their critical skills in public innovation. In addition, governments may provide internship opportunities for students to witness the innerworkings of the government firsthand. During internships, governments can create opportunities for students to play the role of the public entrepreneur, sharing the problems they

[4] https://www.oecd.org/gov/innovative-government/embracing-innovation-in-government.pdf.

are experiencing and asking how the student might solve those problems. Through these trainings, students will build systemic analysis skills that are necessary for future public innovation.

In Israel, as young men and women approach the age of eighteen, they are required to perform mandatory public service, most commonly in the military.[5]While millions around the world at this age would be preparing for their inaugural college experience, their Israeli counterparts gear up for their maiden voyage into the realm of combat.[6] Following their military obligations, many Israeli veterans then pursue higher education at one of Israel's esteemed universities, where they can leverage their skills and experiences to excel in a variety of academic fields.

The Israeli military training silently molds leaders by instilling vital competencies and preparing them for life in a much different way. Once they have completed their military duty and can return to the life of a civilian, Israel has created clear pathways to easily integrate their specialized knowledge with real-world challenges, gaining a distinct advantage in entrepreneurial endeavors over their counterparts from other countries. Thanks to mandatory military service, the Israeli youth receive excellent technical training while also developing a sense of duty, respect, and drive for success.[7,8]

Across the globe, governments have been intensely seeking extraordinary talent, continually honing their strategies to secure the brightest minds. In the quest for talent, the public sector finds itself in a delicate yet fierce competition with the private sector, both vying to attract and retain the most skilled individuals. While the private sector often offers more lucrative financial incentives, the public sector must leverage its own unique strengths, such as opportunities for meaningful impact and public service.

Singapore, with its competitive education landscape, has positioned itself as an attractive destination for talented individuals from around the world. Taking cues from Singapore's trio of prime ministers, their hallmark strategy is applying meritocratic principles widely across organizations and institutions (Bellows, 2009). This approach includes carefully selecting scholarship recipients for overseas education, offering diverse training programs, and

[5] https://www.idf.il/en/mini-sites/our-soldiers/

[6] https://maint.loc.gov/law/help/military-draft/israel.php.

[7] https://www2.deloitte.com/il/en/pages/innovation/article/the_israeli_technological_ecosystem.html.

[8] https://www.forbes.com/sites/julianmitchell/2016/07/11/startup-nation-this-israeli-company-uses-military-principles-to-build-scalable-businesses/?sh=3b0a407343cc.

creating fresh paths for internal mobility and career growth within the public sector (Quah, 2010; Ye, 2021). Additionally, these principles guide the selection of parliamentary candidates, favoring those with proven merit from within the bureaucracy, cultivating a technocratic governance culture (Barr, 2006; Tan, 2012).

Singapore's success story is more than just attracting top talent; it's about nurturing and retaining it. Investing in the growth and development of its brightest minds ensures a dynamic and innovative public sector. This commitment to meritocracy has not only shaped the country's political landscape but also positioned it as a global leader in governance and talent acquisition. Continuously evolving strategies guarantee Singapore's enduring appeal to exceptional individuals, solidifying its status as a hub for brilliance.

Entrepreneurial Culture

David Landes (1969; 1998) argued that culture played a crucial role in impacting entrepreneurship and ultimately long-term economic growth. Indeed, historical analysis of nineteenth-century France reveals that the prevailing cultural attitudes toward entrepreneurship were a major obstacle to economic advancement, stifling innovation and limiting the country's potential for growth. These entrepreneurs in that particular historical context viewed entrepreneurship as a means to uphold family status rather than pursuing innovation and growth. They were security-oriented rather than risk-taking. As a result, their businesses were economically inefficient and technologically conservative.

Traditionally, the public sector is not used to changes or innovation. Although governments around the world have made lots of progress in directing the development of new technologies and innovation through internally sponsored programs, there is still much room for them to actively create a healthy cultural environment to promote public innovation.[9] Notably, not cultivating an environment that is ready for innovation will lose public organizations' competitiveness and will not be an enticing prospect for motivated, creative people to develop their careers. Governments at every level should embark on a cultural metamorphosis, fostering

[9] https://www.weforum.org/agenda/2022/03/should-government-leave-innovation-to-the-private-sector/.

an environment where individuals are empowered to navigate technical uncertainty and embrace the inherent value of experimentation and learning from mistakes. An innovative culture encourages and supports new ideas and is willing to put them to the test in real-life practice. This culture enables two-way dialogue between government and citizens. So how can a cultural environment conducive to public innovation be created?

Competition

Competition is at the core of innovation. Compelled by the imperative of distinguishing themselves from their competitors, entrepreneurs and innovators come up with new ideas and expedite the implementation of the innovations (Baumol et al., 2007).

As Schumpeter (1942) cogently argued, the interplay of entrepreneurial entry and creative destruction furnishes incumbents with incentives to perpetually refine their offerings through the introduction of novel products and services. This perpetual cycle of innovation, growth, and dynamism lies at the heart of entrepreneurial ecosystems, propelling them forward as engines of economic advancement.

Putting this notion into practice, the Bloomberg Philanthropies' Mayors Challenge in the US is a dynamic competition that ignites innovative ideas to enhance cities and the lives of their residents. Novel solutions and positive change become natural byproducts as leaders are encouraged to think creatively.[10]

Portugal played host to GovTech, a public competition in 2018 that joined similar state-sponsored events to endorse and reward forward-thinking startups with a mind to the UN's Sustainable Development Goals. Those include subjects such as women's rights, youth, migrants, and other societal concerns that resonate with current worldwide issues. Supporting the competition was the stated objective of rejuvenating the country's startup ecosystem, propelling sustainable economic growth and opening a new wave of opportunities to align Portugal with the 2030 Agenda. Numerous new technologies from government-commissioned trials were in the marketing, including the ability to incorporate new ideas in the public voting phase using blockchain technology, which facilitated new alternatives

[10] https://www.bloomberg.org/government-innovation/spurring-innovation-in-cities/.

to gathering inventive concepts and harnessing transparent involvement equally, from both citizens and startups.[11] Instead of relying on traditional methods for the vote, it ingenuously turned the voting process into an online game to make it fun for all the participants. Also interestingly, GovTech leveraged Ethereum blockchain technology to ensure the transparency and security of the voting process with the support from Portugal's Administrative Modernization Agency and the Ministry of Foreign Affairs. Participants interacted through a virtual platform, earning GovTech cryptocurrency for various actions.[12]

Innovation Incentives

Incentives play a key role in all organizations. Well-designed incentives increase employee engagement and improve productivity. For public innovation, incentives are also important. Incentives could be in different formats including reward systems for public employees to innovate within and open up other collaborative opportunities for citizens and other sectors.

Singapore's fifteen-year-olds are among the top performers in the Programme for International Student Assessment, which has a lot to do with its public innovation in education.[13] Some of its success can be attributed to the teacher system that values well-qualified teachers and also incorporates elements of meritocracy. Primary and secondary education teachers are paid 60% of their starting salary to attend trainings for three years to prepare them for primary and secondary education. On top of this, teachers are entitled to 100 hours of professional development each year to stay up to date with the latest teaching methods and curriculum updates. The system also provides teachers with multiple career paths, each accompanied by corresponding increases in compensation. Then, just like the rest of the country, teachers are subject to performance appraisals to measure their performance against multiple measures to determine their efficacy and receive pay increases in return for positive results.[14,15]

[11] https://oecd-opsi.org/innovations/govtech/.
[12] https://www.oecd-ilibrary.org/docserver/932780bc-en.pdf.
[13] https://ncee.org/country/singapore/.
[14] https://asiasociety.org/global-cities-education-network/how-singapore-developed-high-quality-teacher-workforce.
[15] https://ncee.org/country/singapore.

Crowd-Powered Open Innovation

Montevideo Decide stands as a novel digital platform that invites the citizens of Montevideo, the capital city of Uruguay, to play a direct role in the shaping of the city and indeed to decide. This dynamic vehicle facilitates diverse levels of participation, empowering the citizenry to debate and propose initiatives, to propose new projects (in fields as diverse as urban life and health, among others), and to intervene in local political processes with direct action. Offering a vital means of immediate citizen engagement by way of the digital sphere, Montevideo Decide guarantees that the making of public policy be democratized and converted into a point of entry for anyone passionate to innovate their city together.[16]

Accessible from any internet-enabled device, the platform embodies inclusivity, welcoming all citizens to participate freely without constraints. Its intuitive interface, tailored to the Uruguayan context and the strategic objectives of the Municipality of Montevideo, embodies the ethos: "Your ideas can transform the city." With modules spanning Citizen Consultations, Debates, Idea Generation, Participatory Budgeting, and Collaboration Spaces, the platform introduces innovative avenues for civic engagement, amplifying citizen voices and fostering a sense of ownership over municipal decision-making processes.[17]

Built on open-source software and part of the global Consul community, Montevideo Decide offers a replicable model adaptable to diverse municipal contexts worldwide. While grounded in the unique context of Montevideo, its core elements including facilitating debates, soliciting ideas, conducting consultations, and promoting participatory budgeting all serve as universally applicable pillars of democratic governance. These practices foster vibrant, inclusive civic engagement and more importantly, help cultivate an entrepreneurial culture in which citizens play an active role in shaping the future of their city.

In a radical shift toward citizen-centricity, Finland launched Kokeilun Paikka, a digital platform igniting a collaborative culture of public service innovation. This platform departs from the traditional top-down model, empowering citizens to become active agents of change. In some regards, it can be thought of as its own self-contained ecosystem. Kokeilun Paikka

[16] https://participa.montevideo.gub.uy/.
[17] https://oidp.net/distinction/en/candidacy.php?id=1218.

serves as a vibrant marketplace where citizens not only envision transformative ideas but also showcase them, garner feedback, secure funding, and connect directly with reform-minded officials. It moves beyond a static model, fostering a dynamic shift from passive recipients to engaged co-creators, actively shaping their communities.[18]

This citizen-centric approach operates as a two-way street. While amplifying grassroots innovations through visibility, resources, experimentation, and mentorship, it simultaneously empowers the government to tackle complex challenges by breaking them down into manageable components through citizen-generated solutions. This collaborative ecosystem nurtures a more responsive and dynamic public sector, one that listens intently, adapts readily, and evolves seamlessly alongside its constituents.[19]

But Kokeilun Paikka's ambition extends beyond mere participation. It harnesses the collective power of the crowd, not just in ideation but also in action. Crowdsourcing unlocks a vast reservoir of ingenious solutions, while crowdfunding empowers citizens to directly invest in projects they believe in, fostering a profound sense of ownership and shared responsibility. This blurring of traditional boundaries ushers in a more inclusive and participatory governance model, where the lines between "them" and "us" begin to dissolve.

Finland seeks to be the world leader in experimentation and innovation by 2025, and they hope that Kokeilun Paikka can help achieve this goal.[20] The success of Kokeilun Paikka hinges on robust citizen engagement, an effective platform design, and an unwavering commitment to collaboration. If these elements coalesce, this platform has the potential to redefine citizen–government relations and pave the way for a more responsive, innovative, and truly citizen-centric public sector. The future of public service development might just be co-created, crowd-funded, and experimented into existence, and Finland is taking the bold first step on this exciting journey.

In Córdoba, Argentina, the government is kickstarting an exciting adventure with an open innovation GovTech strategy. For additional context, the World Bank defines Govtech as "a whole-of-government approach to public sector modernization. It emphasizes three aspects of public sector

[18] https://www.oecd.org/gov/innovative-government/embracing-innovation-in-government.pdf.

[19] https://www.motiva.fi/ratkaisut/kokeileva_kehittaminen/kokeilun_paikka.

[20] https://vnk.fi/-/kokeilunpaikka-fi-on-alusta-yhdessa-tekemiselle-ja-kokeilujen-rahoitukselle.

modernization: citizen-centric, universally accessible public services, and whole-of-government approach to digital government transformation."[21] Córdoba's bold initiative seeks to ignite an entrepreneurial spirit within the government, shaking up established norms and practices while forging dynamic partnerships with startups. Together, with initiatives like these ones we've covered we are poised to reimagine public administration and urban dynamics, fostering a culture of innovation and collaboration that promises to shape the future of our city for the better.[22,23]

Cross-Sector Collaboration

As previously mentioned, it may take a village to raise a child, but it undoubtedly takes a village to innovate. Thereafter, it is in the government's best interest to develop interorganizational partnerships. The traditional paradigm of scaling innovation in the public sector is undergoing a transformative shift. The most successful governments at innovating are the ones who recognize their own weaknesses. They are increasingly embracing collaborative alliances with diverse stakeholders, transcending the limitations of siloed approaches and unlocking previously unimaginable innovations. There is a sort of collaborative alchemy that occurs when these stakeholders come together, where there is an exchange of knowledge while the government seeks to close their skill gaps. Through these newfound partnerships, public services can be more innovative, and public managers can be more responsive to serve the needs of citizens.[24]

The shift toward collaborative problem-solving is driven by a growing recognition of the limitations inherent in siloed approaches. Governments, despite their vast reach, often lack the specialized knowledge and the skills necessary to wield new technical innovations effectively. This necessitates a move beyond internal resources that these organizations have become accustomed to and toward "collaborative intelligence" (Hackman, 2011)—the ability to recognize and leverage external expertise. This manifests in the form of collaborative alliances forged with universities, private companies, and even citizens (Gray & Wood, 1991). These alliances act as crucibles

[21] https://www.worldbank.org/en/programs/govtech.

[22] https://govinsider.asia/intl-en/article/how-cordoba-champions-open-innovation-in-argentina.

[23] https://corlab.cordoba.gob.ar/wp-content/uploads/2024/05/Building-MODERN-Cities-through-Govtech-2.pdf.

[24] https://www.oecd.org/gov/innovative-government/embracing-innovation-in-government.pdf.

for knowledge exchange and innovation, fostering an epistemological convergence that transcends the limitations of individual actors (Kastenhofer, 2007).

All-Sided Partnerships

To demonstrate these points, we can take a trip around the world again to explore how countries are utilizing cross-sector collaboration. In the Pacific where seasonal monsoons are a recurring challenge, Greater Jakarta found a beacon of hope in PetaBencana.id. This platform's strength lies not just in its real-time flood maps powered by social media and crowdsourcing, but in the synergistic partnership birthing it. PetaBencana.id is a prime example of cross-sector collaboration as it included academia (MIT's Urban Risk Lab), the NGO PetaBencana.id, and the Indonesian government's BNPB.[25] Together, the partners co-designed the platform with the people's and emergency responders' best interests in mind, ensuring seamless integration with existing workflows. This collaborative alchemy transcended siloed approaches, leveraging diverse expertise to tackle complex challenges.[26]

PetaBencana.id represents a paradigm shift, for the people of Jakarta while (Stone, 2004) being indicative of the shift toward cross-sector collaboration. For the people of Jakarta, it replaces static, six-hourly PDF maps with real-time insights, empowering both government and citizens with accurate, immediate data (Hidayat, 2020). Furthermore, it provides clear methods to city personnel and citizens to monitor flood events to be able to activate their emergency plans. From the perspective of cross-sector collaboration, it exemplifies the potential of multistakeholder partnerships in public sector innovation, offering a promising path toward building more resilient megacities (Hidayat, 2020).

Lucerne, Switzerland's "digital cooperative" experiment offers a novel twist on cross-sector collaboration, echoing initiatives like PetaBencana.id. Unlike these citizen science platforms, Lucerne's model directly incentivizes data contribution from diverse stakeholders, including citizens with varying digital literacy levels, corporations, and public bodies. This

[25] BNPB, or Badan Nasional Penanggulangan Bencana, is translated to National Disaster Management Agency. The Agency provides relief to citizens who fall victim to the natural disasters from earthquakes, monsoons, and so on.

[26] https://www.oecd.org/gov/innovative-government/embracing-innovation-in-government.pdf.

democratization of data presents a unique challenge in fostering collaboration across disparate groups, as Lucerne acknowledges by exploring innovative engagement strategies and "dataspaces" concepts (Franklin et al., 2005).[27]

Sectorial Competitions

While the technology behind Lucerne's model has garnered positive feedback, the long-term success hinges on addressing the social and organizational dynamics of such cross-collaborations. Meanwhile, Uruguay's IA-CKATON, a government-led initiative designed to promote open innovation and collaboration in AI within the public sector. It acts as a "hackathon" or innovation marathon, inviting participants from diverse sectors to work and compete together to develop AI-based solutions to public challenges. By encouraging healthy competition alongside collaboration, IA-CKATON encourages innovation while potentially mitigating the challenges of diverse stakeholder engagement (El Bcheraoui et al., 2017). In the meantime, the collaborators and participants use a design approach with a clear end goal in mind, which can help alleviate some of the tension that arises from cross-sector collaborative efforts (Bryson et al., 2015).[28]

Both initiatives, situated in geographically distinct contexts (Europe and South America), showcase the burgeoning potential of cross-sector collaboration in driving public sector innovation. Lucerne's digital cooperative, with its focus on data incentives and engagement strategies, offers a unique method to encourage citizen participation, while IA-CKATON's emphasis on healthy competition within collaborative environments presents a valuable alternative. As the research on these initiatives progresses, we can expect further insights into the nuances of fostering successful cross-sector collaboration for tackling urban challenges.

Collaborating with Startups

The trend of city-startup collaboration has been on prominent display with the citizen science movement seen in initiatives like our previous examples, but in America's North Carolina it is extended to leverage the expertise of

[27] https://www.oecd-ilibrary.org/docserver/932780bc-en.pdf?expires=1686681175&id=id&accname=guest&checksum=D5DA3753464E714C67B0100CE520C32C.

[28] Ibid.

local tech talent. Knowledge spillover, or the diffusion of knowledge, has been found to face challenges when people are geographically disbursed (van der Wouden & Youn, 2023). Additionally, citizens like to be involved in shaping their communities when they feel there is a void that is not being addressed (Horlings et al., 2021). As exemplified by Durham, North Carolina's partnership with a VR startup, such collaborations transcend geographical boundaries while providing an opportunity for participatory government by harnessing the unique strengths of each player (Parker, 2011).

Durham's 3D tours of unbuilt projects demonstrate the potential for such partnerships to enhance democratic processes. Democratization of information and civic engagement facilitate meaningful collaboration between governments and citizens, ultimately empowering residents to take a more active role in shaping the future of their communities (Bryson et al., 2015).[29] This example, alongside others like it, highlights the burgeoning potential of cross-sector partnerships in driving urban innovation, fostering citizen participation, and ultimately improving quality of life for residents (Bason, 2010).

Amsterdam's Startup in Residence program transcends mere city-startup collaboration, creating a vibrant co-creation ecosystem (Bason, 2010). Similar to Durham's 3D tours fostering resident engagement through technology, this initiative leverages the power of cross-sector partnerships to tackle pressing urban challenges. However, Amsterdam goes beyond showcasing unbuilt projects, inviting startups to co-develop and pilot solutions alongside city officials and citizens.

This program resonated deeply with Amsterdammers, known for their independent spirit, entrepreneurial flair, and embrace of diverse perspectives, due to its focus on resident-driven innovation and its open, collaborative approach (Bryson et al., 2015). Empowering citizens to actively participate in shaping their city's future fosters a sense of ownership and shared responsibility, a crucial element for driving successful public sector innovation (Bason, 2010). This initiative exemplifies the potential of cross-collaboration to not only generate innovative solutions but also cultivate a more engaged and empowered citizenry, contributing to a more vibrant and responsive urban environment.[30]

[29] https://www.govtech.com/civic/durham-nc-picks-six-startups-for-local-gov-collaboration.html.

[30] https://collaborative-innovators.org/assets/files/Collaborative-Innovation-between-Startups-and-the-Public-Sector.pdf.

Supporting Resources

In cross-sector collaboration, governments may choose to roll up their sleeves and take a more active role in initiatives, working alongside private sector partners to address problems directly. Alternatively, they may assume a more hands-off role, allowing others to take the lead while still providing essential support and resources.

The effectiveness of rolling up their sleeves versus a more hands-off approach depends on the unique circumstances and objectives of each collaboration. Both methods have the potential to yield successful outcomes, but it is crucial to consider the specific context, issue at hand, and the capacities of involved parties when deciding on the appropriate level of government involvement.

Incubator

The first model of supporting resources the government provides we will discuss is the Incubator model. Incubators serve as an opportunity for fledgling businesses to gain crucial elements required for success at their early stages including funding, mentoring, and data access. Recognizing the potential startups can bring to the country, governments around the world have witnessed the value of incubators and looked to incorporate them into their countries, acting as strategic tools to foster entrepreneurial ecosystems and nurture nascent businesses (Abetti, 2004). These incubators provide a supportive environment beyond just physical space, offering a multidimensional package of resources and guidance. Governments play a diverse role in incubator development, ranging from direct funding and infrastructure provision to policy interventions and regulatory frameworks. Some governments actively create and manage incubators, while others incentivize and support private initiatives (Chandra & Fealey, 2009; Li et al., 2020; Soetanto & Jack, 2011). Many incubators offer business development workshops, mentoring programs, access to networks and investors, legal and accounting support, and even shared office space. Brazil's Innovation Barueri, echoing Chandra et al.'s (2009) emphasis on multipronged support, transcends mere space and integrates research, technology, and business development, fostering academia–industry collaboration for impactful solutions. Furthermore, it provides a shared location for academics and businesses to interact and develop solutions while providing socioeconomic benefits for the community. Tailored services like mentorship and research access empower startups, the incubator serves as are a place to nurturing new ventures. Barueri's success showcases the potential of public–private partnerships in driving innovation ecosystems.[31]

For our next example, we move over to the Middle East. Since its inception in the early 1990s, Israel's Technology Incubator program has morphed into a thriving ecosystem fostering high-potential tech startups. This unique approach blends government support with private sector dynamism, offering valuable insights for nations seeking to cultivate innovation.

At the heart of this success lies a two-pronged strategy: financial support and comprehensive services. First, the program boasts over twenty-five privatized incubators nationwide, each offering government funding covering up to 85% of early-stage project costs for two years. This significantly mitigates risk for investors, attracting them to fledgling ventures (Abetti, 2004; Hendratmi & Sukmaningrum, 2018). As a result, over 1,100 projects have successfully graduated from these incubators, with over 45% securing additional investments (Li et al., 2020).

Second, the Israel Innovation Authority, with its annual budget of $400 million, provides robust support through programs such as the R&D Fund, offering grants covering up to 40% of approved R&D program costs.[32] This model helps to reduce the financial risks for entrepreneurs while also fosters a strong innovation ecosystem by connecting startups with mentors, investors, and global markets. As a result, Israel has become a global leader in tech entrepreneurship and public innovation.

Innovation Funds

Innovation funds serve as vital incentives for governmental innovation, contingent on agencies' flexibility in resource allocation and stable funding commitments. While greater spending autonomy enhances innovation outcomes, excessive fragmentation poses risks of organizational silos and diminishes innovation capacity for smaller agencies. Forecast-based financing (FbF) revolutionizes funding paradigms by releasing resources based on forecasted risks, enhancing preparedness and risk management

[31] https://oecd-opsi.org/innovations/innovation-barueri-technological-development-center-research-and-business-incubator/.

[32] https://www2.deloitte.com/il/en/pages/innovation/article/the_israeli_technological_ecosystem.html.

in humanitarian aid. Pioneered by the German Red Cross with government support, FbF has proven transformative, as demonstrated in Uganda, where a scientific flood risk forecast prompted proactive distribution of 5,000 preparatory items to vulnerable communities.[33,34]

Social financing provides another tool that has been used for smart innovative financing. Social impact bonds (SIBs) are a tool in which private investors can fund a project that addresses a social need that has been outlined by the government (Dear et al., 2016, Sinclair et al., 2014). Upon a project's success, the government refunds the investors their invested amount plus additional compensation for the risk associated with the investment. If the project fails to meet its goals, the investor loses their investment, and the government incurs no loss.[35]

The UK has experimented with an SIB pilot program to discover whether a project would help address rehabilitation programs for male prisoners. Recidivism rates dropped by roughly 8%, indicating the project's success as a whole.[36] According to Socialfinance.org, as of 2022, there are thirty-five impact bonds spread across the world representing over $700 million in funding, indicating the trend is on the rise.[37]

An important element on display here is the level of transparency and accountability that comes with these SIBs. Because projects can be monitored and the success can be tracked, there is a reasonable incentive for the project leaders to be successful to receive compensation for their efforts. These types of programs can overall have a positive impact on raising the public's perception of government performance and efficacy.

Public Procurement

In the realm of government procurement, Austria has seized control, leveraging its authority to set market rules for the public sector. This strategic approach is evident in initiatives like the Austrian Action Plan on Public Procurement Promoting Innovation, standing a testament to this ethos that has been strategically incorporated with the broad span of the Austrian

[33] https://www.oecd.org/gov/innovative-government/embracing-innovation-in-government.pdf.
[34] http://www.climatecentre.org/programmes-engagement/forecast-based-financing/.
[35] https://www.oecd.org/gov/innovative-government/embracing-innovation-in-government.pdf.
[36] Ibid.
[37] https://www.socialfinance.org.uk/what-we-do/social-impact-bonds.

Strategy for Research, Technology, and Innovation. Together, they wield procurement as a powerful tool to drive transformative change and shift markets.[38]

In the digital sphere, platforms like the United States Micro-purchase Platform from 18F and Australia's Digital Marketplace are revolutionizing the old procurement approaches that have been in place for generations. Acting almost like e-Bay by utilizing online auctions along with bidirectional collaboration, these platforms to a large extent circumvent traditional procurement constraints to help provide necessary support for agile projects. Australia's Digital Marketplace facilitates government-supplier interaction and fosters innovation through challenges that are delivered by the government. These challenges stand as a testament to radically different times in the procurement space that can deliver better and more cost-effective solutions to the government and ultimately citizens.[39]

Public Policy

An increased number of governments across the globe have initiated open government data policy with increased data availability, accessibility, and reusability. Countries including South Korea, France, and the United Kingdom are the leaders in sharing data with the public. Open government data policies help to promote transparency and accountability. More importantly, it facilitates cross-sector collaborations among citizens, the private sector, the nonprofit sector, and other governmental agencies. Rather than solely relying on the government to make decisions and innovate, opening data allows all parties to participate and be on the same page and greatly contribute to public innovation.

Ask any technology company, and they will tell you that closed data silos stifle innovation. Open access fuels collaboration, prevents duplication, and empowers individuals, organizations, and even nations to build upon each other's ideas. The OECD's OUR Data Index helps identify global leaders and areas for improvement, paving the way for a more innovative and interconnected future.[40]

Another important aspect of data sharing involves what is referred to as sharing innovations. Denmark has attempted to create a method in which

[38] https://www.oecd.org/gov/innovative-government/embracing-innovation-in-government.pdf.
[39] Ibid.
[40] Ibid.

the public sector can share their innovations with one another, allowing each to reuse what may have been best practices and to apply these innovations in a different context. It draws on crowdsourcing from employees to determine innovations that may have been useful to them and encourages them to share their success with other agencies.[41,42]

The actual source code of the government has been targeted as another item to release to the public to help spur further innovations. The People's Code is a government-wide platform to allow people to access government code to ensure its security and functionality. Meanwhile, government employees are encouraged to give back to the open-source community to further development efforts.[43] Different agencies have participated, including the Departments of Agriculture, Commerce, Defense, and more, all hoping to gain feedback from the public on their projects.[44]

Admittedly, public policies do not solely exist to facilitate public innovation; they also play a crucial role in safeguarding the public's interests. One of the key responsibilities of government is to ensure that innovation proceeds in an ethical and responsible manner. This includes mitigating any potential negative effects that new technologies or innovations may have on society.

For instance, governments can use regulations to address the monopolistic behavior of tech giants, which may stifle innovation and limit opportunities for individuals and startups. By implementing and enforcing antitrust laws, governments can promote competition and create a more level playing field for all players in the sector. Recently, the EU opened investigations into Apple, Google, and Meta for suspected noncompliance with the Digital Markets Act (DMA), a broad rulebook that targets Big Tech "gatekeeper" companies.[45] The DMA aims to make digital markets fairer and more contestable. Through fines, investigations, and new regulations, the EU aims to create a more competitive and innovative digital landscape that benefits both consumers and smaller businesses.

The EU has taken steps to regulate the tech sector and promote competition through its Digital Markets Act and Digital Services Act. However, the proposed AI Act has been criticized for its potential impact

[41] https://oecd-opsi.org/toolkits/spreading-innovation/.
[42] https://.www.oecd.org/gov/innovative-government/embracing-innovation-in-government.pdf.
[43] Ibid.
[44] https://code.gov/agencies.
[45] https://www.cbsnews.com/news/eu-apple-google-meta-investigation-new-digital-markets-act-antitrust-law/.

on the EU's competitiveness in the global AI market.[46,47] While the act aims to ensure responsible development and use of AI, critics argue that its strict regulations and compliance requirements could stifle innovation and hinder the growth of AI companies in the EU. As the act continues to evolve, policymakers and industry stakeholders will need to work together to ensure the act strikes the right balance between promoting innovation and protecting citizens' rights.

Management and Leadership

The road to a better tomorrow still has guardrails rather than an open field. Similarly, public innovation needs to have boundaries set up to ensure equal competition and fairness across businesses, nonprofits, citizens, and even the government itself. It's important to understand that collaboration, transparency, and accountability are all paramount to the success of public innovation. Without these in place, any one group involved could overpower another.

For example, if a business receives funding from an SIB, it is important to validate the results reported by that business before reimbursing the venture capitalist. Or, if there was a new innovation lab initiative put in place by the state and a city manager was in charge of delivering the service, there need to be checks in place to ensure the resources promised are delivered. While it can be time-consuming to undertake these additional steps, they help to maintain the public innovation system's integrity and allow it to continue. To that point, smart cities and federal agencies need managers who understand, support, and promote public innovation. They should seek to inspire, nurture, and nudge those who are attempting to be change agents.

Support from the Top

This nurturing and support for innovation should be pervasive throughout entire agency and organizations. It should be a common value and goal for all stakeholders and trickle down from the very top of the organization.

[46] https://consumerchoicecenter.org/the-eus-ai-act-will-stifle-innovation-and-wont-become-a-global-standard/.

[47] https://www.gisreportsonline.com/r/ai-act-eu-regulation-innovation/.

Mokhber et al. (2018) found that transformational leadership was a big driving factor in organizational innovation. Furthermore, this support is found to transcend cultures, to carry a strong proximal impact from managers, and to be applicable to multiple stages of innovation for employees (Lukes & Stephan, 2017).

Leadership should not only be receptive to change but also champion it. Organizational leaders should be encouraging and supportive of public entrepreneurs, providing necessary resources so long as proper evaluations of the innovation have been conducted. Leaders should consistently reinforce the organization's mission to their employees, clearly outline their upcoming initiatives, and actively communicate their support for those who engage with and contribute to those initiatives. By doing so, they foster a sense of shared purpose and create a supportive environment where innovation and initiatives are recognized and rewarded.[48]

Innovation Lab

Innovation labs are blooming across the public sector landscape, sprouting either centrally to address national priorities or within specific agencies to cultivate domain-specific solutions (Tõnurist et al., 2017). These labs take diverse forms, birthing digital tools, policy prototypes, process redesigns, and service delivery interventions—all aimed at enriching the public realm (Lewis & Moultrie, 2005).

Denmark's MindLab, nestled within the central government, exemplifies this approach. Leveraging human-centered design, it tackles national challenges and crafts policy recommendations (Carstensen & Bason, 2012). Similarly, Chile's Laboratorio de Gobierno fosters innovation processes that prioritize user needs, striving to bridge the gap between citizens and the state (Zivkovic, 2018). This lab operates through three channels: (1) spearheading innovation projects for high-demand services, (2) bolstering civil servant innovation capabilities, and (3) incentivizing private sector participation through prototype challenges (Carstensen & Bason, 2012).[49]

[48] https://www.opm.gov/policy-data-oversight/performance-management/reference-materials/historical/promoting-innovation-in-government/.

[49] https://www.oecd.org/gov/innovative-government/embracing-innovation-in-government.pdf.

Beyond national labs, localized efforts are also taking root. France's Futurs Public, housed within the Prime Minister's Office, exemplifies this. This lab operates at a smaller scale, testing solutions for specific public sector challenges and nurturing an "innovation ecosystem" (Carstensen & Bason, 2012). Interestingly, Futurs Public collaborates with NGOs and social entrepreneurs, harnessing diverse expertise (Lewis & Moultrie, 2005). Imagine, for example, partnering with design experts to streamline social benefit applications, or collaborating with social entrepreneurs to pilot personalized disability support. Such cross-pollination can breathe new life into public services, particularly in rural areas where challenges might be unique (Carstensen & Bason, 2012).[50]

New Public Management

In order to effectively support public innovation, public management must provide the necessary structural foundation alongside the efforts of individual leaders of organizations. This is where New Public Management comes into play. While the term "new public management" (NPM) suggests a cutting-edge approach, it is anything but new, having been born in the 1980s (Hood, 1991; Osborne & Gaebler 1992). The 1980s public administration was fraught with bureaucratic inefficiencies, and NPM was portrayed as the silver bullet to solve the problems plaguing these organizations. These problems would be addressed by borrowing private-sector principles and applying them to the public sector where competition, efficiency, and performance-based accountability reign supreme (Dunleavy et al., 2006).

NPM had many strengths that helped make it an attractive choice for public managers. It streamlined processes, incentivized innovation, and brought a focus on taxpayer value (Hood, 1995). But it had a host of glaring issues that were not easily overlooked and ultimately led to criticism from public managers and the academic community. A number of challenges arose during the introduction of the new system, including process silos, limited citizen engagement, and an overly simplistic solution that neglected the nuances of complex social issues (Hood & Scott, 1996).

[50] Ibid.

But perhaps just as car models get refreshed or new interior design trends become fashionable in a home, the predominate managerial philosophy in the private sector also goes through its changes. The major change of course to NPM's relevance lies in the rise of the digital age. As citizens have realized their voices can be heard on social media and people can become stars overnight, this ethos encapsulated the demands of governance. Hence the digital governance age is upon us, and we are still shaping it. While building upon NPM's emphasis on efficiency and transparency, digital governance goes further.

Digital Era Governance

The proliferation of digital technologies has ushered in substantial changes to public administration, often referred to as digital era governance (Dunleavy et al., 2006). E-government and open government initiatives have redefined citizen engagement and service delivery models (Bertot et al., 2010). From automating permit approvals (Williamson, 2016) to leveraging big data for policy insights (Young, 2020), the digital era has seen an emergence of new tools that have helped public leaders and managers streamline processes, optimize resource allocation, and facilitate information dissemination much better than they could have achieved even twenty years ago. Open data initiatives and online platforms can pierce the veil of bureaucracy, fostering greater transparency and accountability. Citizens empowered to access and analyze government data can hold authorities accountable and advocate for informed decision-making (Flyverbom et al., 2019). Furthermore, the digital platforms that have been implemented across many agencies and cities can help bridge the gap between citizens and governance, fostering participation in policy discussions and decision-making. Collaborative online forums and interactive tools can empower individuals to contribute their voices and shape the future of their communities (Nørreklit et al., 2019). Where previously citizens would have had no avenues to perform these tasks, the digital platforms we have discussed in this book now make it possible for citizens and government leaders to build the future together.

While technologies bring new possibilities of transparency, participation, and co-creation with citizens (Linders, 2012), they have also created multifaceted negative impacts on the society including the intrusion of privacy, the misuse large data, and other ethical issues (Meijer & Bolivar, 2016). Digital platforms rely on citizens to voluntarily give up their data in order for them to function. The extensive data collection inherent in digital governance raises concerns about privacy violations, security concerns in the event of nefarious actors, and potential misuse. A 2023 Pew Poll found that 71% of adults in the US are concerned about their privacy,[51] indicating that privacy is a major concern for people in the era of digital governance. Protecting individual data and ensuring responsible data handling practices are crucial in building trust and safeguarding fundamental rights if digital governance is to succeed (Flyverbom et al., 2019). The next point of digital governance is also an intrinsic flaw, which is its reliance on being digital. When considering global contexts, not everyone has equal access to technology and digital literacy skills that are required to be able to make full use of these technical tools, exacerbating existing inequalities. This digital divide, affecting 3.7 billion people globally,[52] can hinder citizen participation and create exclusion zones, undermining a major component that was at the essence of inclusive governance (Young, 2020).

Additionally, when resource allocations are based on algorithms or predictive analytics, it is imperative that the algorithms are fair and do not discriminate based on political affiliation, religion, race, or gender. Without proper disclosure, the lack of transparency in these algorithms could further complicate accountability and trust (Williamson, 2016).

In light of these areas, developing new management approaches for the digital era is essential to the success of public innovation. These approaches should focus on experimentation, new skill development, strategic investments in infrastructure, and comprehensive digital transformation within public administration to fully realize technology's potential and impacts (Margetts & Dunleavy, 2013; Coursey & Norris, 2008).

Agile Methodology

By now, you have likely noticed a common theme that innovation and collaboration often go hand-in-hand. To that point, Agile project management has become increasingly popular in both the private and public sectors for

[51] https://www.pewresearch.org/internet/2023/10/18/how-americans-view-data-privacy/.
[52] https://press.un.org/en/2021/dsgsm1579.doc.htm.

many reasons, often being touted for its collaborative nature and being seen as a more adaptable alternative to traditional sequential "waterfall" methods (Conforto et al., 2014). Rather than acting sequentially, tasks are executed in an iterative manner, with people being the central focus of the methodology, welcoming ever-changing requirements throughout the lifecycle of the project or service. These changes are facilitated through constant close collaboration with customers, end users, or self-organizing teams, and the end result is the frequent delivery of a functional product or service (Beck et al., 2001; Schwaber & Sutherland, 2017).

Having its origins in software development means that technology and innovation were already deeply engrained into its core. Although it began in software development, the Agile principles have found application in various contexts, including new product development, marketing, systems implementation, and service delivery (Leybourne, 2009; Moi & Cabiddu, 2021).

Although contemporary governments increasingly collaborate with partners who use Agile methodologies and have made significant progress, they by and large still lacks the nimbleness and adaptability that is enjoyed by the private sector. Achieving successful Agile transformation requires overcoming cultural barriers that run deep within organizations and establishing new leadership (whether through training or new hiring), streamlined work processes, and the supporting infrastructure capable of handling the new tasks and data that accompany some of the other changes we have discussed (Conboy & Carroll, 2019). Beyond the upper leadership, it is crucial to get all levels of the organization onboard with the change to mitigate risks associated with reduced documentation that is inherent in Agile and prescriptive controls (Conforto et al., 2014).

To further complicate the process, the public sector faces unique challenges in their implementation as well, which is why many government organizations have never undergone the transformation. Stakeholder complexity, legal compliance requirements, and the demand for transparency are all elements that slow down or prevent the transformations altogether. However, if governments can incorporate certain Agile practices within democratic structures, it is believed to show promise in delivering greater citizen value over time.[53]

[53] https://www.mckinsey.com/industries/public-sector/our-insights/implementing-agile-ways-of-working-in-it-to-improve-citizen-experience.

Several government agencies did however take the leap of faith and attempted to adopt Agile. Across the pond, the UK Visas Agency enjoyed some of the performance improvements to its applicant experience and reduced operating costs thanks to the incorporation of Agile methods. In the US, the US Treasury's Federal Reserve Bank of Cleveland implemented Agile for their Pay.gov program. The Bank is responsible for processing payments for over 1,000 federal business lines that total over $160 billion annually. The project experienced substantial turbulence along the way, making the transition span roughly five years, which was longer than the team originally believed. However, the team noticed the payoffs of the switch and believed the gains to be worth the effort.[54]

In sum, entrepreneurial ecosystems are not exclusive to the private sector. Public sector actors need much of the same support and resources that their private sector counterparts do. We have seen how each of the elements of the entrepreneurial ecosystem plays a part in shaping the dynamic environment that the government operates within, and how many elements of the private sector have slowly been seeping into the very fabric of government. Some of these changes have been for the better, others have their own challenges ahead of them. Regardless of the changes though, one thing is for certain—the government *can* change; it just has to have a proper ecosystem in place to successfully do so.

[54] https://techfarhub.usds.gov/assets/files/USDS-TreasuryCaseStudy.pdf.

Chapter 8

Unsung Heroes

Making Public Entrepreneurs

Human history has witnessed many innovative government initiatives and projects spanning from Roman aqueducts in the countryside of Europe to the modern-day e-government. However, none of these innovations would have taken place without public sector entrepreneurs, the unsung heroes behind each public innovation. If they had hesitated for a moment, the ripple would have been cast through time causing the progress of public innovation to slow to a trickle.

Just like any startup founder, public sector leaders and managers face new challenges and uncertainties every day. Contemporary citizens no longer tolerate a government that fails to deliver public service or implements public policies that do not benefit taxpayers (Van de Walle, 2018). The requests from citizens have become increasingly complex from climate change to national security, and the public sector has been unable to keep up with the drastic change in the external environment (Boyne, 2006; Head & Alford, 2015). On top of these complex challenges, there have been government failures in the headlines, including the response to Hurricane Katrina in 2005, the Veteran's Healthcare waiting list in 2014, and more recently many countries' response to the pandemic, all having a direct and critical impact on citizens' lives. These problems and more have led to dramatic drops in trust in the public sector and an overall feeling of dissatisfaction. To make matters worse, there does not seem to be a reversal in sight.

There is a silver lining to all the negative news, however. Public managers around the world have become more committed to innovation over recent years (Bekkers & Tummers, 2018; Osborne & Brown, 2011; Sørensen & Torfing, 2011) and have created new positions such as Chief Innovation Officers (CIO) to be responsible for driving innovation within the public sector.[1]

[1] https://www.govtech.com/archive/will-the-chief-innovation-officer-transform-government.html.

Innovation and Entrepreneurship in the Public Sector. Wendy D. Chen and David B. Audretsch, Oxford University Press. © Oxford University Press (2025). DOI: 10.1093/9780197679470.003.0008

In the US, for instance, the Transportation Security Administration created the CIO position to lead innovative research projects for travelers on the federal level.[2] With positions like this, people could expect to see new technology being implemented to expedite security check-ins at the airport and other innovations to help make travel safer. Similarly, the Department of Labor created a position of the same title. On the Department of Labor side, the CIO position is set to help innovate for the Future of Work, a major initiative that seeks to create a work environment with dignity and fairness for all citizens.[3]

Also, as we have covered in this book, innovation does not only happen at the national level. At the local level, many states and cities have followed suit and created new positions with official titles like Chief Innovation Officer, Government Performance and Innovation Coach, Innovation Stakeholder Change Manager, and Chief Innovation and Technology Officer. They guide and lead organizational innovation through building a culture of innovation, supporting programs on innovation, partnering with external innovators, and implementing cutting-edge technologies like artificial intelligence, cloud computing, and Internet of Things (IoT) devices to improve public service.

Despite the good intentions of many public managers and leaders to make the public sector entrepreneurial, it is not a simple task that can happen overnight. Instead, it is a tailored strategy that employs proven techniques to foster innovation and entrepreneurship in the public dependent on the context. It is as much a science as it is an art.

We are all familiar with modern entrepreneurship in the private sector. Entrepreneurial companies including Apple, Amazon, and Microsoft have revolutionized modern technology and created sensational innovation for the world (Chen et al., 2024). The definition of "entrepreneurship" has been posited by scholars from different perspectives. Schumpeter (1942) coined the term "creative destruction," which refers to a constant and deliberate dismantling of long-standing practices and developing new ones including new ideas, products, and technologies. Inventions such as the railroad and Henry Ford's assembly line are prime examples of creative destruction. He further argued that entrepreneurs were the agents responsible for bringing about creative destruction because they are the individuals who can explore and

[2] https://www.hstoday.us/subject-matter-areas/transportation/steven-parker-sworn-in-as-tsa-chief-innovation-officer/.

[3] https://fedscoop.com/labor-department-chief-innovation-officer/.

take advantage of any opportunities as well as finding their own competitive advantages to develop new products and technologies. Another main characteristic of entrepreneurs lies in their propensity for risk taking. In his seminal 1921 book *Risk, Uncertainty, and Profit,* Frank Knight emphasized that entrepreneurs delt with uncertainties and took risks (Audretsch & Belitski, 2021).

Of course, when we think of entrepreneurship, innovation is not far away. To that point, Drucker (1985) linked innovation with entrepreneurship. To him, entrepreneurship is a systematic process of innovation, and innovation is not exclusive solely to founders of startups but can exist in any type of organization. Further, he elucidated that entrepreneurs are innovators of business management who can either create or enhance existing resources to unlock their potential for growing wealth. Hisrich (1986) argued that entrepreneurs demonstrate initiative and creative thinking. More importantly, they are also able to identify and mobilize resources. Although the definition of entrepreneurship warrants further investigation, in general, entrepreneurship scholars agree that an entrepreneur should be willing to take risks when faced with uncertainties, discover opportunities, identify and mobilize resource strategically, and innovate.

Private sector entrepreneurship is a topic that has been extensively studied and has attracted many different disciplines coming in to examine it from different angles from management, sociology, psychology, education, and more. However, the landscape of public sector entrepreneurship literature is comparatively scarce, with public administration almost exclusively being the sole field to examine it. Understandably, most do not immediately think of innovation and entrepreneurship when they hear terms associated with the government such as "bureaucracy" and "regulation." Nevertheless, we should remind ourselves that the government is a giant entity that controls resources such as publicly owned land, natural resources including forests, parks, and waterways; other infrastructure including roads, bridges, and railways; and public budget and spending. In addition, government is one of the largest employers across all sectors. Using the US government as an example, nearly "24 million people are involved in military, public, and national service at the local, state, and federal levels."[4] The US federal government alone employs more than two million civilians (Congressional Research Service, 2023). Moreover, it has a higher level of highly educated

[4] https://www.brookings.edu/articles/public-service-and-the-federal-government/.

workers than the private sector, meaning that hypothetically they are sitting on a figurative gold mine of potential innovation.[5] Put differently, government has a vast number of resources available for any entrepreneurial endeavors.

Public entrepreneurs, like their counterparts in the private sector, are change agents. They are the government employees who discover opportunities and leverage resources to improve public organizations and address wicked social outcomes despite risks or resistance (Demircioglu & Chowdhury, 2021; Hjorth, 2013). Public entrepreneurs make public services more efficient and effective while concomitantly making governments more responsive. The best public entrepreneurs also have the power to increase public employee job satisfaction and garner greater trust from the public.

Of the existing research on public sector entrepreneurship, most have discussed public sector capabilities (e.g., Klein et al., 2013), government policy initiatives (e.g., Hayter, et al., 2018), new public management (e.g., Moore,

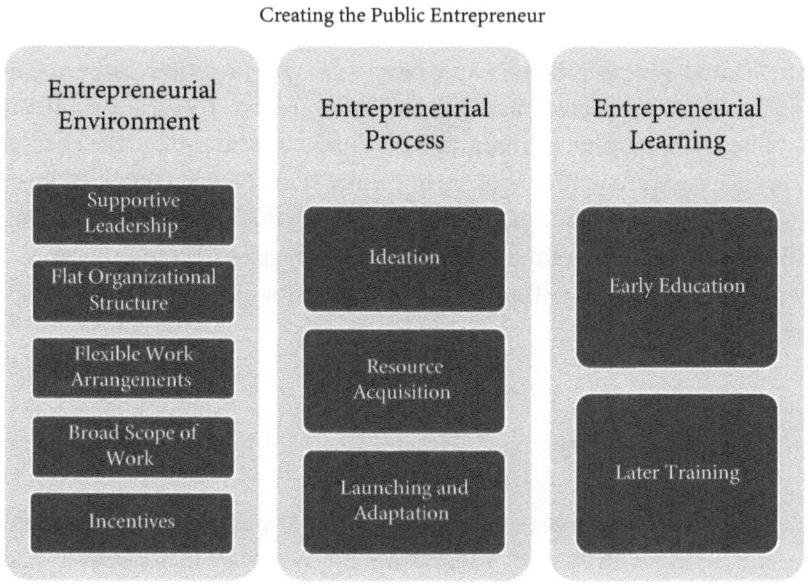

Figure 8.1 Creating the public entrepreneur: a depiction of the three elements key to making a public entrepreneur

[5] Over 60% of the US government workforce has at least a bachelor's degree as of 2022. https://www.bls.gov/opub/ted/2023/private-industry-nonprofit-workers-had-the-highest-levels-of-formal-education-in-2022.htm.

1997; Osborne & Brown, 2005), and the purpose of middle management (e.g., Morris & Jones, 1999; Rainey, 1983). What is missing in the literature is the understanding of how to make public entrepreneurs, which is the focus of this chapter. We build this chapter based on three strands of literature: entrepreneurial environment, entrepreneurial process, and entrepreneurial learning.

To help convey what we will cover in a moment, we have depicted the relationship between each of these concepts and the elements that fall under each of them (Figure 8.1). These concepts are not necessarily linear, but instead elements that go into the creation of a public entrepreneur. Furthermore, they are elements that are not limited to public managers but can be for anyone in government. Then, once we cover entrepreneurial learning, these elements can be applicable to anyone who is interested in beginning the journey of a public entrepreneur.

Entrepreneurial Environment

The famed nineteenth-century orator and speech writer Robert Green Ingersoll once reflected that "Man will never have an idea, except those supplied to him by his surroundings." It cannot be understated the effect that a proper environment conducive to creativity and innovation can have on individuals (Wang et al., 2022). Environment in this context can mean many things and is not just limited to physical workspace. Environment is also extended to work organizational structure, culture, mindsets, and support structures.

Supportive and Entrepreneurial Leadership

Here is a quick anecdote that serves as a tale of two cities. One of the authors recently spoke with two city leaders from the same state in the US—one leading a city with a booming economy, and the other at a much slower growth pace. Both leaders were asked the same question: "Can you please share your vision of the future of the city?" On hearing this question, the leader of the growing city's eyes lit up and they took out a piece of paper to draw a picture of major public innovations that were in the pipeline for the city, with new technologies to be implemented, international events scheduled, foreign investment deals, and other major development plans. When asked the same question, the leader of the slower city grinned, replying, "We don't have any plans. I think the best thing a city leader can do is to keep everything the same." When pushed further to explain their thinking, the leader replied, "Too much work."

Leadership is paramount for organizational success, playing a critical role in molding an organizational environment. Effective leaders are a major driving factor in the shaping of organizational culture, establishing support structures, and guiding strategic decision-making (Kotter, 1996; Schein & Schein, 2016; Yukl, 2013). Leaders who actively champion and nurture innovative ideas imbue their teams with a sense of purpose and motivation, catalyzing a culture of creativity and forward-thinking. They create an environment where employees feel motivated to take ownership of their tasks, make independent decisions, and pursue innovative ideas (Dabić et al., 2021; Yang & Bentein, 2023). The absence of this support system can lead to a lull in government innovation, collapsing under the weight of bureaucracy and regulations.

The two city leaders mentioned above face important decisions every day on how to guide development and improve livability. However, they approach this task differently with one being entrepreneurial and ambitious and the other content with preserving the status quo. These diverging mindsets can have major implications for a city's trajectory.

Entrepreneurs recognize opportunities and dare to take risks and try new things (Porter, 2008). When public leaders constantly say no to new visions potential opportunities are missed, which sends a message to government employees that there is no incentive to come up with new ideas. In contrast, leaders with an entrepreneurial mindset embrace risks as they pursue an ambitious vision of continually improving quality of life (Kuratko et al., 2021; Shepherd & Patzelt, 2018). They are willing to think big and challenge the status quo with visions with no guarantee of success. These leaders exploit new ideas to make their cities a destination for investment, talent, and innovation. Their goals often involve turning urban negatives like deterioration, disparities, or isolation into opportunities. This more adventurous approach better positions cities to compete globally in fast-changing environments.

For example, once a declining textile town, Greenville, South Carolina transformed itself beginning in the 1970s through bold urban initiatives. A catalyst was the Peace Center performing arts complex downtown, with a taskforce initiated by the mayor and funded by a $10 million donation from the Peace family.[6] This surge of activity spurred renewed interest in the city center. Abandoned mills along the Reedy River were repurposed into parks, trails, and residences like Falls Park and others in the West End district.[7,8] Furthermore, as business boomed downtown, the parking problem became apparent for employers who worked with city leaders to form the Downtown Transportation Coalition.[9] Public–private partnerships poured millions into infrastructure and attractions using tools like tax increment financing.[10]

Many successful public leaders point to their teams as being the real enablers behind the scenes making things happen. Studies on Harvard Kennedy School's Innovations in American Government Awards found that government innovations often had high support from the agency leaders (Borins, 2000). They cultivate a supportive system to encourage public entrepreneurship that enables innovation to flourish. More specifically, supportive leaders should welcome and listen to frontline government workers' complaints and ideas. They should emphasize to their employees that failure is merely a steppingstone to growth (Kim, 2010). Additionally, supportive leaders empower their teams by ensuring everyone has the necessary resources, guidance, and mentorship, to not only perform their roles but enabling them to unleash their full potential and contribute meaningfully to the organization's objectives.

Flat Organizational Structure

To enable and encourage innovation, many businesses in the private sector have begun experimenting with alternative arrangements that have allowed for greater flexibility and autonomy for workers, thus enhancing their creativity as well. Flat organizational structure is the antithesis of bureaucracy, in which most or all employees in an organization are viewed as a similar

[6] https://www.peacecenter.org/news/detail/25-years-ago-peace-center-helped-revive-downtown.

[7] https://www.greenvillesc.gov/178/History.

[8] https://scdah.sc.gov/sites/scdah/files/Documents/Historic%20Preservation%20%28SHPO%29/Research/Historic%20Contexts/GreenvilleCity2018.pdf.

[9] https://www.greenvilleonline.com/story/news/2018/04/08/downtown-greenville-job-growth-transportation-park-and-ride-greenlink/492498002/.

[10] https://greenvillejournal.com/syndicated/how-public-private-partnerships-bring-development-to-fruition/.

level and work as equals rather than in a hierarchical manner. It affords employees greater autonomy to determine their own work and responsibilities and has an increased focus on strong communication among teams.

Most governments follow a hierarchical structure, where frontline employees are not responsible for major decision-making. Innovative organizations will seek to garner input from everyone throughout the organization to help develop new ways to do business and achieve the missions set forth. This means that everyone from the head of an agency to the frontline worker is empowered and in fact expected to provide input (Behn, 1995). Their involvement will allow them to understand the big picture of the grander mission. In the context of government, frontline workers would be the ones most experienced dealing with the end customers or service recipients as they witness the processes and hear the complaints the most. With a flat organizational structure, they would be able to provide feedback on the experience and circulate the findings throughout the organization.

One of the benefits of a flat organizational structure is the creativity that it inspires in employees. With the increased autonomy that employees have, they are more likely to have the freedom to explore new ideas and approaches to solving the organization's problems. Accompanying this flat org structure should be an entrepreneurial environment that encourages and rewards the exploration of new ideas and approaches (Brazeal et al., 2014; Fraihat et al., 2023).

Other gains can also be found from implementing a flat organization structure. For one, it has been found that flat organization structure in the public sector has led to efficiency gains.[11] Accompanying those efficiency gains are also improved cost cutting and communication (Rishipal, 2014). However, it is important to still maintain a centralized goal and direction however to avoid aimless idea exploration and new forms of power struggle (Lee, 2022).

Flexible Work Arrangements

Another way that public managers can help improve their organization's creativity and output is through flexible work arrangements. The modern workplace looks drastically different than it did even ten years ago. Some of

[11] https://hbr.org/2021/06/how-to-successfully-scale-a-flat-organization.

that can be attributed to the impact the pandemic had on working arrangement, but it could also be the natural progression of work as technology became more integral into workstreams, allowing for teams to be located virtually anywhere while they work.

Many researchers have combined the terms of "flexible" and "remote" work together. However, for the purposes of this book, we will refer to flexible work as allowing employees to work outside of the office setting and offering flexibility with their work hours. Flexible work arrangements allow for employees to be more productive in their work (Hunter, 2018). In the field of neurophysiology, providing individuals with autonomy increases productivity in groups and has the additional benefit of improving one's mood (Johannsen & Zak, 2020). Additionally, environment plays a big part in productivity, and people have been found to be more productive in comfortable environments (Shobe, 2018). These psychological elements help to explain the rationale behind the productivity gains in these flexible arrangements, and public managers should note that these arrangements are not only beneficial to the workers but to the organization as well.

Furthermore, flexible working arrangements have been found to increase individuals' creativity (Hunter, 2018). In line with the previous findings for productivity, striving for a better work–life balance is crucial in ensuring employees remain motivated and able to provide innovative ideas. This also holds true when observing R&D flexible work arrangements, where creative professionals generally reported higher levels of fulfillment regarding their work outcomes (Hazak et al., 2017).

These flexible work arrangements also lead to more engaged employees overall. In 2023, a survey found that over two-thirds of workers would prefer to quit than return to the office, indicating the importance of flexibility to workers.[12] This sentiment is echoed throughout technical workforce for developers, stating that flexibility is the primary reason to stay in one position or leave another.[13] In other words, in PPP and other collaborative arrangements, this flexibility should be maintained as well.

In the public sector, teleworkers employed by the government have a lower turnover. When given the option to choose, employees who were provided the flexibility to choose where they wanted to work were found to have

[12] https://www.shrm.org/topics-tools/news/benefits-compensation/will-employees-quit-forced-back-office.

[13] https://stackoverflow.blog/2023/11/27/are-remote-workers-more-productive-that-s-the-wrong-question/.

lower turnover (Choi, 2018). Working remotely provides opportunities to have flex time that leads to lower stress levels (Solanki, 2013). To that point, it is crucial that there are supportive strategies resonating from the institutional and managerial level of organizations that flow to employees to ensure they feel supported with their flexibility.

Broader Job Responsibility for Opportunity Discovery

Most modern positions are narrow. Employees are required and expected to work within a narrow framework, resulting in siloed workstreams where they have little visibility into what the rest of the organization is doing. Each small team has a manager, which increases the size of the public sector and creates unnecessary bureaucracy. Governments should make their positions broader rather than narrow, which will not only give public employees a chance to learn about the overall strategic goal of the government but also offer them space to use their imagination and leverage their skills.

When roles are delineated in a broad manner rather than being narrowly defined, individuals who possess a diverse set of skills can undertake various tasks that can afford them insight into the entire organization. In this case, assignments prioritize achieving outcomes rather than adhering strictly to rules or procedures (Kanter, 1988).

For example, in a government department responsible for environmental protection, instead of employees being confined to their specific roles, they should be given opportunities to collaborate across departments. An employee responsible for policy analysis might also participate in field inspections or public outreach campaigns. This approach fosters a deeper understanding of environmental issues and allows employees to develop innovative solutions that effectively address complex challenges, ultimately benefiting the community and the environment.

Governments can also use the job rotation method to expose individuals to different job positions so they can play different roles and explore opportunities at different levels of the government. When they are hired for the organization, they can also receive broader training that could be applicable to multiple different roles they could rotate between. This practice not only enhances employee skills and knowledge but also promotes a more agile and adaptable workforce capable of addressing diverse challenges and meeting evolving public needs.

Create Incentives for Public Innovation

The final point here is about building incentives into the structure of the organization. Studies have suggested that providing group incentives and support for employees results in increased organizational commitment (Park & Kim, 2013). This suggests that when organizations prioritize collaborative incentives and cultivate a culture of support and recognition, employees are more likely to develop strong bonds with the organization, exhibiting higher levels of loyalty, dedication, and engagement in their roles.

In the context of government organizations, enticing incentives can serve as powerful motivators, encouraging government employees to proactively seek out and implement innovative solutions to address complex societal challenges. It is important that leadership forgives mistakes early in the process and rewards long-term progress of programs (Manso, 2017). A crucial lesson here is to acknowledge that rewards for innovation help cultivate a culture where creative thinking is valued over rigid procedures, encouraging employees to develop novel solutions that drive more effective public service delivery.

Encouraging innovation not only helps governments attract and keep talented individuals but also fosters workplaces that genuinely appreciate and celebrate employees' creativity. When governments offer exciting incentives for brainstorming new ideas, they become more competitive in attracting skilled professionals, ensuring they have the right team to drive positive change in society. Moreover, when governments give recognition and rewards for innovative thinking, it makes team members feel valued and connected to their work. When their unique contributions are acknowledged it instills a sense of pride and dedication, leading to greater job satisfaction and enthusiasm for their roles. This positive atmosphere inspires everyone to give their best, resulting in increased productivity and impactful outcomes throughout government agencies.

Notably, sharing about the failures endemic to innovation in an organization can be equally important because they are valuable opportunities for growth and improvement. Researchers have found that discussing the details around innovation failure helps to reduce repeat mistakes (Xiong et al., 2021). When people feel comfortable admitting mistakes it cultivates a culture of continuous improvement, allowing them to take advantage of each unsuccessful attempt as a helpful lesson that can inform more effective problem-solving and strategic decision-making in the future. Moreover, this approach of discussing failures openly enhances team collaborations and signals that teammates are experimenting innovation together.

Entrepreneurial Process

Studies have shown that entrepreneurship is a dynamic process composed of multiple stages. While frameworks may vary in terminology and emphasis, they commonly highlight key phases such as ideation, resource acquisition, and the launch of the venture.

The entrepreneurial journey involves navigating a sequence of pivotal steps, each marked by distinct activities and milestones. Although the progression is often nonlinear, these stages provide structure to the development of a new business endeavor (Omrane & Fayolle, 2011).

At the outset lies the stage of opportunity identification, where entrepreneurs keenly discern untapped market niches or latent potential for innovative products or services. This process is informed by meticulous market research and analysis aimed at identifying prevailing consumer needs and pain points, or "product–market fit" (Cunningham et al., 2022). Additionally, external catalysts such as technological advancements, regulatory changes, or demographic shifts often serve as triggers for identifying entrepreneurial opportunities (Shane & Venkataraman, 2000). Armed with a potential opportunity, the entrepreneur conducts critical analysis on the feasibility of the opportunities. Once they confirm these opportunities are feasible, the next main stage is the procurement of resources.

Resource acquisition is a process involving the procurement of essential physical, financial, human, and knowledge-based inputs necessary for launching operations (Barney & Arikan, 2001, Huang et al., 2010). This includes activities such as securing startup funding, hiring initial employees, and establishing infrastructure and supply chain relationships. Emerging trends include the utilization of government grants and crowdfunding as popular channels for financing (Chen, 2023).

In the last stage, the entrepreneur orchestrates the launch and adaptation of the new venture, bringing the business concept to market. This stage witnesses the initiation of product development and sales, often starting with a small-scale test, minimum viable product (MVP) pilot program before a full-scale rollout (Ries, 2011). It is at this time that organizations can most accurately assess the product-market fit and determine what changes are needed to their business model, product, or strategy. Launch mistakes, while inevitable, serve as invaluable learning opportunities for entrepreneurs to refine their models.

Borrowing from the entrepreneurial process literature, public entrepreneurship shares the same overall stages of development as private entrepreneurship, but there are differences in the exact approach they take for each stage. Most of this is due to the environment in which the two sectors operate and the intrinsic nature of each of them.

Ideation

Public entrepreneurs in the ideation stage must first identify a need or demand from the public. Public entrepreneurs too must familiarize themselves with the current regulatory and technical landscape and note any societal shifts that may serve as an indicator for where innovation is required. Different from private entrepreneurship, however, where private entrepreneurship is likely to be driven by monetary profit, public entrepreneurship is driven by social profit. Put differently, public entrepreneurs are on the hunt for where they can have the greatest level of societal impact or change grounded in the purview of their organization. Also, private entrepreneurs often will have exposure to industry knowledge or have personal experience that has influenced their idea, such as becoming a parent and recognizing a child's needs. While public leaders may have some general high-level knowledge of their organization, they may not necessarily always have specific details to capture the major pain points of their service recipients or internal staff. To that point, it is important to include government employees in the ideation process to create ownership to help carry out the change (Behn, 1995; Eggers & O'Leary, 2009).

Resource Acquisition

Next, both private and public entrepreneurs need funding. But being in the organizational context of a public entities, public entrepreneurs understandably go about this process quite differently. Despite being controversial, taxation is one of the primary means of financing for public services and infrastructure. Individual income taxes, corporate taxes, and sales and property taxes have all been collected for some general government expenditures (Mikesell, 2014; Musgrave, 1959). Debt issuance is another source of government funding, which is usually spent on larger projects. In addition, public–private partnerships allow governments to offload some short-term costs by contracting private firms to deliver services (Grimsey & Lewis, 2002; Ng & Loosemore, 2007). More recently, with the development of technology and online platforms, governments have also raised funds via alternative methods such as crowdfunding or peer-to-peer lending (Chen, 2023; Chen, 2022).

Resources are not only limited to monetary funding; both private and public entrepreneurs form or solidify their crucial relationships at this stage. In the case of public sector entrepreneurs, a lot of times this can manifest in the form of creating new intra or interagency partnerships, nonprofits, or businesses to help them carry out their projects. In the case of co-production, this could also be the time that some formal channels for citizens to engage with the project may be established to ensure their participation throughout the journey (Ansell & Gash, 2008; Gil-Garcia, 2012).

Launching and Adaptation

In the last stage of launching and adaptation, the project once again has some similarities in that both private and public entrepreneurs will need to develop some form of their product, even if it is only an MVP to prove the concept. For private entrepreneurs, this will usually be seeking insights from customers, fine-tuning pricing, and so on. However, for public entrepreneurs, this stage will be rolling out the service to a small group of people, whether they are internal or external to the agency, to test the reception and how useful the service is (Alves, 2013; Brown & Osborne, 2013). Then, based on the feedback received, adaptations will be made to the delivery of the service to help facilitate broader and deeper reach to the users of the project.

Entrepreneurial Learning

Entrepreneurship is a learned skill. By taking a close examination of the founders of the most compelling extreme examples of entrepreneurship, such as Apple's Steve Jobs, Bill Gates of Microsoft, Amazon's Jeff Bezos, and Mark Zuckerberg of Facebook, Chen et al. (2024) first identified a common entrepreneurial learning ecosystem that they share. They then conducted in-depth analyses of a large longitudinal database with 3,116 respondents spanning over twenty years and found that entrepreneurship learning is statistically significant to all types of entrepreneurship. In other words, entrepreneurship education and training provide individuals with exposure to knowledge and skills that help them to recognize and create opportunities and leverage resources.

The same logic applies to the public sector as well. Like their private sector counterparts, public entrepreneurs would benefit from similar education and training that equip them with the knowledge and skills to recognize and create opportunities while leveraging resources. In fact, innovative governments may educate people from early on by rebranding the view of public administration, not depicting it as a place of no innovation or just a place to have good job security, but rather a place to make meaningful impact in the world. Government offers a unique opportunity to combine expertise with a sense of purpose, drive real-world impact, and shape the future of communities while working on high-stakes problems that affect millions of lives. By harnessing this entrepreneurial learning ecosystem, the public sector can tap into the same skills, passion, and drive that propel private sector innovators forward, using these resources to amplify their ideas, scale their solutions, and create lasting change.

Further, governments can also use the internal training of public innovation to engage public employees and foster public entrepreneurs. Those are the individuals who already have chosen a public sector career. Additional professional training would help them develop their skills further to contribute to public innovation and entrepreneurship.

To conclude, with increased public needs to meet and growing societal challenges, there has been a higher demand to turn public employees to public entrepreneurs. While traditional bureaucratic structures in governments tend to stifle innovation, fostering entrepreneurial individuals could revitalize the public and push human society to a new level of innovation. Interestingly, although the public's trust in the federal government is relatively low and the dissatisfaction with the government is high, a 2022 US poll conducted by the Partnership for Public Service and Freedom Consulting shows that 62% of Americans "has a positive view of the nation's 2 million public servants."[14] Therefore, this is an opportune time for the public sector

[14] https://ourpublicservice.org/blog/the-publics-support-of-public-servants/.

to enhance public entrepreneurship. This chapter lays out multiple strategies for the public sector to make public entrepreneurs based on three main pieces of literature examining the antecedents to entrepreneurship. With the right approach and preparation, we have the opportunity to create even more original stories for our modern-day unsung heroes.

Chapter 9
Challenges and Opportunities of Public Innovation and Entrepreneurship

Previous chapters have celebrated the amazing successes that the public sector across the globe has achieved in innovation efforts. We have also identified all the effective practices and strategies that have led to those successes. Additionally, we have covered the history of public innovation and the circumstances that have helped shape the government and consequently the world we live in today.

However, the road to paradise is not always paved in gold. It is critical to remember the countless times governments have failed in their innovation. For instance, after several policies that incentivized the inhabitation and cultivation of the Midwest including Oklahoma, Texas, Kansas, New Mexico, and Colorado, the four generations of farming led to severe topsoil erosion that left the land unable to cope with the droughts of the 1930s. The result was the Dust Bowl, a series of devastating dust storms that ravaged the American and Canadian prairies, serving as a sobering reminder of the consequences of unsustainable farming practices and the disregard for environmental factors, as chronicled by environmental historian Donald Worster (2014).

Millions of tons of fertile topsoil were stripped away by the relentless winds, leaving the land barren and unable to be farmed (Lee & Gill, 2015). The resulting loss of vegetation and topsoil disrupted the delicate ecosystem, with declining biodiversity resulting in further soil erosion, creating a destructive cycle that exacerbated the already monumental crisis (Williams, 2011). The human health toll was a massive shock to the country who was already in the middle of the Great Depression, with an estimated 7,000 lives lost to dust-related illnesses. The government attempted to help alleviate the pain caused to the farmers, with estimates placing the total aid to be around $1 billion (1930s dollars) (Warrick, 1980). However, the damage was already done. Hundreds of thousands of residents, dubbed "Dust Bowl refugees," were forced to abandon their homes and farms, embarking on a massive

Innovation and Entrepreneurship in the Public Sector. Wendy D. Chen and David B. Audretsch, Oxford University Press. © Oxford University Press (2025). DOI: 10.1093/9780197679470.003.0009

westward migration that would become a defining moment in American history (Egan, 2006).

It was a harsh wake-up call to the downtrodden country, serving as a stark reminder that ignoring environmental factors in government initiatives can have catastrophic consequences (Hansen & Libecap, 2004). The harrowing experience of the time was captured in arts such as John Steinbeck's book *Grapes of Wrath* and the iconic photo *Migrant Mother* taken by Dorothea Lange.

In what follows, we are going to explore some of the primary points of failure that most commonly plague organizations in their pursuit of public innovation. Then, we will discuss potential opportunities and remedies to these challenges from the perspective of looking to the future.

Challenges

According to our research, some of the main challenges that often apply to the public sector include its risk aversion culture, bureaucracy and inefficient process, stringent regulations, lack of technological knowledge, complications in public private partnerships, change management issues, and power struggles. These obstacles not only hinder innovation but also create significant barriers to the effective implementation of new policies and programs.

Risk Aversion Culture

When many people think of governments, at least modern stable governments, the characteristics of being risk-taking and avant-garde do not come to mind. Instead, governments will typically prefer pathways of stability and lean towards being risk averse. There are several reasons for this avoidance of risk including the complex decision-making structures in the public sector, the fear of mistakes, lack of leadership support, and in some circumstances the limited resources available to the specific agency or department (Bason, 2010). Furthermore, on a personnel level, employees and managers may fear the additional workload that accompany these changes and as a result favor the status quo present in the organization.

At the top levels of government, elected politicians and public managers have strong incentives to avoid risk, as failures or delivery issues tend to receive intensive scrutiny from oversight bodies and media outlets (Borins, 2001; O'Toole, 1997; Sørensen & Torfing, 2011). High-profile blunders could generate unflattering headlines that seriously damage careers or reelection prospects. This political reality understandably makes those in leadership positions of civic administrations inherently inclined against enacting new initiatives with uncertain outcomes.

Furthermore, there is little evidence of risk/reward structures in place for public employees to branch out and try new things. This is reinforced by the hierarchical bureaucracies and policies that put them at risk in the event of experimentation for transparency violations or scandals and planning periods that do not have room to account for these innovative initiatives. In essence, there is little opportunity for creative endeavors to flourish and to be approved should they be raised (Osborne & Brown, 2011).

Similar to the culture of risk aversion is the resistance to change that can be found throughout the public sector. As evidenced by the government's reluctance to adopt or support blockchain,[1] there is a fear of the unknown that drives decisions in the public sector. As in the case of blockchain, the added levels of transparency could offer greater insight into the incompetence of governments. In the meantime, the growing fear of being replaced by technology such as AI provides an additional barrier to the government championing change.[2]

Bureaucracy and Inefficient Process

The bureaucracy itself that exists throughout the government is in and of itself a challenge to innovation (Hirst et al., 2011). The operation of public sector is process-oriented. Governments rely heavily on standard operating procedures and other official government forms to carry out their business. Typically, governments operate in a repeatable routine fashion where large processes are broken up into relatively small tasks and each task is delegated to an employee. Then, once one employee completes their task, it is passed on to the next person in the workflow. This system works well when

[1] https://www.investopedia.com/articles/forex/042015/why-governments-are-afraid-bitcoin.asp.

[2] https://www.oecd-ilibrary.org/docserver/932780bc-en.pdf.

they are utilized for performing routine tasks and maintaining control over processes. They favor compliance with the status quo over disruptive or novel approaches to doing business (Wilson, 2000). With this fundamental approach so deeply ingrained in the essence of organizations, it makes it difficult to break free from the defining constraints (Bason, 2010). However, the bureaucratic system is not conducive to creativity (Thompson, 1965). Any new initiative will be subjected to an extensive approval process requiring input from multiple levels of management, which can draw out the overall time required to reach a decision.

Government Regulation

In other instances, regulation can cause the government to trip over itself. Regulatory frameworks tend to evolve at a slower pace than companies can in the private sector, as governments typically require legislative processes to make changes that are inherently time-consuming. Moreover, the government spends additional time and resources on maintaining compliance with extensive regulations that can divert resources and attention away from innovation initiatives, as being compliant with regulations takes precedent over investing in research and development (Fabrizio & Di Minin, 2008).

This regulation can be outward or inward facing, meaning that it could be regulation applicable to citizens or to the government. For example, in Venezuela, it takes an average of 230 days to form a business while in others, such as New Zealand, it is as little as a day.[3,4] If barriers of entry are impenetrable for newcomers, innovation can at a national scale consequently suffer.

Organizations rely on rules and structures, using them to define the confines in which they operate and their own vision of self (Osborne & Brown, 2011). Being overly administrative puts a limit on innovation and the experimentation that is necessary for organizations to be innovative, including pilot programs, and additional research (Bason, 2010). Additionally, the lack of reward structures for venturing out to attempt to innovate can lead to a lack of innovation and poorer work performance (Jin & Rainey, 2020; Tep, 2015; Si et al., 2020). These limitations provide little reason for

[3] https://www.reuters.com/article/idUSKBN19R0DC/.
[4] https://www.weforum.org/agenda/2019/10/starting-business-fastest-countries/.

employees to risk their current position or to take on additional workload for little gain.

Furthermore, governments rarely have additional funding reserved for experiments, having most of it already locked up in other projects dictated by their regulations. These strict planning and budget cycles provide little room to deviate from their current service delivery much less risking losing future budget allocations based on untested concepts (Aghion et al., 2009). In the meantime, operating in short political windows and election cycles make agencies gravitate toward lower-risk options to allocate their resources toward to avoid future scandals or questions. Finally, government regulations can impede the progress of technical innovation, leading to slower and more expensive R&D efforts and making it harder for newcomers who may have new answers to government problems to go to market (Aghion, 2023; de la Potterie, 2011; Shin et al., 2022). These regulations can take many forms, from additional red tape paperwork to professional licensing, approvals, and additional tax burdens. All these issues result in a public sector that is too rigid to deviate from their status quo.

Digital Divide

Throughout this book we have touched on technology and its utilization by governments quite a bit. However, there are implicit challenges inherent in technology, especially for organizations that do not have the core knowledge or understanding to navigate those challenges. This can be shared with the recipients of services as well, commonly referred to as the "digital divide," where individuals would not have the necessary skills to know how to implement the new services into their daily routines (Meijer, 2015).

Technological innovations and implementations are complex and can be costly in terms of both the underlying technology and the high-skilled labor necessary to implement that technology. To further complicate the matter, the public sector is presented with an overwhelming number of options that they may not fully understand. Considering the costs associated with these projects, it can be difficult to ascertain the benefits and improvements these investments can provide, leading to a "paralysis by analysis" cycle the government undergoes to decide whether to progress forward with an innovation or not (Bason, 2010).[5]

[5] https://washingtonexec.com/2023/12/lmis-kimberly-stambler-on-breaking-the-federal-paralysis-by-analysis-innovation-cycle/.

When governments do implement technology without a comprehensive understanding of what exactly they are implementing, there can be additional dire consequences as well. Back in 2002, the British government was forced to shut down its online tax filing system due to a critical security flaw that allowed citizens to see each other's tax information. With millions of taxpayers relying on the online platform for filing their taxes, the shutdown resulted in widespread panic and eroded public trust in the government's digital infrastructure. The incident underscored the urgent need for robust cybersecurity protocols and highlighted the potential risks associated with the rapid digitization of public services without adequate safeguards in place.[6]

Despite the widespread access to the internet, ICT infrastructure still poses a challenge to many governments, especially local ones. Cities in more rural areas and especially those in developing countries lag behind cities with greater resources in terms of deploying modern technologies as many rely on existing ICT infrastructure. With poor bandwidth and internet access, these cities are prevented from realizing the many benefits from e-government, AI, and so on (Ndou, 2004).[7]

The digital divide exists not only within the government but also across society. As we all know, for e-government programs to be successful, citizens and residents need to possess at least a certain level of digital literacy to navigate online platforms and access services. However, many people, particularly older citizens, may lack the necessary digital skills necessary to be able to make full use of these platforms (Rasi-Heikkinen & Doh, 2023). Marginalized communities including rural regions are most commonly impacted by the digital divide, limiting or at times even eliminating access to e-government platforms and other digital public resources (Manoharan, 2014). Similarly, there are gaps in digital literacy and skills. In response to this pressing issue, the European Union is actively exploring initiatives to promote digital inclusion, as seen in conferences such as Building Inclusive Pathways for Enhanced Digital Services, which aims to address the complex challenges of digital inequality and foster a more inclusive digital environment.[8]

[6] https://ash.harvard.edu/files/government_innovation_around_the_world.pdf.

[7] https://publicadministration.un.org/egovkb/en-us/Reports/UN-E-Government-Survey-2020.

[8] https://www.esn-eu.org/news/bridging-digital-divide-collaborative-approach-digital-inclusion-europe.

In contrast to the digital disparities that exist in many parts of the world, South Korea's digital odyssey is a testament to the transformative power of human ingenuity, where the boundary between technology and society is blurred and the future is forged. First, the Korean Information Infrastructure project, launched in 1994, was an ambitious initiative to connect the entire country with broadband. This government-led initiative partnered with Korea Telcom to "connect 80 urban centers, government institutions, and establish a national backbone."[9,10]

Furthermore, digital education and smart city initiatives have been precision-tuned to unlock the potential of its citizens, equipping them with the skills and tools to navigate the intricate web of the digital world. The results paid off, as evidenced by cities like Songdo, which promoted sustainability, efficiency, and creativity to enrich their citizens' well-being. In doing so, South Korea elevated the lives of its citizens while simultaneously recalibrating the narrative of what it means to be a connected society, offering a compelling precedent for other nations as they strive to overcome the complex challenges of digital inequality.[11]

Complications in Public–Private Partnerships

Public–private partnerships (PPP) provide a great way for the government to overcome some of the obstacles they would be vulnerable to, especially in the realm of technology. But PPPs also carry with them some of their own challenges, and they are not always technical in nature. It is noteworthy that the government does not share the same culture as startups and many small businesses. Governments have a bureaucratic and hierarchical structure and are often constrained by political and economic considerations. Small businesses and startups, on the other hand, are often more agile, flexible, and quick to respond to new market opportunities. They also have fresh ideas and are the most likely to keep abreast of new knowledge while being able to disseminate new ideas through their customer base. In the event that a partnership is formed, there can be a cultural mismatch between the parties that causes the two sides to be more likely to reach an impasse. These situations can be frequent as well because governments value their processes,

[9] https://sites.google.com/site/internethistoryasia/book2/south-korea-snapshot-2000.
[10] https://www.eff.org/deeplinks/2020/02/why-south-korea-global-broadband-leader.
[11] Ibid.

rules, and bureaucracies, which may not always be congruent with the partner organization that may value innovation, flat organization structures, and unique team dynamics (OECD, 2017; Schenkel et al., 2016; Xu et al., 2022).[12]

To illustrate the differences in culture and structure, let's use the fictional country of Aerius's Aviation Authority (AAA) underneath the Ministry of Transportation as an example. Say Avery is a new employee who is tasked with monitoring the air traffic delays caused by a pilot shortage across the whole country. First, Avery's boss, Cynthia, tells her the location of all the data the agency has and is told to prepare a report for her every week. Avery then begins learning the data available to her and begins her analysis, quickly finding the data has only been saved in a shared email inbox. She then must spend most of her time sifting through emails to find which ones are relevant, all the while providing updates to Cynthia on her status. Once Avery completes the task, she reports it to Cynthia, who then reports it to her superior. The next week, Avery repeats the whole process again and that process continues for several months.

In contrast, a startup consulting company named Zephyr Consulting is much nimbler. Zephyr wins a contract to revamp Avery's job, making it easier for her to process her work. The consultants quickly organize to have a project manager, two business analysts, and three developers to solve her issues. On some days the project manager, Dan, is gathering requirements to understand AAA's needs. Other times, Dan oversees the development efforts and occasionally even lends a hand to help develop the end product. Then once a week, Dan must provide a report on progress for the project by pulling up the team's scrum board to see where they are at. There are no limits to the role Dan does in this example, and there are not predefined processes per se to which he must adhere.

As aforementioned, startups and other businesses operate in more flexible environments. In general, they tend to be result and efficiency driven. The public sector's rigid structures are generally viewed as a hurdle and foreign to the companies that partner with them. In other words, the public sector is not adaptable. Therefore, once a promising solution is identified, the government needs to adapt it to fit the institutional context and requirements of public service. In reality, many partnerships between government and startups fail.

[12] https://www.oecd.org/gov/innovative-government/embracing-innovation-in-government.pdf.

Information asymmetry on the side of startups is another problem. A great number of startups may have solutions to public problems, but they have no idea how to reach a government agency and who specifically they should speak to without the proper inroads. Compared to large businesses who may already have contacts with the government or who have already partnered with government before, startups are obviously put at a disadvantage. Even when a startup discovers what it should prepare to collaborate with the government, they will have to go through lengthy paperwork and rigid procedures and wait a long amount of time, which with limited resources may drain the company.

Moreover, PPPs carry with them a certain level of risk from both parties. For one, PPPs are often laden with issues stemming from multiple stakeholders, large investments, and information asymmetry between the parties (Carbonara et al., 2015; Xiong et al., 2018). To further complicate the issue, PPPs do not always have proper risk management strategies put in place, leading to failed outcomes (Hood & McGarvey, 2002; Macwan & Pitroda, 2018). The challenges faced by PPPs are frequently compounded by issues such as inadequate or infrequent levels of communication and proper coordination among stakeholders, conflicting objectives, and limited accountability mechanisms for either partner involved. These factors contribute to the complexity and uncertainty surrounding PPP projects.

Another obstacle arises when partners in these relationships attempt to migrate their outdated legacy systems to the new platforms created for them by their partners. This is especially true when government organizations require their legacy data to be utilized in the new system, requiring a mass migration of data that may not be immediately compatible with the new system. Although efforts were put underway back in 2013 in the US to help address these issues, the execution of the executive order was not carried out thoroughly and was limited in scope, meaning there were no data standards identified and in essence the order had no impact on actual government data as of 2023.[13] Since then, there have been efforts to standardize data in the government,[14] but without any enforcement or organized execution, the effort will likely face challenges. Carrying out any sort of upgrade process requires careful attention to detail to avoid wasting valuable resources, and

[13] https://www.gao.gov/products/gao-24-106164.
[14] https://resources.data.gov/standards/.

many details need to be discussed regarding specific workflows, fields, users, and so on in order for the project to be successful. This is especially true when there are no proper preparations in place and rules government must follow to ensure their systems are futureproof.

Overlooked Change Management

The next topic examines the failures that might not necessarily result from the intrinsic qualities of government but rather the execution of implementing change. Once a government agency decides to undergo changes, a proper change management strategy should be put in place to ensure success. However, many implementations of new innovation still fail due to overlooking this process. Many projects fail due to a lack of shared understanding between organizations, which can especially be true as well when there are multiple organizations going through change at once (Ansell & Gash 2008). This can be a symptom of siloed work verticals the government operates in, a lack of understanding of new technology or processes, or lack of openly listening to other stakeholders (Cinar et al., 2019).

Related to this is the lack of governance put in place related to the change, more specifically network governance. The problem here lies with partners who are undergoing change together not effectively aligning their actions to ensure the successful completion of the innovation (Sørensen & Torfing 2011). In other times, they may not be actively engaged or participating in the change. An example of this occurred with the Health Information Technology for Economic and Clinical Health (HITECH) Act of 2009. The HITECH Act was designed to promote the adoption and meaningful use of Electronic Health Records (EHRs) by healthcare providers. However, despite the good intentions of the policy, there were significant challenges in implementation due to a lack of coordination between various stakeholders such as healthcare providers, EHR vendors, government agencies, and patients (Gold & McLaughlin, 2016).

One major issue was the lack of interoperability among different EHR systems. Healthcare providers often used different EHR systems that were all designed by different vendors using proprietary formats. This meant that the systems could not easily communicate or share data with each other leading to a lack of coordination, inefficiencies, data fragmentation, and errors in patient care. Additionally, there were privacy and security concerns surrounding the transmission and sharing of sensitive health information electronically. The failure to address these concerns adequately undermined public trust and slowed down the adoption of EHRs (Adler-Milstein & Jha, 2014; Blumenthal, 2010).

Power Struggles

In some instances of innovation, the public managers engage in turf fights with one another over who owns what part of the organization or process. First, we will examine internal turf wars. In these examples, the bureaucrats throughout the government are constantly vying for control over their piece of the pie, believing they should have the final say in matters (Bannister, 2005; Finke, 2020; Haughton et al., 1997). When this comes to head in times of change, the challenges identified previously in the chapter such as lack of shared understanding and delayed decision-making can come into play.

The power struggles can be external as well, where bureaucrats and politicians act without the consultation of the public. An example could be the Flint water crisis spanning 2014–2015. In Flint, Michigan, emergency managers appointed by the state government made the decision to switch the city's water source without proper consultation or consideration of the concerns raised by local residents. By doing so the city's drinking water became contaminated with lead, leading to major health risks. The lack of citizen involvement and disregard for community concerns led to a public health disaster and a loss of trust in the decision-making process.[15]

The federal level in the US provides another example where citizens and businesses felt disenfranchised by the government with the enactment of the Clean Power Plan (CPP) in 2015. The plan fell under the purview of the EPA and was established to reduce carbon emissions from existing powerplants while trying to point the nation toward clean energy, which although being promoted as a long-term solution for the world, it was still found to be less efficient and more costly than traditional energy.[16,17,18] Once implemented, it was met with controversy due to its crippling impacts on the lives of citizens

[15] https://www.nrdc.org/stories/flint-water-crisis-everything-you-need-know.

[16] https://elements.visualcapitalist.com/how-much-land-power-us-solar/.

[17] https://www.politico.com/news/2024/02/21/democrats-climate-action-utility-bills-00142316.

[18] https://www.theverge.com/2023/9/26/23889066/climate-change-international-energy-agency-roadmap-hydrogen-carbon-capture.

and economic impact on industry.[19,20] In the end, the Supreme Court struck down the Act, stating that the EPA did not have the statutory authority to enact or enforce the CPP.[21]

However, challenges also breed opportunities. If we go back to the Dust Bowl example, from the ashes of this disaster arose a renewed commitment to sustainable farming practices. Further public innovations including the establishment of the Soil Conservation Service (now the Natural Resources Conservation Service) and the adoption of more environmentally friendly land management techniques, such as crop rotation and contour plowing, were born out of the harsh lessons learned during the Dust Bowl era.

Future Opportunities

As the rest of the world continues to evolve, the public sector will need to adapt along with it or risk plateauing or even regressing behind. The needs of the world continue to change as well. For instance, during a time before AI existed, there would have been no need for policies related to regulating or governing AI technologies. Innovation breeds innovation, and therefore the public sector will always need to maintain pace to ensure society operates as fairly and efficiently as possible.

Adoption of New Approaches

Just as user expectations of products rise for each release of a new cell phone, the public will have increasingly higher expectations of the public sector as they get used to new offerings. Much of this stems from advancements in technology and a plethora of information readily available at people's fingertips. Gone are the days of governments only maintaining peace and building roads. Complex challenges such as economic problems, environment, and public health call for governmental solutions. Social media has amplified the impact of individuals' voices, leading to an increased demand for greater government accountability and transparency to ensure the will of the people is being met.

[19] https://www.heritage.org/environment/report/the-many-problems-the-epas-clean-power-plan-and-climate-regulations-primer.

[20] https://www.nbcnews.com/business/energy/states-industry-groups-sue-block-obamas-clean-power-plan-n450216.

[21] https://www.supremecourt.gov/opinions/21pdf/20-1530_n758.pdf.

But public managers need not feel helpless in addressing these daunting tasks. New approaches have been developed to allow public managers to obtain feedback much sooner as they test solutions in small, cross-functional teams (Bason, 2010). Public managers are increasingly realizing the value of nimble, iterative problem-solving approaches and service provisions. Traditional bureaucratic government structures and siloed divisions are slow to react, lack adaptability, and prove ill-equipped for tackling complex challenges (Bason, 2010; Scott & Gong, 2021). In response, public administrators are exploring new ways to organize their workforce into smaller cross-departmental teams.

When people with diverse skill sets and viewpoints come together, they can tackle complex issues in a more integrated and innovative way, rather than being limited by individual silos of expertise (Agranoff & McGuire, 2003; Emerson et al., 2012). Using this approach, these interdisciplinary teams offer more innovative and comprehensive solutions. Additionally, they retain freedom to rapidly experiment, prototype, and test potential remedies, unhindered by excessive bureaucracy or lengthy ratification cycles. This agile modus encourages iterative learning, continuous betterment, and dexterity responding to fluctuating conditions or emerging insights (Bason, 2010; Sørensen & Torfing, 2011).

Through the strategic integration of diverse departments and placing a heavy emphasis on collaboration, public administrations can unlock a dynamic of collective creativity, foster agile innovation, and seize opportunities for transformative growth (Agranoff & McGuire, 2003; Emerson et al., 2012). When complemented by adequate autonomy support and accountability metrics, such innovative structuring yields opportunities to reimagine policies, operations, and public services delivery (Sørensen & Torfing, 2011).

Overcome Risk Aversion

The proclivity towards risk aversion carries with it some dire consequences that should they play out could lead to even worse outcomes than the act of taking that risk. Government agencies must cultivate an environment where "safe-to-fail" experiments are possible, and successes are publicly recognized to overcome risk aversion (Ahern, 2011). Government agencies can have R&D teams that focus primarily on evaluating their own business processes and initiatives and go through constant rounds of feedback to iterate on their approaches. Along with this would be clear implementation processes and committees to guide the new initiatives that result from these changes and conduct risk assessments of the proposed changes. On a personal career level, there should be some form of incentive for employees to attempt to improve their programs and clear guidelines that are put in place that still protect the agency from exposure to determined risk that could jeopardize the agency or country.

Continued Technological Innovations

Technological advances will continue to be a focal point in public innovation. It is known that technology does not always yield the results that we look for. Adoption of emerging technologies by the public sector is more or less associated with additional social, sustainable, and ethical implications.[22] Therefore, governments in the future should increasingly monitor the use of technology and how it could help service delivery. For instance, there should be a comprehensive assessment of each adoption of technology and its real impact, including a variety of decentralized digital tools.[23] In the meantime, despite many problems that technology has caused, governments ought to narrow the digital divide by improving technological skills and continue leveraging technology for good. Some of the technology that could benefit the public sector includes AI, data standards, and blockchain to aid in improving overall efficiency.

Leveraging technology also helps to enhance user-centered design. Information technology and various digital tools such as online platforms, websites, social media, and blockchain technology allow governments to directly reach citizens and invite them to participate in innovating together. These digital platforms have become the modern place of social discourse, and governments can learn to turn social discourse into actionable policy initiatives.

In the realms of AI, governments have begun implementing advanced chat bots in their service delivery to increase efficiency. Singapore's Ministry of Communications and Information launched the Gov.sg chatbot on Facebook Messenger, enabling citizens and visitors to easily access information

[22] https://www.oecd-ilibrary.org/docserver/932780bc-en.pdf.
[23] Ibid.

about government agencies. Similarly, the Travel For London government agency created an AI-powered Facebook messenger chatbot TravelBot to help update transportation information such as bus arrivals.[24]The government can also use AI to assist with the internal processing of forms. The UK government issues over five million passports and the US issues over one million green cards per year.[25,26] AI could assist with checking the data being processed, validating it across different agency databases, and facilitating the delivery of the physical card to users. This type of technology is specific to agencies but can be replicated across the government to help all tiers become more efficient.

Governments also stand to benefit greatly from the standardization of their data. As we have discussed in this book, the government operates in silos and as a result their data is very fragmented. The government can seek to standardize their data in a way that makes sense so that there can be greater interoperability between government entities and look to further facilitate the standardization of electronic medical records.

Another important technology is blockchain, which stands to have a positive impact on government (Chen & Murtazashvili, 2023). Blockchain can be leveraged to enhance the security of any data exchanges, which can be especially helpful when the government is managing and exchanging personal identifiable information. Furthermore, blockchain can be leveraged to help protect the integrity of elections, which will continue to be a controversial topic as countries become more politically polarized. It also has the potential to provide great opportunities to enhance transparency for governments and it can be extended to virtually all aspects of government to provide visibility into approval processes, fund transfers, and votes that occur behind the closed doors of government agencies.

For use cases more specific to the health domain, blockchain can help with the management and monitoring prescription drugs. For instance, counterfeiting prescription drugs has caused tens of thousands of lives each other, and it happens mostly in more impoverished and less developed countries (Medina et al., 2016; Tagde et al., 2021). Mongolia is one of the places that has high number of counterfeiting drug frauds. Its government has

[24] https://blog.vsoftconsulting.com/blog/15-governments-agencies-that-use-chatbots.
[25] https://www.gov.uk/government/organisations/hm-passport-office/about.
[26] https://www.boundless.com/immigration-resources/the-green-card-explained/.

partnered with FarmaTrust, a blockchain company to track each batch of medicine and monitor the supply chain process.[27]

In the case of emergency and crisis management, blockchain also has the potential to alleviate some of the challenges due to its secure channels of communication and rapid transmission of data. In instances of disaster where normal systems may have a centralized point of failure, blockchains decentralized nature can allow for the continuation of emergency response. Further, when it is necessary to allow resources to flow to individuals directly to alleviate the burden of resource distribution, blockchain can help facilitate these transactions in times of crises such as war and natural disasters (Chen & Murtazashvili, 2023). It can also be leveraged during war time to help provide relief to war victims, as has been evidenced in assisting in the war in Ukraine through partnerships between governments and nonprofits (Chen & Murtazashvili, 2024).

Strategic Public–Private Partnerships

As previously mentioned, innovation often takes place at the intersection of multiple disciplines and diverse realms of knowledge, and the public sector around the world has been increasingly fostering collaboration and knowledge-sharing networks to exchange ideas and expertise and to achieve the same innovation goals together. However, although public-private partnerships bring tremendous benefits to government, they also create new challenges for the public sector, one of them being the overall cultural mismatch with private sector partners. Therefore, in order to achieve successful innovations for public private partnerships, the government needs to relax the environment and foster a mutual understanding to enable innovation. The private sector is typically more nimble and able to keep abreast with the latest managerial trends and technology. Although the government operates in a different environment, it can leverage knowledge from the private sector through collaborative frameworks, incorporating best practices and leveraging innovation to inform its own operational strategies. For instance, we touched on the adoption of Agile methodologies earlier, yet this represents only one the various techniques and methodologies at the disposal of

[27] https://medium.com/@farmatrust/oecd-selects-farmatrusts-mongolia-project-as-key-public-sector-trend-de64710e64ef.

government. Working with private sector partners can allow the government to have knowledge spillover from the private sector and even ask for their partners to help them adapt to the industry best practices.

In terms of future cross-sector collaboration, government should always be the steerer in determining the priorities of innovation with the caveat that they are constantly soliciting the feedback of the public on their priorities. Citizen science has been a growing trend indicating that citizens want to get involved with scientific pursuits and have their own research agendas, and figuring out new ways to incorporate them into the scientific fold including new research directives or projects can be a way to foster new innovations (Özden & Velibeyoğlu, 2023; Sampaio & Rault, 2022). To ensure this is the case, e-governance platforms can include sections where the public would like to see innovation occur and allow them to craft the innovation goals of governments.

Government should strive to maintain an equal balance between increasing its internal capacity for innovation and providing external resources for private innovation. Public leaders should strive to avoid the negative consequences, such as corruption and picking winners and losers, at each step of the joint innovation efforts demonstrated in the previous chapters.

While there have been increased collaborations between the public sector and small businesses, the number of small businesses doing business with the government has plummeted roughly 40% since 2010.[28] That said, although the government recognizes the importance of these businesses, there is still much more work to be done to ensure that the government is not picking favorites but instead is giving all businesses an equal shot at competition (Aligica & Tarko, 2014; Mitchell, 2012). In order to raise awareness within the public sector to increase public entrepreneurship, governments may also consider designing new courses or collaborate with industries or universities to build new programming to educate public employees.

In sum, the government faces a plethora of challenges and blunders in their pursuit of providing a better tomorrow for everyone. But as Ralph Waldo Emerson put it, "every wall is a gate." When faced with challenges, there is always an opportunity beneath the problem. With those words, governments should seek first to acknowledge the areas that they could still improve and work on those weak points. Then, by overcoming risk aversion, embracing innovative partnerships, and leveraging new technologies, they can find effective ways to overcome every obstacle in their way.

[28] https://nationalequityatlas.org/federalcontracts.

Chapter 10
Conclusion and Contributions

The past few decades have witnessed unprecedented growth in human history, the likes of which the human race has never seen. But with this growth has come a malaise that casts shadows over all those below it. From economic recessions and regional war conflicts to climate crises and global pandemics, the world has experienced various threats and hardships in recent history. These challenges have formed a byzantine, interrelated web with no straightforward solution. They also make public sector innovation more important and urgent than ever before. Governments can address challenges in more effective ways through pioneering new solutions, which ultimately leads to better service delivery that meets the evolving needs of the public. However, research has consistently shown that innovation is not an inherent trait of government organizations.

Can the public sector be innovative? Has it ever been innovative? How can the government be more innovative? How can we ensure the government innovates for the public good? These are the questions that we make efforts to answer throughout the entirety of this book.

Taking an interdisciplinary approach, we have covered a plethora of literature that has contributed to the greater understanding of public innovation, ranging from domains including public administration, public policy, entrepreneurship, economics, computer science, ecology, and many more. Drawing upon previous theories from many of these disciplines, we have sought to expand the understanding of theories including connective action, participatory democracy, and entrepreneurial ecosystem, among others, and how they can all be intertwined with one another.

Aiming to bridge the gaps between theories and real-life practice of public innovation, we examine many innovation cases using different data sources covering governments on all geographic extents, including local, national, and global scales throughout our analysis, providing readers with an enlightening trip around the world to examine public innovation through both a geographic and temporal lens. These approaches enable *Innovation and*

Innovation and Entrepreneurship in the Public Sector. Wendy D. Chen and David B. Audretsch, Oxford University Press. © Oxford University Press (2025). DOI: 10.1093/9780197679470.003.0010

Entrepreneurship in the Public Sector to make unique contributions to academic literature and provide significant lessons for contemporary and future public innovators.

First and foremost, we hope that we have shattered the illusion that the government is but a mere machine, incapable of formulating or producing its own innovation. Governments have been operating in a variety of contexts, either behind the scenes or at the forefront to help lead the way to new heights for civilization. In this book, we carefully explore the variety of roles that governments have played throughout the world for public innovation, including resource provider, innovation enabler, and collaborator. For instance, it is a resource provider for internal innovation facilitated by organizations such as federal labs or research parks such as Research Triangle Park in North Carolina in the US. Yet it is precisely in these areas where the government can shine brightest—bridging gaps and leveling playing fields—by offering life-giving support to entrepreneurs and innovators, whose nascent ideas have the power to reshape the very fabric of society. What we can see from this is that governments have the opportunity to wear many different hats, not only taking a passive role and assuming the other sectors will decide on a path themselves. Instead, under the assumption that government will act on behalf of the people, they can play an entrepreneurial role, aiding those around them in fostering innovation.

Next, when we are enamored by all the new technology adoptions in the public sector, it is critical to remind ourselves that innovation exists in areas beyond technology, and governments have the capacity to innovate in a variety of ways. While this book does highlight a lot of exhilarating examples of technological innovations in the public sphere, we also debunk the myth that innovation is only limited to technological or scientific discoveries. By examining public innovation through a historical perspective, this book presents the successes of public sector innovation ranging from workforce specialization that served as the underpinnings to the industrial revolution, to the very foundations of modern society including democracy itself. Indeed, society has come a long way from the times of agrarian societies and god-kings, and these times were merely blips on the timeline of civilization that connects us all.

Thanks to the interconnected nature of our world, places are no longer shrouded behind the veil of distance, hiding backstage in a show with all the world treading the boards in their grand performance for one another.

Instead, problems have become amplified and more evident as issues can become viral sensations that spread across our social media channels. To tackle these challenges, our research on public innovation demonstrates the importance of collaboration. In *Innovation and Entrepreneurship in the Public Sector*, we explore the different approaches that governments have taken to work together with the private sector and other entities. We have seen how government has collaborated with the private sector to form public private partnerships to build impressive feats of engineering such as the National Highway System and the Transcontinental Railroad. We have also seen it foster collaboration between all three sectors in the UK through its Industrial Strategy Challenge Fund. These are just some examples highlighting the interconnectedness of sectors with government often spearheading these efforts. We want to underscore again the importance of government getting the right stakeholders involved in the innovation process, while always having citizens in mind for the end goal. Perhaps equally important to getting the right stakeholders involved is ensuring that the execution of carrying out innovation is thoroughly thought through and properly scoped.

Besides coproducing innovation with the private sector, one of the critical roles that governments can play is to be an innovation enabler by creating a supportive bottom-up policy environment for individual citizens to innovate for society. We saw this in the case of Montevideo Decide, which empowers its citizens to make vital decisions regarding the city. Or in the case of the United States Agriculture Department when the government invited farmers and everyday citizens to participate in public discussions from home to discuss regulations for organic farming. The end goal for all of these is a way for citizens to be involved in helping to shape the policies of their governments, allowing for the potential benefits of the wisdom of the crowds to take root in the soil of their society.

Throughout the journey of this book, we did of course cover the great benefits of public innovation, but we also discovered that public innovation is not always a rosy picture. This book offers a balanced view to evaluate public innovation. In particular, we lay out some significant side effects of public innovation such as what happens when government interests did not take citizens into consideration. The Dutch government's goal to reduce greenhouse gases was at odds with local farmers, resulting in massive protests. China and India both suffered consequences for building dams on their rivers, leading to new sets of problems. Situations like these emphasize the importance of having a well formulated plan with contingencies in mind, all while ensuring the proper stakeholders are involved in the decision-making process.

In addition, diverging from prior research on public innovation, we argue that one cannot examine public innovation without considering entrepreneurship. To help bridge this gap, entrepreneurship was interwoven throughout the book. We have discussed government support for startups such as the Israeli Yozma Programme, which offers incentives for foreigners to support their domestic startups. In the meantime, in Argentina, the Córdoba Smart City initiative provides startups with the ability to gain real-world experience of providing solutions to the government while the government gains additional support in the tackling of their own challenges.[1,2]

These are some examples that show how government plays a crucial role in the survival of startups, helping to foster an environment in which they can contribute to the goals of government while providing new employment opportunities for citizens. This book emphasizes that entrepreneurship is no longer confined to the realm of startups; rather, it is a vital catalyst for public leadership, empowering leaders to transform their institutions into vibrant, innovative hubs of growth. To that point, we contribute to the public innovation field by providing direct and actionable insights on how to make public entrepreneurs including building an entrepreneurial environment through supportive leadership, flat organizational structure, flexible work arrangements, broad scope of work, and other incentives. In developing our strategies to cultivate public entrepreneurs, we draw not only from theories of entrepreneurial environments but also apply theoretical frameworks related to the entrepreneurial process and learning.

New positions have sprouted up in organizations, such as TSAs or the Department of Labor's Chief Innovation Officer. Other efforts have included providing employees more freedom to work remotely and fostering a supportive environment that encourages experimentation and safety in failure. Many would understand these as mantras that are crucial to the success of innovative companies in Silicon Valley, but seem almost out of place in the rigid, risk-averse culture of government. Notably, it is imperative that

[1] https://whatworkscities.bloomberg.org/cities/cordoba-argentina/.
[2] https://oecd-opsi.org/innovations/cordoba-smart-city-fund/.

public leaders focus on the needs of their employees while providing ample opportunities for new initiatives to arise.

Innovators and entrepreneurs take risks in uncertain times, with their own calculation of risk and reward. In the private sector, entrepreneurs can make many of their mistakes during the innovation process while facing little to no facing public criticism. In contrast, the stakes of public innovation are much higher as the services are usually on wide display to the entire world. In the public sector setting, due to the potential impact mistakes could have on the public, public employees are hesitant to make any mistakes. What may be a relatively minor mistake could make front-page news. Nevertheless, it is important to know that mistakes and failure are inherent to innovation. When even the slightest hint of punishment befalls those daring enough to innovate, whether real or merely perceived, it sends a clear message to frontline workers: the bureaucratic status quo reigns supreme and daring to explore new ideas comes at a steep cost. To that point, it is important that this lesson does not get engraved in public workers minds so that innovation can thrive.

Furthermore, we emphasize the collaborative nature of public innovation, understanding that silos lead to failure and that the cross-pollination of ideas is crucial to thriving societies. We build upon the entrepreneurial and innovation ecosystem theory, highlighting government's position in the system while providing empirical insights into the functioning of the ecosystem. We demonstrate the importance of creating inclusive ecosystems that lower the barriers of entry for all. Additionally, we highlight ecosystems that tap into the existing regional specialization, such as in the case of Planet M in Detroit and its accelerating impact on innovation in the realm of mobility.[3] Building these ecosystems that fully consider stakeholders and spatial context is crucial to achieving sustainable innovation.

Finally, we contribute to understanding the challenges facing public innovation and what future opportunities lie ahead. We saw how government regulation can lead to crippling processes that stifle new businesses from forming such as in the case of Venezuela and how bureaucracies excel at stability and repeatable processes but struggle in times of innovation and change. We see lots of opportunities for government to modernize, becoming more agile in new structural shifts and through the adoption of

[3] https://www.michiganbusiness.org/press-releases/2018/07/planetm-and-plug-and-play-partner--for-mobility-matchmaking-event

new technologies. New opportunities await in the form of AI, blockchain, digital platforms, and more to assist the government with its delivery of services and processes, and it's imperative that the government takes the time to properly assess these opportunities and their potential impacts on delivery.

A growing number of challenges are on the rise, but as Mark Twain said, "History doesn't repeat, but it often rhymes." In many ways, the problems we face today are as old as civilization itself. They are merely the evolution of older challenges, a sort of archaea that has been with us all along but morphed into different shapes. Indeed, these problems have been with us all along—not because of the rise of new technologies or governments, but because they're rooted in our shared humanity.

With the knowledge and tools shared in this book, you have the power to transform challenges into opportunities and make a lasting impact on the world. Remember to look for collaboration and innovation opportunities to join hands with the private sector, universities, and citizens to bring about positive change. Government holds the key to unlocking new technologies through its support of the private sector and universities in the form of grants and various forms of collaborative governance.

The future is bright for public innovation, with societal shifts that demand greater public participation along with new organizational structures, methods, institutions, and technology that can help facilitate these changes. We expect to see these trends continue, with greater emphasis placed on government doubling down on each of their roles from facilitator to resource provider. We also expect to see AI playing a pivotal role, aiding governments in addressing concerns while balancing the additional privacy and ethical concerns that are inherent in the field. Meanwhile, we have primarily seen many of these innovations take place at the city or regional level. We would expect over time for many of these innovations to eventually roll up to state or federal levels, offering new opportunities for citizens to participate in their government.

A word of caution, however, would be that the innovation government carries out must strongly align with the will of the people. Research areas, initiatives, and collaborations must all be transparent, ethical, democratic, and be thoroughly vetted to prohibit conflicts of interest between government leaders and collaborators. Future studies could potentially dive into the ever-shifting landscape as we see some of these new initiatives roll out and the ramifications felt by the public.

The public sector has many challenges ahead, but thankfully there are many pathways to addressing large challenges that have been cleared by technology and others before. Some pathways may lead to success while others to failure. But it's this experimentation that has led us to where we are today. There will be inherent risk through the process of this public entrepreneurship, just as a startup founder could attest to. But should the public entrepreneur ever wonder which path to choose, the people can always guide them.

References

Chapter 1

Arundel, A., Bloch, C., & Ferguson, B. (2019). Advancing innovation in the public sector: Aligning innovation measurement with policy goals. *Research Policy*, 48(3), 789–798.

Aschauer, D. A. (1989). Is public expenditure productive? *Journal of Monetary Economics*, 23(2), 177–200.

Audretsch, D. B., Colombelli, A., Grilli, L., Minola, T., & Rasmussen, E. (2020). Innovative start-ups and policy initiatives. *Research Policy*, 49 (10), 104027.

Autio, E., Kenney, M., Mustar, P., Siegel, D., & Wright, M. (2014). Entrepreneurial innovation ecosystems and context. *Research Policy*, 43 (7), 1097–1108.

Bekkers, V. J. J. M., Edelenbos, Jurian., & Steijn, A. J. (2011). *Innovation in the public sector: Linking capacity and leadership*. Palgrave Macmillan.

Covin, J. G., & Slevin, D. P. (1989). Strategic management of small firms in hostile and benign environments. *Strategic Management Journal*, 10(1), 75–87.

Djankov, S., La Porta, R., Lopez-de-silanes, F., & Shleifer, A. (2002). The regulation of entry. *Quarterly Journal of Economics*, 117(1), 1–37.

Hanushek, E. A., & Woessmann, L. (2012). Do better schools lead to more growth? Cognitive skills, economic outcomes, and causation. *Journal of Economic Growth*, 17(4), 267–321.

Jacknis, N. (2011). Government's role in facilitating an innovative economy. *International Journal of Innovation Science*, 3(3), 107–116.

Karlson, N., Sandström, C. & Wennberg, K. (2021). Bureaucrats or markets in innovation policy? – a critique of the entrepreneurial state. *Review of Austrian Econonomics*, 34, 81–95.

Mazzucato, M. (2013). *The Entrepreneurial State: Debunking Public vs. Private Sector Myths*. Anthem Press.

Osborne, D., Gaebler, T. A. (1992). *Reinventing government: How the entrepreneurial spirit is transforming the public sector*. Basic Books.

Patriotta, G., & Siegel, D. (2019). The context of entrepreneurship. *Journal of Management Studies*, 56(6), 1194–1196.

Schumpeter, J. A. (1942). *Capitalism, socialism, and democracy*. Harper.

Stiglitz, J. E. (2000). The contributions of the economics of information to twentieth century economics. *Quarterly Journal of Economics*, 115(4), 1441–1478.

Chapter 2

Ames, E., & Rosenberg, N. (1968). The Enfield Arsenal in theory and history. *The Economic Journal*, 78(312), 827–842.

Assmann, J. (2001). *The search for God in Ancient Egypt.* Cornell University Press.

Bai, L. (2005). *Shaping the ideal child: Children and their primers in late imperial China.* Hong Kong University Press.

Bonner, S. (2012). *Education in Ancient Rome: From the elder Cato to the younger Pliny.* Routledge.

Brinkley, D. (2009). *The wilderness warrior: Theodore Roosevelt and the crusade for America.* Harper Collins.

Brownlee, W. E. (2004). *Federal taxation in America: A short history.* Cambridge University Press.

Canevaro, M. (2017). The rule of law as the measure of political legitimacy in the Greek city states. *Hague Journal on the Rule of Law*, 9, 211–236.

Chandler, A. D. (1977). *The visible hand: The managerial revolution in American business.* Harvard University Press.

Clark, B., & Foster, J. B. (2002). George Perkins Marsh and the transformation of Earth. *Organization & Environment*, 15(2), 164–169.

Deming, D. (2020). The aqueducts and water supply of Ancient Rome. *Ground Water*, 58(1), 152–161.

Dupree, A. H. (1986). *Science in the federal government.* Johns Hopkins University Press.

Finley, M. I. (1999). *The ancient economy.* University of California Press.

Fishback, P. V. (2014). The impact of New Deal spending and lending during the Great Depression. *NBER Reporter*, (3), 11–14.

Frank, J. (2019). Athenian democracy and its critics. *Ethnic and Racial Studies*, 42(8), 1306–1312.

Gasman, D. (1971). The scientific origins of national socialism: Social Darwinism in Ernst Haeckel and the German monist league. Elsevier.

Grady, J. (2015). Matthew Fontaine Maury, father of oceanography: A biography, 1806–1873. McFarland & Company.

Haque, Z. (1976). Origin and development of Ottoman Timar system: A bibliographical essay. *Islamic Studies*, 15(2), 123–134.

Herodotus (1920). *The history of Herodotus* (translated by A. D. Godley). Harvard University Press

Hooks, G. 1990. The rise of the Pentagon and the U.S. state building: The defense program as industrial policy. *American Journal of Sociology*, 96(2), 358–404.

Hudson, M. (2023). *The collapse of Antiquity: Greece and Rome as civilization's oligarchic turning point.* Islet.

Ihsanoglu, E. (2024). *Science, technology and learning in the Ottoman Empire: Western influence, local institutions, and the transfer of knowledge.* Taylor & Francis.

Kahn, D. E. (2005). The royal succession in the 25th dynasty. *Der Antike Sudan. Mitteilungen der Sudanarchäologischen Gesellschaft zu Berlin e.* V., (16), 143–163.

Khan, B. Z. (2005). *The democratization of invention: Patents and copyrights in American economic development, 1790–1920.* Cambridge University Press.

Lawson, J., & Silver, H. (2013). *A social history of education in England.* Routledge.

Leick, G. (2001). *Mesopotamia: The invention of the city.* Penguin Books.

McCullough, D. (2001). *Mornings on horseback: The story of an extraordinary family, a vanished way of life and the unique child who became Theodore Roosevelt.* Simon & Schuster.

Montazeri, S. S. R., Tame, M., & Sharifi, S. (2022). A comparative study of the functions of Asha and Ma'at. *Journal of Comparative Theology*, 13(27), 71–84.

Morris, C. R. (2012). *The dawn of innovation: The first American industrial revolution.* PublicAffairs.

Murray, F. (2002). Innovation as co-evolution of scientific and technological networks: exploring tissue engineering. *Research Policy*, 31(8), 1389–1403.

Nevins, A. (1962). The origins of the land-grant colleges and state universities: A brief account of the Morrill Act of 1862 and its results. Civil War Centennial Commission.

Podany, A. H. (2013). *The ancient near east: A very short introduction.* Oxford University Press.

Schwantes, C. A. (1996). *The Pacific Northwest: An interpretive history.* University of Nebraska Press.

Schwuchow, S. C., & Tridimas, G. (2022). The political economy of Solon's law against neutrality in civil wars. *Public Choice*, 192(3–4), 249–272.

Sellars, R. W. (1997). *Preserving nature in the national parks: A history.* Yale University Press.

Stover, J. F. (1961). *American railroads.* University of Chicago Press.

Taylor, D. E. (2016). *The rise of the American conservation movement: power, privilege, and environmental protection.* Duke University Press.

Trebilcock, C. (1969). Review of The American system of manufactures: The report of the committee on the machinery of the United States 1855 and the special reports of George Wallis and Joseph Whitworth 1854, edited by Nathan Rosenberg. *The Journal of Economic History*, 30(2), 471–472.

Watts, S. (2005). *The people's tycoon: Henry Ford and the American century.* Vintage Books.

Williams, R. L. (1991). *The origins of federal support for higher education: George w. Atherton and the land-grant college movement.* Penn State University Press.

Yılmaz, M. Ş. (2006). *Koca Nişancı" of Kanuni: Celalzade Mustafa Çelebi, Bureaucracy and Kanun in the reign of Süleyman the Magnificent (1520–1566).* Bilkent Universitesi (Turkey).

Chapter 3

Adediran, F. E., Okunade, B. A., Daraojimba, R. E., Adewusi, O. E., Bukola, A., & Igbokwe, J. C. (2024). Blockchain for social good: A review of applications in humanitarian aid and social initiatives. *International Journal of Science and Research Archive*, 11(1), 1203–1216.

Agrawal, A., Gans, J., & Goldfarb, A. (2018). *Prediction machines: The simple economics of artificial intelligence.* Harvard Business Review Press.

Ajina, A., Christiyan, J.K., Bhat, D. N., & Saxena, K. (2023). Prediction of weather forecasting using artificial neural networks. *Journal of applied research and technology*, 21(2), 205–211.

Alketbi, A., Nasir, Q., & Talib, M. A. (2018, February). Blockchain for government services—Use cases, security benefits and challenges. In *2018 15th Learning and Technology Conference (L&T)* (pp. 112–119). IEEE.

Allen, D. W. (2017). Discovering and developing the blockchain cryptoeconomy. *SSRN*, 1–26.

Allessie, D., Sobolewski, M., Vaccari, L., & Pignatelli, F. (2019). Blockchain for digital government. Luxembourg: *Publications Office of the European Union*, 8–10.

Almirall, E., Wareham, J., Ratti, C., Conesa, P., Bria, F., Gaviria, A., & Edmondson, A. (2016). Smart cities at the crossroads: New tensions in city transformation. *California Management Review*, 59(1), 141–152.

Alvarez, R. M., Hall, T. E., & Trechsel, A. H. (2009). Internet voting in comparative perspective: The case of Estonia. *Political Science & Politics*, 42(3), 497–505.

Androniceanu, A. (2023). The new trends of digital transformation and artificial intelligence in public administration. *Administratie si Management Public*, 40, 147–155.

Angwin, J., Larson, J., Mattu, S., & Kirchner, L. (2016, May 23). Machine bias. *ProPublica.*

Anthopoulos, L., & Fitsilis, P. (2010, July). From digital to ubiquitous cities: Defining a common architecture for urban development. In *2010 Sixth International Conference on Intelligent Environments* (pp. 301–306). IEEE.

Arsène, S. (2021). The social credit system in China. *Reseaux*, 225(1), 55–86.

Asher, M., Leston-Bandeira, C., & Spaiser, V. (2019). Do parliamentary debates of e-petitions enhance public engagement with parliament? An analysis of Twitter conversations. *Policy & Internet*, 11(2), 149–171.

Barocas, S., & Nissenbaum, H. (2014). Big data's end run around anonymity and consent. In *Privacy, Big Data, and the Public Good* (pp. 44–75). Cambridge University Press.

Bochsler, D. (2009). Can the internet increase political participation? An analysis of remote electronic voting's effect on turnout. In *An Analysis of Remote Electronic Voting's Effect on Turnout (August 5, 2009). APSA 2009 Annual Meeting, Toronto* (pp. 3–6).

Buterin, V. (2014). A next-generation smart contract and decentralized application platform. https://ethereum.org/en/whitepaper/

Cantwell, J., & Janne, O. (1999). Technological globalisation and innovative centres: The role of corporate technological leadership and locational hierarchy. *Research Policy*, 28(2–3), 119–144.

Caragliu, A., Del Bo, C., & Nijkamp, P. (2011). Smart cities in Europe. *Journal of Urban Technology*, 18, 65–82.

Cerrudo, C. (2015). An emerging US (and world) threat: Cities wide open to cyber attacks. *Securing Smart Cities*, 9.

Chen, W., & Murtazashvili, I. (2023). Blockchains for emergency and crisis management. *Public Administration Review*, 83(5), 1409–1414.

Chen, W., & Murtazashvili, I. (2024). Is cryptoaltruism transforming the nonprofit sector? Lessons from the Ukrainian nonprofits during the Russia-Ukraine War. *Chinese Public Administration Review*, 15(1), 36–46.

Choi, J. W. (2014). E-government and corruption: A cross-country survey. *World Political Science*, 10(2), 217–236.

Citron, D. K. (2008). Technological due process. *Washington University Law Review*, 85(6), 1249–1313.

Colebatch, H. K. (1998). *Policy*. Open University Press.

Conradie, P., & Choenni, S. (2014). On the barriers for local government releasing open data. *Government Information Quarterly*, 31, S10–S17.

Coppi, G., & Fast, L. (2019). *Blockchain and distributed ledger technologies in the humanitarian sector*. HPG Commissioned Report.

Coursey, D., & Norris, D. F. (2008). Models of e-government: Are they correct? An empirical assessment. *Public Administration Review*, 68(3), 523–536.

Cruickshank, P., & Smith, C. F. (2009). Self-efficacy as a factor in the evaluation of epetitions. *Proceedings of EDEM*, 223–232.

Deloitte (2020). Study on public sector data strategies, policies and governance: ANNEX Case studies. https://joinup.ec.europa.eu/sites/default/files/custom-page/attachment/2020-07/Study%20on%20public%20sector%20data%20strategies%2C%20policies%20and%20governance%20%E2%80%93%20ANNEX%20Case%20studies.pdf.

De Massis, A., Audretsch, D., Uhlaner, L., & Kammerlander, N. (2018). Innovation with limited resources: Management lessons from the German Mittelstand. *Journal of Product Innovation Management*, 35(1), 125–146.

Draai, E., & Taylor, D. (2009). Public participation for effective service delivery: A local government perspective. *Journal of Public Administration*, 44(si-1), 112–122.

Dudycz, H., & Piątkowski, I. (2018). Smart mobility solutions in public transport based on analysis chosen smart cities. *Informatyka Ekonomiczna. Prace Naukowe Uniwersytetu Ekonomicznego we Wrocławiu*, 2(48), 19–35.

Eggers, W., Schatsky, D., & Viechnickl, P. (2017). AI-augmented government: Using cognitive technologies to redesign public sector work. https://www2.deloitte.com/us/en/insights/focus/cognitive-technologies/artificial-intelligence-government.html.

Ehin, P., Solvak, M., Willemson, J., & Vinkel, P. (2022). Internet voting in Estonia 2005–2019: Evidence from eleven elections. *Government Information Quarterly*, 39(4), 101718.

Elbahnasawy, N. G. (2014). E-government, internet adoption, and corruption: an empirical investigation. *World Development*, 57, 114–126.

Eskelinen, J., Garcia Robles, A., Lindy, I., Marsh, J., & Muente-Kunigami, A. (2015). Citizen-driven innovation: A guidebook for city mayors and public administrators. World Bank.

Ferretti, T. (2022). An institutionalist approach to AI ethics: Justifying the priority of government regulation over self-regulation. *Moral Philosophy and Politics*, 9(2), 239–265.

Fischer, C., Hirsbrunner, S. D., & Teckentrup, V. (2022). Producing open data. *Research Ideas and Outcomes*, 8, e86384.

Floridi, L., Cowls, J., Beltrametti, M., Chatila, R., Chazerand, P., Dignum, V., ... & Vayena, E. (2018). AI4People—an ethical framework for a good AI society: Opportunities, risks, principles, and recommendations. *Minds and Machines*, 28, 689–707.

Fox, J. (2007). The uncertain relationship between transparency and accountability. *Development in Practice*, 17(4–5), 663–671.

Fraczkiewicz-Wronka, A., & Szymaniec, K. (2013). The application of the Resource-Based View (RBV) for public hospitals performance. *Organization and Management*, 5158, 149–162.

Gallagher, J. (2010). *Reimagining Detroit: Opportunities for redefining an American city*. Wayne State University Press.

Germanakos, P., Samaras, G., & Christodoulou, E. (2005). Multi-channel delivery of services–The road from egovernment to mgovernment: Further technological challenges and implications. *Proceedings of the first European Conference on Mobile Government* (Euro mGov), Mobile Government Consortium International LLC, 210-220. http://www.grchina.com/mobility/lab/Archives/EuromGov2005/PDF/22_R362GP.pdf

Giffinger, R., Fertner, C., Kramar, H., Kalasek, R., Pichler-Milanovic, N., & Meijers, E. J. (2007). Smart cities. Ranking of European medium-sized cities. Final Report. https://www.smart-cities.eu/download/smart_cities_final_report.pdf

Grönman, J., Rantanen, P., Sillberg, P., Pohjola, T., & Jönkkäri, T. (2023). Challenges of combining open and commercial data sources in visitor mobility estimations. In *2023 46th MIPRO ICT and Electronics Convention (MIPRO)* (pp. 935–940). IEEE.

Hall, T., & Hubbard, P. (1996). The entrepreneurial city: New urban politics, new urban geographies? *Progress in Human Geography*, 20(2), 153–174.

Holden, A., Braun, S., Lee, L. Phelps, A., & Samuelson, R. (2017). *Catalyzing public sector innovation: Defining your role in the innovation ecosystem*. Deloitte Insights. https://www2.deloitte.com/us/en/insights/industry/public-sector/catalyzing-public-sector-innovation-initiatives.html.

Holder, S. (2020) *In San Diego, "smart" streetlights spark surveillance reform*. Bloomberg. https://www.bloomberg.com/news/articles/2020-08-06/a-surveillance-standoff-over-smart-streetlights.

Hollands, R. G. (2008). Will the real smart city please stand up? *City*, 12(3), 303–320.

Innes, J. E., & Booher, D. E. (2004). Reframing public participation: strategies for the 21st century. *Planning Theory & Practice*, 5(4), 419–436.

Ionescu, R. V., Zlati, M. L., & Antohi, V. M. (2023). Smart cities from low cost to expensive solutions under an optimal analysis. *Financial Innovation*, 9(60), 1-34.

Isaksen, K. (2023). Good suggestion—but no! Innovation as the struggle between different roles and perceptions in a municipal organisation. *Journal of Innovation Management*, 11(4), 54–70.

Ismagilova, E., Hughes, L., Rana, N. P., & Dwivedi, Y. K. (2022). Security, privacy and risks within smart cities: Literature review and development of a smart city interaction framework. *Information Systems Frontiers*, 24(2), 393-414.

Jafar, U., Aziz, M. J. A., & Shukur, Z. (2021). Blockchain for electronic voting system—review and open research challenges. *Sensors*, 21(17), 5874.

Janssen, M., Charalabidis, Y., & Zuiderwijk, A. (2012). Benefits, adoption barriers and myths of open data and open government. *Information Systems Management*, 29(4), 258–268.

Jessop, B. (1998). The narrative of enterprise and the enterprise of narrative: Place marketing and the entrepreneurial city. In Tim Hall and Phil Hubbard (Eds.) *The*

Entrepreneurial City: Geographies of Politics, Regime and Representation (pp. 77–99). Wiley.

Kattel, R., & Takala, V. (2023). The case of the UK's government digital service: The professionalisation of a paradigmatic public digital agency. *Digital Government: Research and Practice*, 28(4), 1–15.

Kao, K. T. (2024). From Robodebt to responsible AI: Sociotechnical imaginaries of AI in Australia. *Communication Research and Practice*, 10(3), 387–397.

Kotsialou, G., & Riley, L. (2018). Incentivising participation in liquid democracy with breadth-first delegation. *arXiv preprint* arXiv:1811.03710.

Lee, H. (2023). Collaborative governance platforms and outcomes: An analysis of Clean Cities coalitions. *Governance*, 36(3), 805–825.

Lemieux, V. L. (2016). Trusting records: Is Blockchain technology the answer? *Records Management Journal*, 26(2), 110–113.

Leston-Bandeira, C. (2019). Parliamentary petitions and public engagement: An empirical analysis of the role of e-petitions. *Policy & Politics*, 47(3), 415–436.

Lin, L. Y. H., & Milhaupt, C. J. (2023). China's corporate social credit system: The dawn of surveillance state capitalism? *The China Quarterly*, 256, 835-853.

Lindner, R., & Riehm, U. (2009). Electronic petitions and institutional modernization: International parliamentary e-petition systems in comparative perspective. *JeDEM: eJournal of eDemocracy and Open Government*, 1(1), 1–11.

Lorentzen, A. (2008). Knowledge networks in local and global space. *Entrepreneurship and Regional Development*, 20(6), 533–545.

Lukensmeyer, C. J. (2017). Civic tech and public policy decision making. *PS: Political Science & Politics*, 50(3), 764–771.

Maciag, M. (2017, August). How smart is your city? *Governing Magazine*. https://www.governing.com/topics/urban/gov-cities-smart-city-data.html.

Malatesta, D., & Smith, C. R. (2014). Lessons from resource dependence theory for contemporary public and nonprofit management. *Public Administration Review*, 74(1), 14–25.

McCorry, P., Shahandashti, S. F., & Hao, F. (2017). A smart contract for boardroom voting with maximum voter privacy (conference paper). In Aggelos Kiayias ed., *Financial Cryptography and Data Security: International Conference on Financial Cryptography and Data Security*, 10322, 357–375.

McKenna, D. (2011). UK local government and public participation: Using conjectures to explain the relationship. *Public Administration*, 89(3), 1182–1200.

Meijer, A., & Bolívar, M. P. R. (2016). Governing the smart city: A review of the literature on smart urban governance. *International Review of Administrative Sciences*, 82(2), 392–408.

Merton, R. K. (1968). The Matthew effect in science: The reward and communication systems of science are considered. *Science*, 159(3810), 56–63.

Nam, T., & Pardo, T. A. (2011). Conceptualizing smart city with dimensions of technology, people, and institutions. *Proceedings of the 12th Annual International Digital Government Research Conference: Digital Government Innovation in Challenging Times*, 282–291.

Naranjo-Zolotov, M., Oliveira, T., Casteleyn, S., & Irani, Z. (2019). Continuous usage of e-participation: The role of the sense of virtual community. *Government Information Quarterly*, 36(3), 536–545.

Nikiforova, A., & Zuiderwijk, A. (2022). Barriers to openly sharing government data: Towards an open data-adapted innovation resistance theory. *Proceedings of the 15th International Conference on Theory and Practice of Electronic Governance*, 215-220.

Nilsson, N. J. (2009). *The quest for artificial intelligence.* Cambridge University Press.

Norris, D. F., & Moon, M. J. (2005). Advancing e-government at the grassroots: Tortoise or hare? *Public Administration Review*, 65(1), 64–75.

Norris, P. (2001). *Digital divide: Civic engagement, information poverty, and the Internet worldwide.* Cambridge University Press.

OECD. (2019). State of the art in the use of emerging technologies in the public sector. https://www.sipotra.it/wp-content/uploads/2019/09/State-of-the-art-in-the-use-of-emerging-technologies-in-the-public-sector.pdf.

Ølnes, S., Ubacht, J., & Janssen, M. (2017). Blockchain in government: Benefits and implications of distributed ledger technology for information sharing. *Government Information Quarterly*, 34(3), 355–364.

Oni, A., Ayo, C. K., Oni, S., & Duruji, M. (2015, June). Electronic petition and democratic participation in Nigeria. *Proceedings of the 15th European Conference on Digital Government*, 223–231.

Ostrom, E. (1990). *Governing the commons: The evolution of institutions for collective action.* Cambridge University Press.

Paden, B., Čáp, M., Yong, S. Z., Yershov, D., & Frazzoli, E. (2016). A survey of motion planning and control techniques for self-driving urban vehicles. *IEEE Transactions on Intelligent Vehicles*, 1(1), 33–55.

Parenti, C., Noori, N., & Janssen, M. (2022). A smart governance diffusion model for blockchain as an anti-corruption tool in smart cities. *Journal of Smart Cities and Society*, 1(1), 71–92.

Park, S., Specter, M., Narula, N., & Rivest, R. L. (2021). Going from bad to worse: From internet voting to blockchain voting. *Journal of Cybersecurity*, 7(1), tyaa025.

Pasquale, F. (2015). *The black box society: The secret algorithms that control money and information.* Harvard University Press.

Pereira, R. & Pereira, M. (2022). Challenges, open research issues and tools in big data analytics Covid-19. *International Journal for Research in Applied Science and Engineering Technology*, 10, 2649–2659.

Raphael, C., Bachen, C. M., & Hernandez-Ramos, P. F. (2012). Flow and cooperative learning in civic game play. *New Media & Society*, 14(8), 1321–1338.

Rawls, J. (1999). *A theory of justice* (rev. ed.). Harvard University Press.

Reddick, C. G., & Frank, H. A. (2007). The perceived impacts of e-government on U.S. cities: A survey of Florida and Texas City managers. *Government Information Quarterly*, 24(3), 576–594.

Ritchie, K. L., Cartledge, C., Growns, B., Yan, A., Wang, Y., Guo, K., ... & White, D. (2021). Public attitudes towards the use of automatic facial recognition technology in criminal justice systems around the world. *PloS One*, 16(10), e0258241.

Russell, S. J., & Norvig, P. (2010). *Artificial intelligence: A modern approach* (3rd ed.). Pearson Education.

Salha, R. A., El-Hallaq, M. A., & Alastal, A. I. (2019). Blockchain in smart cities: Exploring possibilities in terms of opportunities and challenges. *Journal of Data Analysis and Information Processing*, 7(3), 118–139.

Sanka, A. I., & Cheung, R. C. (2019). Blockchain: Panacea for corrupt practices in developing countries. *2019 2nd International Conference of the IEEE Nigeria Computer Chapter (NigeriaComputConf)* (pp. 1–7). IEEE.

Schaffers, H., Komninos, N., Pallot, M., Trousse, B., Nilsson, M., & Oliveira, A. (2011). Smart cities and the future internet: Towards cooperation frameworks for open innovation. In Domingue, J., et al. Eds. *The Future Internet*. Vol. 6656, (pp. 431–446. Springer.

Schrock, A. (2018). *Civic tech: Making technology work for people*. Rogue Academic.

Shahaab, A., Maude, R., Hewage, C., & Khan, I. (2020). Blockchain-a panacea for trust challenges in public services? A socio-technical perspective. *Journal of the British Blockchain Association*, 3(2), 1–10.

Shang, Q., & Price, A. (2019). A blockchain-based land titling project in the republic of georgia: Rebuilding public trust and lessons for future pilot projects. *Innovations: Technology, Governance, Globalization*, 12(3–4), 72–78.

Sieber, R. E., & Johnson, P. A. (2015). Civic open data at a crossroads: Dominant models and current challenges. *Government Information Quarterly*, 32(3), 308–315.

Sintomer, Y., Herzberg, C., & Röcke, A. (2008). Participatory budgeting in Europe: Potentials and challenges. *International Journal of Urban and Regional Research*, 32(1), 164–178.

Solymosi, R., Buil-Gil, D., Ceccato, V., Kim, E., & Jansson, U. (2023). Privacy challenges in geodata and open data. *Area*, 55(4), 456–464.

Springall, D., Finkenauer, T., Durumeric, Z., Kitcat, J., Hursti, H., MacAlpine, M., & Halderman, J. A. (2014). Security analysis of the Estonian internet voting system. *Proceedings of the 2014 ACM SIGSAC Conference on Computer and Communications Security*, 703–715.

Stahl, B. C., & Wright, D. (2018). Ethics and privacy in AI and big data: Implementing responsible research and innovation. *IEEE Security & Privacy*, 16(3), 26–33.

Sun, N., Tao, Y., Leng, X., & Li, J. (2023). Social credit and corporate leverage: Evidence from a natural experiment in China. *Managerial and Decision Economics*, 44(7), 3962–3978.

Topol, E. J. (2019). *Deep medicine: How artificial intelligence can make healthcare human again*. Basic Books.

Trechsel, A. H., & Vassil, K. (2010). *Internet voting in Estonia: A comparative analysis of four elections since 2005*. Report for the Council of Europe.

Troisi, O., & Grimaldi, M. (2022). Guest editorial: Data-driven orientation and open innovation: the role of resilience in the (co-)development of social changes. *Transforming Government: People, Process and Policy*, 16(2), 165–171.

United Nations. (2020). *UN e-government survey 2020*. UNON Publishing Services Section. https://publicadministration.un.org/egovkb/en-us/Reports/UN-E-Government-Survey-2020.

Van Bunderen, L., Greer, L. L., & Van Knippenberg, D. (2018). When interteam conflict spirals into intrateam power struggles: The pivotal role of team power structures. *Academy of Management Journal*, 61(3), 1100–1130.

Vassil, K., Solvak, M., Vinkel, P., Trechsel, A. H., & Alvarez, M. (2016). The diffusion of internet voting. Usage patterns of internet voting in Estonia between 2005 and 2015. *Government Information Quarterly*, 33(3), 453–459.

Vinkel, P. (2015). *Remote electronic voting in Estonia: legality, impact and confidence*. TUT Press.

Webler, T., Tuler, S., & Krueger, R. O. B. (2001). What is a good public participation process? Five perspectives from the public. *Environmental Management*, 27, 435–450.

Wolpert, D. (2003). Theory of collective intelligence. In *Collectives and the design of complex systems* (pp. 43–106). Springer.

Xie, X., & Wang, H. (2020). How can open innovation ecosystem modes push product innovation forward? An fsQCA analysis. *Journal of Business Research*, 108, 29-41.

Zhang, A., & Guo, X. (2008). Study on motivation mechanism of citizens' participation under the conditions of e-government. In *2008 International Conference on Management of e-Commerce and e-Government* (pp. 140–143). IEEE.

Zheng, Y. (2016). The impact of E-participation on corruption: a cross-country analysis. *International Review of Public Administration*, 21(2), 91–103.

Ziosi, M., Hewitt, B., Juneja, P., Taddeo, M., & Floridi, L. (2024). Smart cities: Reviewing the debate about their ethical implications. *AI & Society*, 39, 1185–1200.

Zuiderwijk, A., & Janssen, M. (2014). Open data policies, their implementation and impact: A framework for comparison. *Government Information Quarterly*, 31(1), 17–29.

Zyskind, G., Nathan, O., & Pentland, A. S. (2015). Enigma: Decentralized computation platform with guaranteed privacy. *arXiv* preprint arXiv:1506.03471.

Chapter 4

Ansell, C., & Gash, A. (2008). Collaborative governance in theory and practice. *Journal of Public Administration Research and Theory*, 18(4), 543–571.

Ansell, C., & Gash, A. (2018). Collaborative platforms as a governance strategy. *Journal of Public Administration Research and Theory*, 28(1), 16–32.

Armanios, D. E., Eesley, C. E., Li, J., & Eisenhardt, K. M. (2017). How entrepreneurs leverage institutional intermediaries in emerging economies to acquire public resources. *Strategic Management Journal*, 38(7), 1373–1390.

Audretsch, D. B., & Link, A. N. (2012). Entrepreneurship and innovation: public policy frameworks. *The Journal of Technology Transfer*, 37(1), 1–17.

Austin, J. E., & Seitanidi, M. M. (2012). Collaborative value creation: A review of partnering between nonprofits and businesses: Part I. value creation spectrum and collaboration stages. *Nonprofit and Voluntary Sector Quarterly*, 41(5), 726–758.

Bason, C. (2010). *Leading public sector innovation: Co-creating for a better society.* Bristol University Press.

Bates, T., & Robb, A. (2016). Impacts of owner race and geographic context on access to small-business financing. *Economic Development Quarterly*, 30(2), 159–170.

Bingham, L. B., Nabatchi, T., & O'Leary, R. (2005). The new governance: Practices and processes for stakeholder and citizen participation in the work of government. *Public Administration Review*, 65(5), 547–558.

Boadway, R. (2001). Inter-governmental fiscal relations: The facilitator of fiscal decentralization. *Constitutional Political Economy*, 12, 93–121.

Borneman, W.R. (2010). *Rival rails: The race to build America's greatest transcontinental railroad.* Random House.

Bovaird, T. (2007). Beyond engagement and participation: User and community coproduction of public services. *Public Administration Review*, 67(5), 846–860.

Brandsen, T., & Honingh, M. (2018). Definitions of co-production and co-creation. In Taco Brandsen and Marlies Honingh eds. *Co-Production and Co-Creation* (pp. 9–17). Routledge.

Bridoux, F., & Stoelhorst, J. W. (2022). Stakeholder governance: Solving the collective action problems in joint value creation. *Academy of Management Review*, 47(2), 214–236.

Brush, C., Edelman, L. F., Manolova, T., & Welter, F. (2019). A gendered look at entrepreneurship ecosystems. *Small Business Economics*, 53, 393–408.

Brush, C., Greene, P., Balachandra, L., & Davis, A. (2018). The gender gap in venture capital-progress, problems, and perspectives. *Venture Capital*, 20(2), 115–136.

Bryson, J. M., Crosby, B. C., & Stone, M. M. (2015). Designing and implementing cross-sector collaborations: Needed and challenging. *Public Administration Review*, 75(5), 647–663.

Coleman, S., Cotei, C., & Farhat, J. (2016). The debt-equity financing decisions of US startup firms. *Journal of Economics and Finance*, 40(1), 105–126.

Copeland, B. J. (2010). *Colossus: The secrets of Bletchley Park's code-breaking computers.* Oxford University Press.

Corthay, L. (2009). Local taxes, regulations, and the business environment: Finding the right balance. *Investment Climate in Practice*, 5. Business operations and taxation note. World Bank. http://documents.worldbank.org/curated/en/280301468158062866/Local-taxes-regulations-and-the-business-environment-finding-the-right-balance.

Costa, K., & Shah, S. (2013). Government's role in pay for success. *Community Development Investment Review*, 9(1), 91–096. Federal Reserve Bank of San Francisco.

D'Este Cukierman, P., & Fontana, R. (2008). What drives the emergence of entrepreneurial academics? A study on collaborative research partnerships in the UK, *SSRN*, 16(4), 257–270.

Dalgaard, C. J., Kaarsen, N., Olsson, O., & Selaya, P. (2022). Roman roads to prosperity: Persistence and non-persistence of public infrastructure. *Journal of Comparative Economics*, 50(4), 896–916.

Díez-Vial, I., & Fernández-Olmos, M. (2015). Knowledge spillovers in science and technology parks: how can firms benefit most? *Journal of Technology Transfer*, 40, 70–84.

Dilger, R. J. (2018). *SBA's 8(a) Program: Overview, history, and current issues.* Congressional Research Service Report R44844.

Dobbin, K. B., & Lubell, M. (2021). Collaborative governance and environmental justice: Disadvantaged community representation in California sustainable groundwater management. *Policy Studies Journal*, 49(2), 562–590.

Duran, X. (2013). The first US transcontinental railroad: Expected profits and government intervention. *Journal of Economic History*, 73(1), 177–200.

Eddleston, K. A., Ladge, J. J., Mittedness, B. R., & Balachandra, L. (2016). Do you see what I see? Signaling effects of gender and firm characteristics on financing entrepreneurial ventures. *Entrepreneurship Theory and Practice*, 40(3), 489–514.

Emerson, K., & Nabatchi, T. (2015). Evaluating the productivity of collaborative governance regimes: A performance matrix. *Public Performance & Management Review*, 38(4), 717–747.

Fairlie, R. W., & Robb, A. M. (2008). *Race and entrepreneurial success: Black-, Asian-, and white-owned businesses in the United States.* MIT Press.

Feld, B. (2012). *Startup communities: Building an entrepreneurial ecosystem in your city.* Wiley.

Fogel, R. W. (1964). *Railroads and American economic growth: Essays in econometric history.* Johns Hopkins University Press.

Fung, A. (2006). Varieties of participation in complex governance. *Public Administration Review*, 66(1), 66–75.

Goldstein, B. E. (Ed.). (2012). *Collaborative resilience: Moving through crisis to opportunity.* MIT Press.

Greenblatt, J. L., & Donovan, A. (2013). The promise of pay for success. *Community Development Investment Review*, 9(1), 19–22.

Greenhalgh, T., Raftery, J., Hanney, S., & Glover, M. (2016). Research impact: A narrative review. *BMC Medicine*, 14(78), 123–135.

Hadaya, P., & Cassivi, L. (2012). Joint collaborative planning as a governance mechanism to strengthen the chain of IT value co-creation. *Journal of Strategic Information Systems*, 21(3), 182–200.

Hawkins, T., Gravier, M., & Randall, W. S. (2018). Socio-economic sourcing: Benefits of small business set-asides in public procurement. *Journal of Public Procurement*, 18(3), 217–239.

Howley, C., Campbell, J., Cowley, K., & Cook, K. (2022). Pathways and structures: Evaluating systems changes in an NSF INCLUDES alliance. *American Journal of Evaluation*, 43(4), 632–646.

Innes, J. E., & Booher, D. E. (2010). *Planning with complexity: An introduction to collaborative rationality for public policy.* Routledge.

Kania, J., & Kramer, M. (2011). Collective Impact. *Stanford Social Innovation Review*, 9(1), 36–41.

Kania, J., & Kramer, M. (2013). Embracing emergence: How collective impact addresses complexity. *Stanford Social Innovation Review*.

Kramer, D. (2016). National labs are nurturing clean-energy startups. *Physics Today*, 69(7), 3334.

Ladd, H. F., & Yinger, J. (1994). The case for equalizing aid. *National Tax Journal*, 47(1), 211–224.

Le Ber, M. J., & Branzei, O. (2010). Towards a critical theory of value creation in cross-sector partnerships. *Organization*, 17(5), 599–629.

Leeuw, F. L. (2020). *Can governments learn? Comparative perspectives on evaluation and organizational learning*. Routledge.

Levitt, R. E., Scott, W. R., & Garvin, M. J. (Eds.). (2019). *Public–private partnerships for infrastructure development: Finance, stakeholder alignment, governance*. Edward Elgar Publishing.

Lose, T. (2021). Institutionalised business incubation: A frontier for accelerating entrepreneurship in African countries. *Academy of Entrepreneurship Journal*, 27, 1–10.

Manikas, I., Malindretos, G., & Moschuris, S.J. (2019). A community-based agro-food hub model for sustainable farming. *Sustainability*, 11(4), 1017.

Marlow, S., & Martinez Dy, A. (2018). Annual review article: Is it time to rethink the gender agenda in entrepreneurship research? *International Small Business Journal*, 36(1), 3–22.

Mazzucato, M. (2015). *The entrepreneurial state: Debunking public vs. private sector myths* (rev. ed.). Public Affairs.

Motoyama, Y., & Knowlton, K. (2017). Examining the connections within the startup ecosystem: A case study of St. Louis. *Entrepreneurship Research Journal*, 7(1), 1–32.

Nabatchi, T., Sancino, A., & Sicilia, M. (2017). Varieties of participation in public services: The who, when, and what of coproduction. *Public Administration Review*, 77(5), 766–776.

NIH Collaboratory. (2020). Principles and guidelines for pragmatic studies. https://www.nihcollaboratory.org/.

NIH Collaboratory. (2021). Enhancing health outcomes through collaborative research. https://www.nihcollaboratory.org/reports/.

NIH Collaboratory. (2022). Transformative approach to large-scale clinical investigations: Overview. https://www.nihcollaboratory.org/.

Odame, H. S., Okeyo-Owuor, J. B., Changeh, J. G., & Otieno, J. O. (2020). The role of technology in inclusive innovation of urban agriculture. *Current Opinion in Environmental Sustainability*, 43, 106–111.

Osborne, S. P. (Ed.). (2000). *Public-Private Partnerships: Theory and Practice in International Perspective*. Routledge.

Ostrom, E. (1996). Crossing the great divide: Coproduction, synergy, and development. *World Development* 24(6), 1073–1087.

Pato, M. L., & Teixeira, A. A. (2016). Rural entrepreneurship: The tale of a rare event. *Journal of Place Management and Development*, 9(2), 183–205.

Pestoff, V. (2006). Citizens and co-production of welfare services. *Public Management Review*, 8(4), 503–519.

Pestoff, V. (2012). Co-production and third sector social services in Europe: Some concepts and evidence. *Voluntas*, 23, 1102–1118.

Peters, B. G. (1998). Managing horizontal government: The politics of coordination. *Public Administration*, 76(2), 295–311.

Petersen, O. H., Baekkeskov, E., Potoski, M., & Brown, T. L. (2019). Measuring and managing ex ante transaction costs in public sector contracting. *Public Administration Review*, 79(5), 641–650.

Porter, M. E., & Kramer, M. R. (2011). Creating shared value. *Harvard Business Review*, 89(1-2), 62–77.

Price, S. E., & Siegel, D. S. (2019). Assessing the role of the federal government in the development of new products, industries, and companies: Case study evidence since World War II. *Annals of Science and Technology Policy*, 3(4), 348–437.

Ramsay, A. M. (1920). A Roman postal service under the Republic. *Journal of Roman Studies*, 10, 79–86.

Ramsay, A. M. (1925). The speed of the Roman imperial post. *Journal of Roman Studies*, 15(1), 60–74.

Robinson, J. A, & Acemoglu, D. (2012). *Why nations fail: The origins of power, prosperity, and poverty*. Random House.

Rossi, F., Rosli, A., & Yip, N. (2017). Academic engagement as knowledge co-production and implications for impact: Evidence from knowledge transfer partnerships. *Journal of Business Research*, 80, 1–9.

Sager, T. (2009). Responsibilities of theorists: The case of communicative planning theory. *Progress in Planning*, 72(1), 1–51.

Seddon, T., Billett, S., & Clemans, A. (2004). Politics of social partnerships: A framework for theorizing. *Journal of Education Policy*, 19(2), 123–142.

Siemiatycki, M. (2012). The global experience with infrastructure public–private partnerships. *Planning & Environmental Law*, 64(9), 6–11.

Sridarran, P., Keraminiyage, K., & Amaratunga, D. (2016). Building community resilience within involuntary displacements by enhancing collaboration between host and displaced communities: A literature synthesis. In *Proceedings of the CIB World Building Congress*. Tampere University of Technology.

Thompson, D., & Lopez Barrera, S. (2019). Building collaborative governance and community resilience under socio-spatial rural disparities and environmental challenges. *Community Development Practice*, 23, 8–16.

Vries, P. de, & Yehoue, E. B. (2013). *The Routledge companion to public–private partnerships*. Routledge.

Wang, L., & Latham, M. (2001). The role of railroad in the development of the American west: Railroad, migration and urban growth. *Chinese Geographical Science*, 11, 223–232.

Wang, H., Xiong, W., Wu, G., & Zhu, D. (2018). Public–private partnership in public administration discipline: A literature review. *Public Management Review*, 20(2), 293–316.

White, R. (2011). *Railroaded: The transcontinentals and the making of modern America*. Norton.

Wondolleck, J. M., & Yaffee, S. L. (2000). *Making collaboration work: Lessons from innovation in natural resource management.* Island Press.

Worley, C. G., & Breyley Parker, S. (2011). Building multi-stakeholder sustainability networks: The Cuyahoga Valley initiative. In *Organizing for sustainability* (pp. 187–214). Emerald Group Publishing.

Yeshua-Katz, D., & Efrat-Treister, D. (2021). "Together in the tech trenches": A view of Israel's innovation culture. *Innovation*, 23(3), 337–353.

Zelekha, Y., Avnimelech, G., & Sharabi, E. (2014). Religious institutions and entrepreneurship. *Small Business Economics*, 42(4), 747–767.

Zwarenstein, M., Treweek, S., Gagnier, J. J., Altman, D. G., Tunis, S., Haynes, B., Oxman, A., & Moher, D. (2008). Improving the reporting of pragmatic trials: an extension of the CONSORT statement. *The BMJ*, 377(7680), 1223–1226.

Chapter 5

Avritzer, L. (2006). The challenges of institutionalizing participatory democracy: The case of participatory budgeting in Porto Alegre. *International Journal of Urban and Regional Research*, 30(1), 1–20.

Baierle, S. (2003). The Porto Alegre Thermidor: Brazil's' participatory budget at the crossroads. *Socialist Register*, 39, 305–328.

Baroudi, S., & Benghida, S. (2022). Blockchain in Dubai: Toward a sustainable digital future. In *Contemporary research in accounting and finance: Case studies from the MENA region* (pp. 253–271). Springer Nature.

Bason, C. (2010). *Leading public sector innovation: Co-creating for a better society.* Bristol University Press.

Butler, D., Adonis, A., & Travers, T. (1994). *Failure in British Government: The Politics of the Poll Tax.* Oxford University Press.

Cabannes, Y. (2004). Participatory budgeting: A significant contribution to participatory democracy. *Environment and Urbanization*, 16(1), 27–46.

Cabannes, Y., & Lipietz, B. (2018). Revisiting the democratic promise of participatory budgeting in light of competing political, good governance and technocratic logics. *Environment and Urbanization*, 30(1), 67–84.

Chambers, S. (2003). Deliberative democratic theory. *Annual Review of Political Science*, 6, 307–326.

Chen, W. (2022). A systematic literature review of reward-based crowdfunding. In *Developments in Entrepreneurial Finance and Technology* (pp. 146–181). Edward Elgar Publishing.

Chen, W. D. (2023). Crowdfunding for social ventures. *Social Enterprise Journal*, 19(3), 256–276.

Chen, W. D., & Murtazashvili, I. (2023). Blockchains for emergency and crisis management. *Public Administration Review*, 83(5), 1409–1414.

Chen, W. D., & Murtazashvili, I. (2024). Is cryptoaltruism transforming the nonprofit sector? Lessons from the Ukrainian nonprofits during the Russia-Ukraine War. *Chinese Public Administration Review*, 15(1), 36–46.

Clarkin, J. E. (2014). An empirical analysis of the missions, funding sources, and survival of social ventures. In *Theory and empirical research In social entrepreneurship* (pp. 191-220). Edward Elgar Publishing.

Cabannes, Y. (2004). Participatory budgeting: A significant contribution to participatory democracy. *Environment and Urbanization*, 16(1), 27–46.

Cohen, J. (1989). Deliberation and democratic legitimacy. In *The good polity: Normative analysis of the state* (pp. 17–34). Basil Blackwell.

Denhardt, R. B., & Denhardt, J. V. (2015). The new public service revisited. *Public Administration Review*, 75(5), 664–672.

Estellés-Arolas, E., & González-ladrón-de-guevara, F. (2012). Towards an integrated crowdsourcing definition. *Journal of Information Science*, 38(2), 189–200.

Gerber, E. M., & Hui, J. (2013). Crowdfunding: Motivations and deterrents for participation. *ACM Transactions on Computer-Human Interaction*, 20(6), 1–32.

Gilman, H. R. (2016). Engaging citizens: Participatory budgeting and the inclusive governance movement within the United States. Ash Center for Democratic Governance and Innovation, Harvard Kennedy School.

Khan, S. N., Shael, M., & Majdalawieh, M. (2019, July). Blockchain technology as a support infrastructure in e-government evolution at Dubai economic department. In *Proceedings of the 1st International Electronics Communication Conference* (pp. 124–130).

Manzoor, A. (2020). Crowdfunding for non-profits: Opportunities and challenges. In *Start-Ups and SMEs: Concepts, Methodologies, Tools, and Applications*, (pp. 376–390). IGI Global.

Marquetti, A., Schonerwald da Silva, C. E., & Campbell, A. (2012). Participatory economic democracy in action: Participatory budgeting in Porto Alegre, 1989–2004. *Review of Radical Political Economics*, 44(1), 62–81.

Mollick, E. (2014). The dynamics of crowdfunding: An exploratory study. *Journal of Business Venturing*, 29(1), 1–16.

Nguyen, C., Tahmasbi, N., de Vreede, T., de Vreede, G. J., Oh, O., & Reiter-Palmon, R. (2016). A definition of community crowdsourcing engagement and application. In *Blurring the boundaries through digital innovation: Individual, organizational, and societal challenges* (pp. 283–296). Springer International.

Ordanini, A., Miceli, L., Pizzetti, M., & Parasuraman, A. (2011). Crowd-funding: Transforming customers into investors through innovative service platforms. *Journal of Service Management*, 22(4), 443–470.

O'Reilly, T. (2011). Government as a platform. *Innovations: Technology, Governance, Globalization*, 6(1), 13–40.

Ostrom, E. (1990). *Governing the commons: The evolution of institutions for collective action*. Cambridge University Press.

Pateman, C. (1970). *Participation and democratic theory*. Cambridge University Press.

Piper, L. (2014). How participatory institutions deepen democracy through broadening representation: The case of participatory budgeting in Porto Alegre, Brazil. *Theoria*, 61(139), 50–67.

Polterovich, V. M. (2014). Why reforms fail. *Journal of the New Economic Association*, 23(3), 169–173.

Rainero, C., & Brescia, V. (2018). The participatory budgeting towards a new governance and accountability. *International Journal of Management Sciences and Business Research*, 7(2), 54–67.

Rezende, F. D. (2002). Why do administrative reforms fail? *Revista Brasileira de Ciências Sociais*, 17(50), 123–142.

Saari, D. G. (2003). Unsettling aspects of voting theory. *Economic Theory*, 22, 529–555.

Sintomer, Y., Herzberg, C., & Röcke, A. (2008). Participatory budgeting in Europe: Potentials and challenges. *International Journal of Urban and Regional Research*, 32(1), 164–178.

Stiver, A., Barroca, L., Minocha, S., Richards, M., & Roberts, D. (2015). Civic crowdfunding research: Challenges, opportunities, and future agenda. *New Media & Society*, 17(2), 249–271.

Surowiecki, J. (2004). *The wisdom of crowds: Why the many are smarter than the few and how collective wisdom shapes business, economies, societies and nations.* Doubleday.

Theodoulou, S. Z. & Roy, R. K. (2016). *Public administration: A very short introduction.* Oxford University Press.

Troise, C. (2020). Discovering the underlying dynamics of crowdfunding networks: entrepreneurs' ties, crowdfunders' connections and community spin-offs. *Journal of Enterprising Communities: People and Places in the Global Economy*, 14(2), 277–298.

Utzig, P. (2002). *Citizens as partners: Information, consultation and public participation in policy-making.* OECD Publications.

West, J., & Bogers, M. (2017). Open innovation: Current status and research opportunities. *Innovation*, 19(1), 43–50.

Wolpert, D. (2003). Theory of collective intelligence. In Kagan Turner and David Wolpert (Eds.), *Collectives and the design of complex systems* (pp.43–106). Springer.

Chapter 6

Berman, P. (1998). The Three Gorges: Dam Energy, the Environment, and the New Emperors. *Education about Asia*, 3(1), 27–35.

Dresser, R. (2009). Priority setting in biomedical research. *The Virtual Mentor*, 11(4), 322–325.

Gillum, L. A., Gouveia, C., Dorsey, E. R., Pletcher, M., Mathers, C. D., McCulloch, C. E., & Johnston, S. C. (2011). NIH Disease Funding Levels and Burden of Disease. *PloS One*, 6(2), e16837–e16837.

Hane, M., & Perez, L. (2013). *Modern Japan: A historical survey.* Westview Press.

Hegde, D. & Sampat, B. (2015). Can Private Money Buy Public Science? Disease Group Lobbying and Federal Funding for Biomedical Research. *Management Science*, 61(10), 2281–2298.

Hersey, J. (1989). *Hiroshima.* Vintage.

Jordan, S. R. (2014). The innovation imperative: An analysis of the ethics of the imperative to innovate in public sector service delivery. *Public Management Review*, 16(1), 67–89.

López-Pujol, J., & Ren, M. X. (2009). Biodiversity and the Three Gorges Reservoir: a troubled marriage. *Journal of Natural History*, 43(43–44), 2765–2786.

Meijer, A., & Thaens, M. (2020). The dark side of public innovation. *Public Performance & Management Review*, 44(1), 1–19.

Mizoguchi, T., & Van Quyen, N. (2014). Corruption in public procurement market. *Pacific Economic Review*, 19(5), 577–591.

Osborne, S. P., & Brown, L. (2005). *Managing change and innovation in public service organizations.* Routledge.

Rhodes, R. (1986). *The making of the atomic bomb.* Simon & Schuster.

Rodriguez, M. A., & García, R. (2013). First, do no harm: The US sexually transmitted disease experiments in Guatemala. *American Journal of Public Health*, 103(12), 2122–2126.

Selden, K. I., & Selden, M. (1989), *The atomic bomb: Voices from Hiroshima and Nagasaki.* M. E. Sharpe.

Sharma, S., Sengupta, A., & Panja, S. (2019). Mapping corruption risks in public procurement: Uncovering improvement opportunities and strengthening controls. *Public Performance & Management Review*, 42(4), 947–975.

Van Eschenbach, A., & Hall, R. (2013). FDA approvals are a matter of life and death. *Missouri Medicine*, 110(2), 110–111.

Chapter 7

Abetti, P. A. (2004). Government-supported incubators in the Helsinki region, Finland: Infrastructure, results, and best practices. *Journal of Technology Transfer*, 29(1), 19–40.

Acs, Z. J., Stam, E., Audretsch, D. B., & O'Connor, A. (2017). The lineages of the entrepreneurial ecosystem approach. *Small Business Economics*, 49(1), 1–10.

Agren, G. I., & Bosatta, E. (1998). *Theoretical ecosystem ecology: Understanding element cycles.* Cambridge University Press.

Avnimelech, G., & Teubal, M. (2004). Venture capital start-up co-evolution and the emergence & development of Israel's new high tech cluster: Part 1: Macro-background and industry analysis. *Economics of Innovation and New Technology*, 13(1), 33–60.

Barr, M. D. (2006). Beyond technocracy: The culture of elite governance in Lee Hsien Loong's Singapore. *Asian Studies Review*, 30(1), 1–18.

Baumol, W. J., Litan, R. E., & Schramm, C. J. (2007). *Good capitalism, bad capitalism, and the economics of growth and prosperity.* Yale University Press.

Bason, C. (2010). *Leading public sector innovation: Co-creating for a better society.* Bristol University Press.

Beck, K., Beedle, M., van Bennekum, A., Cockburn, A., Cunningham, W., Fowler, M., & Thomas, D. (2001). *Manifesto for Agile Software Development.* Agile Alliance.

Bellows, T. J. (2009). Meritocracy and the Singapore political system. *Asian Journal of Political Science*, 17(1), 24–44.

Bertot, J. C., Jaeger, P. T., & Grimes, J. M. (2010). Using ICTs to create a culture of transparency: E-government and social media as openness and anti-corruption tools for societies. *Government Information Quarterly*, 27(3), 264–271.

Blanck, M., & Ribeiro, J. L. D. (2021). Smart cities financing system: An empirical modelling from the European context. *Cities*, 116, 103268.

Bryson, J. M., Crosby, B. C., & Stone, M. M. (2015). Designing and implementing cross-sector collaborations: Needed and challenging. *Public Administration Review*, 75(5), 647–663.

Carstensen, H. V., & Bason, C. (2012). Powering collaborative policy innovation: Can innovation labs help. *The Innovation Journal: The Public Sector Innovation Journal*, 17(1), 1–26.

Carter, L., & Bélanger, F. (2005). The utilization of e-government services: Citizen trust, innovation and acceptance factors. *Information Systems Journal*, 15(1), 5–25.

Chandra, A., & Fealey, T. (2009). Business incubation in the United States, China and Brazil: A comparison of role of government, incubator funding and financial services. *International Journal of Entrepreneurship*, 13, 67–86.

Chen, W., Acs, Z. & Terjesen, S. (2024). Adolescent entrepreneurial learning ecosystem and a tech entrepreneurial career—inspiration from the black swan stories. *Small Business Economics*, 62(3), 1157-1176.

Conboy, K., & Carroll, N. (2019). *Implementing large-scale Agile frameworks: Challenges and recommendations*. IEEE.

Conforto, E. C., Salum, F., Amaral, D., Silva, S., & Almeida, L. (2014). Can Agile project management be adopted by industries other than software development? *Project Management Journal*, 45(3), 21–34.

Coursey, D., & Norris, D. F. (2008). Models of e-government: Are they correct? An empirical assessment. *Public Administration Review*, 68(3), 523–536.

Dear, A., Helbitz, A., Khare, R., Lotan, R., Newman, J., Sims, G., & Zaroulis, A. (2016), Social impact bonds: The early years. *Social Finance*. https://www.socialfinance.org.uk/assets/documents/sibs-early-years.pdf.

Dunleavy, P., Margetts, H., Bastow, S., & Tinkler, J. (2006). New public management is dead—long live digital-era governance. *Journal of Public Administration Research and Theory*, 16(3), 467–494.

El Bcheraoui, C., Palmisano, E. B., Dansereau, E., Schaefer, A., Woldeab, A., Moradi-Lakeh, M., Salvatierra, B., Hernandez-Prado, B., & Mokdad, A. H. (2017). Healthy competition drives success in results-based aid: Lessons from the Salud Mesoamérica Initiative. *PLoS One*, 12(10), e0187107.

Flyverbom, M., Deibert, R., & Matten, D. (2019). The governance of digital technology, big data, and the internet: New roles and responsibilities for business. *Business & Society*, 58(1), 3–19.

Franklin, M., Halevy, A., & Maier, D. (2005). From databases to dataspaces: A new abstraction for information management. *ACM Sigmod Record*, 34(4), 27–33.

Gray, B., & Wood, D. J. (1991). Collaborative alliances: Moving from practice to theory. *Journal of Applied Behavioral Science*, 27(1), 3–22.

Hackman, J. R. (2011). *Collaborative intelligence: Using teams to solve hard problems.* Berrett-Koehler Publishers.

Hendratmi, A., & Sukmaningrum, P. S. (2018). Role of government support and incubator organization to success behaviour of woman entrepreneur: Indonesia Women Entrepreneur Association. *Polish Journal of Management Studies*, 17(1), 105–115.

Hidayat, H. Y. (2020). Petabencana. Id in flood disaster management: An innovation in collaborative governance-based early warning system in Indonesia. *Jurnal Kebijakan dan Administrasi Publik*, 24, 61–78.

Hood, C. (1991). A public management for all seasons? *Public Administration*, 69(1), 3–19.

Hood, C. (1995). The "new public management" in the 1980s: Variations on a theme. Accounting, *Organizations and Society*, 20(2), 93–109.

Hood, C., & Scott, C. (1996). Bureaucratic regulation and new public management in the United Kingdom: Mirror-image developments. *Journal of Law and Society*, 23, 321–345.

Horlings, L. G., Lamker, C., Puerari, E., Rauws, W., & van der Vaart, G. (2021). Citizen engagement in spatial planning, shaping places together. *Sustainability*, 13(19), 11006.

Isenberg, D. (2010). How to start an entrepreneurial revolution. *Harvard Business Review*, 88(6), 40–50.

Kastenhofer, K. (2007). Converging epistemic cultures? A discussion drawing on empirical findings. *Innovation*, 20(4), 359–373.

Kenney, M. (2000). *Understanding Silicon Valley: The anatomy of an entrepreneurial region*. Stanford University Press.

Landes, D. S. (1969). *The unbound Prometheus: Technological change and industrial development in Western Europe from 1750 to the present.* Cambridge University Press.

Landes, D. S. (1998). *The wealth And poverty of nations: Why some are so rich and some so poor.* Norton.

Lehmann, E. E., Seitz, N., & Wirsching, K. (2017). Smart finance for smart places to foster new venture creation. *Economia e Politica Industriale*, 44, 51–75.

Lewis, M., & Moultrie, J. (2005). The organizational innovation laboratory. *Creativity and innovation management*, 14(1), 73–83.

Leybourne, S. A. (2009). Improvisation and Agile Project Management: A Comparative Consideration. *International Journal of Managing Projects in Business*, 2(4), 519–535.

Li, C., Ahmed, N., Qalati, S. A., Khan, A., & Naz, S. (2020). Role of business incubators as a tool for entrepreneurship development: the mediating and moderating role of business start-up and government regulations. *Sustainability*, 12(5), 1822.

Linders, D. (2012). From e-government to we-government: Defining a typology for citizen coproduction in the age of social media. *Government Information Quarterly*, 29(4), 446–454.

Lukes, M., & Stephan, U. (2017). Measuring employee innovation: A review of existing scales and the development of the innovative behavior and innovation support inventories across cultures. *International Journal of Entrepreneurial Behavior & Research*, 23(1), 136–158.

Margetts, H., & Dunleavy, P. (2013). The second wave of digital-era governance: a quasi-paradigm for government on the Web. *Philosophical Transactions of the Royal Society of London. Series A: Mathematical, Physical, and Engineering Sciences*, 371(1987), 20120382–20120382.

Meijer, A., & Bolívar, M. P. R. (2016). Governing the smart city: A review of the literature on smart urban governance. *International Review of Administrative Sciences*, 82(2), 392–408.

Moi, L., & Cabiddu, F. (2021). An agile marketing capability maturity framework. *Tourism Management*, 86, 104347.

Mokhber, M., Khairuzzaman, W., & Vakilbashi, A. (2018). Leadership and innovation: The moderator role of organization support for innovative behaviors. *Journal of Management & Organization*, 24(1), 108–128.

National Academies of Sciences, Engineering, and Medicine (2017). Smart financing strategies. In *Global Health and the Future Role of the United States* (pp. 241-290). National Academies Press.

Nørreklit, L., Jack, L., & Nørreklit, H. (2019). Moving towards digital governance of university scholars: Instigating a post-truth university culture. *Journal of Management and Governance*, 23, 869–899.

Osborne, S. P., & Gaebler, T. (1992). *Reinventing government: How the entrepreneurial spirit is transforming the public sector*. Addison-Wesley.

Parker, G. M. (2011). *Team players and teamwork: New strategies for developing successful collaboration*. Wiley.

Quah, J. S. (2010). The public service commission. In *Public administration Singapore-style* (pp. 71–96). Emerald Group Publishing.

Schwaber, K., & Sutherland, J. (2017). *The Scrum Guide*. Scrum.org.

Sinclair, S., McHugh, N., Huckfield, L., Roy, M., & Donaldson, C. (2014). Social impact bonds: Shifting the boundaries of citizenship. In *Social Policy Review* (pp. 119–136). Policy Press.

Soetanto, D. P., & Jack, S. L. (2011). Networks and networking activities of innovative firms in incubators: An exploratory study. *International Journal of Entrepreneurship and Innovation*, 12(2), 127–136.

Stam, E. (2015). Entrepreneurial ecosystems and regional policy: A sympathetic critique. *European Planning Studies*, 23(9), 1759–1769.

Stone, F. (2004). Deconstructing silos and supporting collaboration. *Employment Relations Today*, 31(1), 11–18.

Tan, K. P. (2012). The ideology of pragmatism: Neo-liberal globalisation and political authoritarianism in Singapore. *Journal of Contemporary Asia*, 42(1), 67–92.

Tõnurist, P., Kattel, R., & Lember, V. (2015). Discovering innovation labs in the public sector. The Other Canon, Foundation and Tallinn University of Technology Working Papers in Technology Governance and Economic Dynamics. TUT Ragnar Nurkse School of Innovation and Governance, 61. https://ideas.repec.org/p/tth/wpaper/61.html.

Tõnurist, P., Kattel, R., & Lember, V. (2017). Innovation labs in the public sector: what they are and what they do? *Public Management Review*, 19(10), 1455–1479.

van der Wouden, F., & Youn, H. (2023). The impact of geographical distance on learning through collaboration. *Research Policy*, 52(2), 104698.

Williamson, B. (2016). Digital education governance: data visualization, predictive analytics, and "real-time" policy instruments. *Journal of Education Policy*, 31(2), 123–141.

Ye, R. (2021). Schooling for government: institutionalised sponsored mobility and trajectories of public service scholarship recipients in Singapore (1979–2018). *Journal of Education and Work*, 34(4), 518–532.

Yen, W. T. (2020). Taiwan's COVID-19 management: Developmental state, digital governance, and state-society synergy. *Asian Politics & Policy*, 12(3), 455–468.

Young, M. M. (2020). Implementation of digital-era governance: The case of open data in US cities. *Public Administration Review*, 80(2), 305–315.

Zivkovic, S. (2018). Systemic innovation labs: A lab for wicked problems. *Social Enterprise Journal*, 14(3), 348–366.

Chapter 8

Alves, H. (2013). Co-creation and innovation in public services. *The Service Industries Journal*, 33(7–8), 671–682.

Ansell, C., & Gash, A. (2008). Collaborative governance in theory and practice. *Journal of Public Administration Research and Theory*, 18(4), 543–571.

Audretsch, D. B., & Belitski, M. (2021) Frank Knight, uncertainty and knowledge spillover entrepreneurship. *Journal of Institutional Economics*, 17(6), 1005–1031.

Barney, J. B., and Arikan, A. M. (2001). The resource-based view: Origins and implications. In *The Blackwell handbook of strategic management* (pp. 124–188), Wiley-Blackwell.

Behn, R. D. (1995). Creating an innovative organization: Ten hints for involving frontline workers. *State & Local Government Review*, 27(3), 221–234.

Bekkers, V., & Tummers, L. (2018). Innovation in the public sector: Towards an open and collaborative approach. *International Review of Administrative Sciences*, 84(2), 209–213.

Borins, S. (2000). Loose cannons and rule breakers, or enterprising leaders? Some evidence about innovative public managers. *Public Administration Review*, 60(6), 498–507.

Boyne, G. A. (2006). Strategies for public service turnaround: Lessons from the private sector? *Administration & Society*, 38(3), 365–388.

Brazeal, D. V., Schenkel, M. T., & Kumar, S. (2014). Beyond the organizational bounds in CE research: Exploring personal and relational factors in a flat organizational structure. *Journal of Applied Management and Entrepreneurship*, 19(2), 78–106.

Brown, L., & Osborne, S. P. (2013). Risk and innovation: Towards a framework for risk governance in public services. *Public Management Review*, 15(2), 186–208.

Chen, W. D. (2022). A systematic literature review of reward-based crowdfunding. In *Developments in entrepreneurial finance and technology* (pp. 146–181). Edward Elgar Publishing.

Chen, W. D. (2023). Crowdfunding for social ventures. *Social Enterprise Journal*, 19(3), 256–276.

Chen, W. D., Acs, Z., & Terjesen, S. (2024). Adolescent entrepreneurial learning ecosystem and a tech entrepreneurial career—inspiration from the black swan stories. *Small Business Economics*, 62(3), 1157-1176.

Choi, S. (2018). Managing flexible work arrangements in government: Testing the effects of institutional and managerial support. *Public Personnel Management*, 47(1), 26–50.

Congressional Research Service (2023). Current federal civilian employment by state and congressional district. https://crsreports.congress.gov/product/pdf/R/R47716.

Cunningham, J. A., Lehmann, E. E., & Menter, M. (2022). The organizational architecture of entrepreneurial universities across the stages of entrepreneurship: a conceptual framework. *Small Business Economics*, 59(1), 11–27.

Dabić, M., Stojčić, N., Simić, M., Potocan, V., Slavković, M., & Nedelko, Z. (2021). Intellectual agility and innovation in micro and small businesses: The mediating role of entrepreneurial leadership. *Journal of Business Research*, 123, 683–695.

Demircioglu, M. A., & Chowdhury, F. (2021). Entrepreneurship in public organizations: The role of leadership behavior. *Small Business Economics*, 57(3), 1107–1123.

Drucker, P. F. (1985). *Innovation and entrepreneurship: Practice and principles.* Harper & Row.

Eggers, W., & O'Leary, J. (2009). *If we can put a man on the moon: Getting big things done in government.* Harvard Business School Press.

Fraihat, B. A. M., Alhawamdeh, H., Younis, B., Alkhawaldeh, A. M. A., & Al Shaban, A. (2023). The effect of organizational structure on employee creativity: The moderating role of communication flow: a survey study. *International Journal of Academic Resource in Economics & Management Sciences*, 12(2), 2226–3624.

Gil-Garcia, J. R. (2012). Towards a smarter state? Inter-agency collaboration, information integration, and beyond. *Information Polity*, 17(3), 269–280.

Grimsey, D., & Lewis, M. K. (2002). Evaluating the risks of public private partnerships for infrastructure projects. *International Journal of Project Management*, 20(2), 107–118.

Hayter, C. S., Link, A. N., & Scott, J. T. (2018). Public-sector entrepreneurship. *Oxford Review of Economic Policy*, 34(4), 676–694.

Hazak, A., Männasoo, K., & Virkebau, M. (2017). Effects of work arrangements on creative R&D work outcomes. *Eastern European Economics*, 55(6), 500–521.

Head, B. W., & Alford, J. (2015). Wicked problems: Implications for public policy and management. *Administration & Society*, 47(6), 711–739.

Hisrich, R. D. (1986). *Entrepreneurship, intrapreneurship, and venture capital: The foundation of economic renaissance.* Lexington Books.

Hjorth, D. (2013). Public entrepreneurship: Desiring social change, creating sociality. *Entrepreneurship and Regional Development*, 25(1–2), 34–51.

Huang, K. P., Wang, C. H., Tseng, M. C., & Wang, K. Y. (2010). A study on entrepreneurial orientation and resource acquisition: The effects of social capital. *African Journal of Business Management*, 4(15), 3226–3231.

Hunter, P. (2018). Remote working in research: An increasing usage of flexible work arrangements can improve productivity and creativity. *EMBO Reports*, 20(1), e47435.

Johannsen, R., & Zak, P. J. (2020). Autonomy raises productivity: An experiment measuring neurophysiology. *Frontiers in Psychology*, 11, https://www.frontiersin.org/journals/psychology/articles/10.3389/fpsyg.2020.00963/full

Kanter, R. M. (1988). When a thousand flowers bloom: Structural, collective and social conditions for innovation in organization. *Research in Organizational Behavior*, 10, 169–211.

Kim, Y. (2010). Improving performance in US state governments: Risk-taking, innovativeness, and proactiveness practices. *Public Performance & Management Review*, 34(1), 104–129.

Klein, P. G., Mahoney, J. T., McGahan, A. M., & Pitelis, C. N. (2013). Capabilities and strategic entrepreneurship in public prganizations. *Strategic Entrepreneurship Journal*, 7(1), 70–91.

Knight, F. H. (1921). *Risk, uncertainty and profit*. Houghton Mifflin.

Kotter, J. P. (1996). *Leading change*. Harvard Business Review Press.

Kuratko, D. F., Fisher, G., & Audretsch, D. B. (2021). Unraveling the entrepreneurial mindset. *Small Business Economics*, 57(4), 1681–1691.

Lee, S. (2022). The myth of the flat start-up: Reconsidering the organizational structure of start-ups. *Strategic Management Journal*, 43(1), 58–92.

Manso, G. (2017). Creating incentives for innovation. *California Management Review*, 60(1), 18–32.

Mikesell, J. L. (2014). *Fiscal administration: Analysis and applications for the public sector*. Wadsworth.

Moore, M. H. (1997). *Creating public value: Strategic management in government*. Harvard University Press.

Morris, M. H., & Jones, F. F. (1999). Entrepreneurship in established organizations: The case of the public sector. *Entrepreneurship Theory and Practice*, 24(1), 71–91.

Morris, M. H., Allen, J., Schindehutte, M., & Avila, R. (2006). Balanced management control systems as a mechanism for achieving corporate entrepreneurship. *Journal of Managerial Issues*, 18, 468–493.

Musgrave, R. A. (1959). *The theory of public finance; A study in public economy*. McGraw-Hill.

Ng, A., & Loosemore, M. (2007). Risk allocation in the private provision of public infrastructure. *International Journal of Project Management*, 25(1), 66–76.

Omrane, A., & Fayolle, A. (2011). Entrepreneurial competencies and entrepreneurial process: A dynamic approach. *International Journal of Business and Globalisation*, 6(2), 136–153.

Osborne, S. P., & Brown, L. (2011). Innovation, public policy and public services delivery in the UK: The word that would be king? *Public Administration*, 89(4), 1335–1350.

Osborne, S. P., & Brown, L. (2005). *Managing change and innovation in public service organizations*. Routledge.

Park, R., & Kim, J. (2013). Individual employees' responses to group incentives: The moderating role of innovation. *Journal of Business and Psychology*, 28, 175–187.

Porter, M. E. (2008). *On competition*. Harvard Business Press.

Rainey, H. G. (1983). Public agencies and private firms: Incentive structures, goals, and individual roles. *Administration & Society*, 15, 207–242.

Ries, E. (2011). *The lean startup: How today's entrepreneurs use continuous innovation to create radically successful businesses.* Crown.

Rishipal, D. (2014). Analytical comparison of flat and vertical organizational structures. *European Journal of Business and management*, 6(36), 56–65.

Schein, E. H., & Schein, P. A. (2016). *Organizational culture and leadership.* Wiley.

Schumpeter, J. A. (1942). *Capitalism, socialism, and democracy.* Harper.

Shane, S., & Venkataraman, S. (2000). The promise of entrepreneurship as a field of research. *Academy of Management Review*, 25(1), 217–226.

Shepherd, D. A., & Patzelt, H. (2018). *Entrepreneurial cognition: Exploring the mindset of entrepreneurs.* Springer Nature.

Shobe, K. (2018). Productivity driven by job satisfaction, physical work environment, management support and job autonomy. *Business and Economics Journal*, 9(2), 1–9.

Solanki, K. R. (2013). Flextime association with job satisfaction, work productivity, motivation & employees stress levels. *Journal of Human Resource Management*, 1(1), 9–14.

Sørensen, E., & Torfing, J. (2011). Enhancing collaborative innovation in the public sector. *Administration & Society*, 43(8), 842–868.

Van de Walle, S. (2018). Explaining citizen satisfaction and dissatisfaction with public services. In *The Palgrave handbook of public administration and management in Europe* (pp. 227–241). Palgrave Macmillan.

Wang, N., Cui, D., Geng, C., & Xia, Z. (2022). The role of business environment optimization on entrepreneurship enhancement. *Journal of Economic Analysis*, 1(2), 66–81.

Xiong, Z., Wang, P., & Wu, C. (2021). How to encourage innovation failure knowledge sharing in virtual research organization: An incentive mechanism based on game theory. *Computational and Mathematical Organization Theory*, 28(3), 1–21.

Yang, J., & Bentein, K. (2023). Entrepreneurial leadership and employee creativity: a multilevel mediation model of entrepreneurial self-efficacy. *Management Decision*, 61(9), 2645–2669.

Yukl, G. (2013). *Leadership in organizations.* Pearson.

Chapter 9

Adler-Milstein, J., & Jha, A. K. (2014). Health information exchange among US hospitals: Who's in, who's out, and why? *Healthcare: The Journal of Delivery Science and Innovation*, 2 (1), 26–32.

Aghion, P., Bergeaud, A., & Van Reenen, J. (2023). The impact of regulation on innovation. *American Economic Review*, 113(11), 2894–2936.

Aghion, P., David, P. A., & Foray, D. (2009). Science, technology and innovation for economic growth: Linking policy research and practice in "STIG Systems." *Research Policy*, 38(4), 681–693.

Agranoff, R., & McGuire, M. (2003). *Collaborative public management: New strategies for local governments.* Georgetown University Press.

Ahern, J. (2011). From fail-safe to safe-to-fail: Sustainability and resilience in the new urban world. *Landscape and Urban Planning*, 100(4), 341–343.

Aligica, P. D., & Tarko, V. (2014). Crony capitalism: Rent seeking, institutions and ideology. *Kyklos*, 67(2), 156–176.

Ansell, C., & Gash, A. (2008). Collaborative governance in theory and practice. *Journal of Public Administration Research and Theory*, 18(4), 543–571.

Bannister, F. (2005). E-government and administrative power: The one-stop-shop meets the turf war. *Electronic Government, an International Journal*, 2(2), 160–176.

Bason, C. (2010). *Leading public sector innovation: Co-creating for a better society*. Bristol University Press.

Blumenthal, D. (2010). Launching hitech. *New England Journal of Medicine*, 362(5), 382–385.

Borins, S. (2001). Encouraging innovation in the public sector. *Journal of Intellectual Capital*, 2, 310–319.

Carbonara, N., Costantino, N., Gunnigan, L., & Pellegrino, R. (2015). Risk management in motorway PPP projects: Empirical-based guidelines. *Transport Reviews*, 35(2), 162–182.

Chen, W., & Murtazashvili, I. (2023). Blockchains for emergency and crisis management. *Public Administration Review*, 83(5), 1409–1414.

Chen, W., & Murtazashvili, I. (2024). Is cryptoaltruism transforming the nonprofit sector? Lessons from the Ukrainian nonprofits during the Russia-Ukraine War. *Chinese Public Administration Review*, 15(1), 36–46.

Cinar, E., Trott, P., & Simms, C. (2019). A systematic review of barriers to public sector innovation process. *Public Management Review*, 21(2), 264–290.

de la Potterie, B. (2011). Europe should stop taxing innovation. *World Patent Information*, 33(1), 16–22.

Egan, T. (2006). *The worst hard time: The untold story of those who survived the great American Dust Bowl*. Houghton Mifflin.

Emerson, K., Nabatchi, T., & Balogh, S. (2012). An integrative framework for collaborative governance. *Journal of Public Administration Research and Theory*, 22(1), 1–29.

European Parliament (2020). Public sector innovation: Concepts, trends and best practices. https://www.europarl.europa.eu/RegData/etudes/BRIE/2020/651954/EPRS_BRI(2020)651954_EN.pdf.

Fabrizio, K. R., & Di Minin, A. (2008). Commercializing the laboratory: Faculty patenting and the open science environment. *Research Policy*, 37(5), 914–931.

Finke, D. (2020). Turf wars in government administration: Interdepartmental cooperation in the European Commission. *Public Administration*, 98(2), 498–514.

Gold, M., & McLaughlin, C. (2016). Assessing HITECH implementation and lessons: 5 years later. *The Milbank Quarterly*, 94(3), 654–687.

Hansen, Z. K., & Libecap, G. D. (2004). Small farms, externalities, and the Dust Bowl of the 1930s. *Journal of Political Economy*, 112(3), 665–694.

Haughton, G., Peck, J., & Strange, I. (1997). Turf wars: The battle for control over English local economic development. *Local Government Studies*, 23(1), 88–106.

Hirst, G., Van Knippenberg, D., Chen, C.-H., & Sacramento, C. A. (2011). How does bureaucracy impact individual creativity? A cross-level investigation of team contextual influences on goal orientation—creativity relationships. *Academy of Management Journal*, 54(3), 624–641.

Hood, J., & Mcgarvey, N. (2002). Managing the risks of public–private partnerships in Scottish local government. *Policy Studies*, 23(1), 21–35.

Jin, R. Q., & Rainey, H. G. (2020). Positive in public service: Government personnel, constrained incentives, and positive work attitudes. *International Public Management Journal*, 23(1), 25–56.

Lee, J. A., & Gill, T. E. (2015). Multiple causes of wind erosion in the Dust Bowl. *Aeolian Research*, 19, 15–36.

Macwan, J., & Pitroda, J. (2018). Risk management in PPP projects: A review. *International Journal of Constructive Research in Civil Engineering*, 4(4), 14–19.

Manoharan, A. (Ed.). (2014). *E-government and websites: A public solutions handbook.* Routledge.

Medina, E., Bel, E., & Suñé, J. M. (2016). Counterfeit medicines in Peru: a retrospective review (1997-2014). *BMJ Open*, 6(4), e010387.

Meijer, A. (2015). E-governance innovation: Barriers and strategies. *Government Information Quarterly*, 32(2), 198–206.

Mitchell, M. D. (2012). The pathology of privilege: The economic consequences of government favoritism. Mercatus Research.

Ndou, V. (2004). E-government for developing countries: Opportunities and challenges. *The Electronic Journal of Information System in Developing Countries.*, 18(1), 1–24.

OECD. Embracing innovation in government global trends. (2017). https://www.oecd.org/gov/innovative-government/embracing-innovation-in-government.pdf.

Osborne, S. P., & Brown, L. (2011). Innovation in public services: Engaging with risk. *Public Money & Management*, 31(1), 4–6.

O'Toole, L. J. (1997). Implementing public innovations in network settings. *Administration & Society*, 29, 115–138.

Özden, P., & Velibeyoğlu, K. (2023). Citizen science projects in the context of participatory approaches: The case of Izmir. *Journal of Design for Resilience in Architecture and Planning*, 4(1), 31–46.

Rasi-Heikkinen, P., & Doh, M. (2023). Older adults and digital inclusion. *Educational Gerontology*, 49(5), 345–347.

Rohde, L. (2002). Security breach on U.K. tax site halts online filing. *Network World.* https://link.gale.com/apps/doc/A87106593/EAIM?u=anon~29a8b1d0&sid=sitemap&xid=40033424.

Sampaio, E., & Rault, V. (2022). Citizen-led expeditions can generate scientific knowledge and prospects for researchers. *PLoS Biology*, 20(11), e3001872.

Schenkel, M., & Brazeal, D. V. (2016). The effect of pro-entrepreneurial architectures and relational influences on innovative behavior in a flat organizational structure. *Journal of Business and Entrepreneurship*, 27(2), 93.

Scott, I., & Gong, T. (2021). Coordinating government silos: challenges and opportunities. *Global Public Policy and Governance*, 1(1), 20–38.

Shin, J., Kim, Y., & Kim, C. (2022). A study on the relationship between government regulations and innovation efficiency in information and communication technology (ICT) industry. *International Journal of Software Innovation*, 10(1), 1–12.

Si, D. K., Wang, Y., & Kong, D. (2020). Employee incentives and energy firms' innovation: Evidence from China. *Energy*, 212, 118673.

Sørensen, E., & Torfing, J. (2011). Enhancing collaborative innovation in the public sector. *Administration & Society*, 43(8), 842–868.

Tagde, P., Tagde, S., Bhattacharya, T., Tagde, P., Chopra, H., Akter, R., Kaushik, D., & Rahman, M. H. (2021). Blockchain and artificial intelligence technology in e-Health. *Environmental Science and Pollution Research*, 28(38), 52810–52831.

Tep, O. (2015). *Exploring the importance of employee incentives and their effectiveness in improving quality performance in a Cambodian public organization*. Phd diss., University of Wellington.

Thompson, V. A. (1965). Bureaucracy and innovation. *Administrative Science Quarterly*, 10(1), 1–20.

Warrick, R. A. 1980. Drought in the Great Plains: A case study of research on climate and society in the USA. In *Climatic constraints and human activities* (pp. 93–123). Pergamon Press.

Williams, E. (2011). Dust Bowl meets Great Depression: Environmental tools & tales of the Dust Bowl. https://scholarship.tricolib.brynmawr.edu/server/api/core/bitstreams/6395bce5-c328-4b12-a631-f6819baafd88/content.

Wilson, J. Q. (2000). *Bureaucracy: What government agencies do and why they do it*. Basic Books.

Worster, D. (2014). *Dust Bowl the southern Plains in the 1930s* (25th ed.). Oxford University Press.

Xiong, W., Zhao, X., & Wang, H. (2018). Information asymmetry in renegotiation of public–private partnership projects. *Journal of Computing in Civil Engineering*, 32(4), 04018028.

Xu, F., Wu, L., & Evans, J. (2022). Flat teams drive scientific innovation. *Proceedings of the national Academy of Sciences*, 119(23), e2200927119.

Index

For the benefit of digital users, indexed terms that span two pages (e.g., 52–53) may, on occasion, appear on only one of those pages.